Mike Meyers' CompTIA A+® Guide to 801: Managing and Troubleshooting PCs Lab Manual

Fourth Edition

(Exam 220-801)

About the Authors

Mike Meyers, lovingly called the "AlphaGeek" by those who know him, is the industry's leading authority on CompTIA A+ certification. He is the president and co-founder of Total Seminars, LLC, a provider of PC and network repair seminars, books, videos, and courseware for thousands of organizations throughout the world. Mike has been involved in the computer and network repair industry since 1977 as a technician, instructor, author, consultant, and speaker. Author of numerous popular PC books and videos, Mike is also the series editor for the highly successful Mike Meyers' Certification Passport series, the Mike Meyers' Computer Skills series, and the Mike Meyers' Guide To series, all published by McGraw-Hill.

Scott Strubberg is a master teacher in computer maintenance and networking. He began his career in IT as a consultant and technician, earning the CompTIA A+, CompTIA Network+, and CompTIA Security+ certifications along the way. Scott taught in the public school system for over half a decade and, after joining Total Seminars, has led computer training courses all over the United States. Scott has worked as a mentor to countless teachers and takes great pleasure in inventing labs that make learning computer and networking subjects entertaining as well as productive.

Aaron Verber graduated from the University of Wisconsin, Eau Claire, with a focus on the spoken and sung word, and turned a passion for computers and a love of English into a career in computer training. Aaron has edited numerous books on computer maintenance, troubleshooting, and networking, including the best-selling *All-in-One CompTIA A+ Exam Guide* by Michael Meyers. Aaron puts his CompTIA A+ certification to good use crafting informative and creative labs suitable for all learners.

About the Technical Editor

Christopher A. Crayton (MCSE, MCP+I, CompTIA A+, CompTIA Network+) is an author, technical editor, technical consultant, security consultant, and trainer. Formerly a computer and networking instructor at Keiser College (2001 Teacher of the Year), Chris has also worked as network administrator for Protocol and at Eastman Kodak Headquarters as a computer and network specialist. Chris has authored several print and online books on topics ranging from CompTIA A+ and CompTIA Security+ to Microsoft Windows Vista. Chris has provided technical edits and reviews for many publishers, including McGraw-Hill, Pearson Education, Charles River Media, Cengage Learning, Wiley, O'Reilly, Syngress, and Apress.

Mike Meyers' CompTIA A+® Guide to 801: Managing and Troubleshooting PCs Lab Manual

Fourth Edition

(Exam 220-801)

Mike Meyers
Scott Strubberg
Aaron Verber

New York   Chicago   San Francisco
Lisbon   London   Madrid   Mexico City
Milan   New Delhi   San Juan
Seoul   Singapore   Sydney   Toronto

McGraw-Hill books are available at special quantity discounts to use as premiums and sales promotions, or for use in corporate training programs. To contact a representative, please e-mail us at bulksales@mcgraw-hill.com.

**Mike Meyers' CompTIA A+® Guide to 801: Managing and Troubleshooting PCs Lab Manual,
Fourth Edition (Exam 220-801)**

1234567890   QDB QDB   1098765432

ISBN   978-0-07-179517-3
MHID   0-07-179517-0

Sponsoring Editor
   Timothy Green

Editorial Supervisor
   Patty Mon

Project Manager
   Yashmita Hota,
      Cenveo Publisher Services

Acquisitions Coordinator
   Stephanie Evans

Technical Editor
   Christopher Crayton

Copy Editors
   William McManus
   Lisa McCoy

Proofreader
   Claire Splan

Indexer
   Ted Laux

Production Supervisor
   George Anderson

Composition
   Cenveo Publisher Services

Illustration
   Cenveo Publisher Services

Art Director, Cover
   Jeff Weeks

To students young and old who keep the faith that with hard work and diligence, you will succeed.

Contents at a Glance

Contents

Acknowledgments

The crew at Total Seminars contributed mightily to this edition. Our editor in chief, Scott Jernigan, helped manage the flow of the textbook and provided direction for the accompanying lab manual. Michael Smyer and Ford Pierson provided stellar art, editing, and help with labs. Doug Jones and Dave Rush, fellow instructors at Total Seminars, added great feedback and support on the many labs in this book.

Our acquisitions editor, Tim Green, and his trusty assistant, Stephanie Evans, did a superb job managing priorities and adding tons of encouragement and praise as the book unfolded. Thanks!

Chris Crayton, our technical editor, did a great job on this edition. Thank you for helping make this book happen.

On the McGraw-Hill side, the crew once again demonstrated why McGraw-Hill is the best in show as a publisher. With excellent work and even better attitude, this book went smoothly together.

Our project manager, Yashmita Hota, and her excellent team were wonderful to work with (*again*, for Mike and Aaron, and *for the first time*, for Scott). Quiet competence is totally *not* overrated, and you and your team have it to spare. Thank you!

To the copy editor, page proofer, and indexer, superb work in every facet. Thank you for being the best.

Additional Resources for Teachers

This lab manual supplements the *Mike Meyers' CompTIA A+ Guide to 801: Managing and Troubleshooting PCs, Fourth Edition (Exam 220-801)*. The textbook includes an instructor Web page available online at:

www.mhprofessional.com/certification801

McGraw-Hill Professional's Web site hosts the instructor support materials for this textbook, providing resources for teachers in a format that follows the organization of the textbook and lab manual.

This site includes the following:

- Answer keys to the Mike Meyers' 801 Lab Manual activities

- Answer keys to the end-of-chapter activities in the 801 textbook

- Access to test bank files and software that allow you to generate a wide array of paper- or network-based tests, and that feature automatic grading. The test bank includes:

  - Hundreds of practice questions and a wide variety of question types categorized by exam objective, enabling you to customize each test to maximize student progress

  - Blackboard cartridges and other formats may also be available upon request; contact your sales representative

- Engaging PowerPoint slides on the lecture topics that include full-color artwork from the book

- Instructor's manual that contains learning objectives, classroom preparation notes, instructor tips, and a lecture outline for each chapter

Please contact your McGraw-Hill sales representative for details.

Chapter 1

The Path of the PC Tech

Lab Exercises

Well, now you've really done it. The fact that you hold this lab manual in your hands says one thing loud and clear—you're deadly serious about getting that CompTIA A+ certification! Good. Even though the CompTIA A+ 220-801 exam is considered entry level, you need to take it seriously if you want to pass.

Because you're serious, I'm going to let you in on a secret: The key to passing this is preparation. When I say "preparation," I'm not talking about studying, although studying is important! I'm talking about *preparing to study*. You need to know exactly how to study for this exam, and you need to have the right tools to get that studying done. Sure, you have a textbook and a lab manual, but you're not ready to hit the books just yet.

In this chapter, you'll learn how to start studying for the CompTIA A+ 220-801 exam. First, you'll organize what you need to study. Second, you'll explore how the CompTIA A+ certification helps move you toward more advanced certifications. Finally, you'll get some ideas on how to gather equipment so that you can reinforce what you read with real hardware and software. So stay serious, roll up your sleeves, and start preparing to study for the CompTIA A+ 801 exam!

 60 MINUTES

Lab Exercise 1.01: Preparing to Study

Back in the 1980s, there was a popular TV show called *The A-Team*, starring George Peppard and Mr. T. It wasn't the greatest TV show, but I always remember one repeated line: "I love it when a plan comes together!" I want you to feel like that while you prepare for your CompTIA A+ certification. In fact, just for fun, let's call ourselves the "A+ Team" as we get ready to knock those exams right into next week's episode!

Learning Objectives

This lab helps you lay out a logical path for your studies. To do this, you need to deal with three issues: determining your weak points, checking your study habits, and scheduling the exam.

At the end of this lab, you'll be able to

- Identify the CompTIA A+ topics you need to learn

- Develop a good study plan

- Schedule the CompTIA A+ exams

Lab Materials and Setup

The materials you need for this lab are

- A PC with Internet access

- A phone

Getting Down to Business

Total Seminars has been teaching CompTIA A+ certification for years. We've developed a handy template that will show you what you need to study and how much time you need to devote to preparing for the CompTIA A+ 801 exam. These tables are shown in the *Mike Meyers' CompTIA A+ Guide to 801: Managing and Troubleshooting PCs* textbook, but with extra steps added to help you determine the topics you need to study.

Step 1   For each skill listed in the table that follows, circle the number that corresponds to the amount of experience you have: None, Once or Twice, Every Now and Then, or Quite a Bit. You'll use that number to calculate the total number of hours you need to study for the exam.

Tech Task	Amount of Experience			
	None	Once or Twice	Every Now and Then	Quite a Bit
Installing an adapter card	6	4	2	1
Installing and configuring hard drives	12	10	8	2
Installing modems and NICs	8	6	6	3
Connecting a computer to the Internet	16	10	8	4
Installing printers and scanners	16	8	4	2
Installing RAM	8	6	4	2
Installing CPUs	8	7	5	3

Tech Task	Amount of Experience			
	None	Once or Twice	Every Now and Then	Quite a Bit
Building complete systems	12	10	8	6
Using Windows XP	6	6	4	2
Using Windows Vista	8	6	4	2
Using Windows 7	8	6	4	2
Configuring sound	2	2	1	0
Using a volt-ohm meter	4	3	2	1

Great! You now have a good feel for the topics you need to study. Now you need to determine the total study time. First, add up the numbers you've circled. Then add the result to the number from the following table that corresponds to your experience. The grand total is the number of hours you should study to be ready for the exam.

Months of Direct, Professional Experience...	Hours to Add to Your Study Time...
0	50
Up to 6	30
6 to 12	10
Over 12	0

A total neophyte usually needs around 120 hours of study time. An experienced tech shouldn't need more than 30 hours.

You'll need to spend _____ hours studying for the CompTIA A+ 220-801 exam.

Step 2   Go to the Computing Technology Industry Association (CompTIA) Web site and download a copy of the exam objectives for the CompTIA A+ 220-801 exam. As of this writing, you can find them here:

http://certification.comptia.org/Training/testingcenters/examobjectives.aspx

You have to fill out a short form (requiring your name, e-mail address, and country of residence) before you can view the objectives. Bear in mind, however, that CompTIA changes its Web site more often than TV networks invent new reality shows, so be prepared to poke around if necessary! Compare what you circled in the tables to the CompTIA A+ exam objectives. Note that any single tech task in the table covers more than one exam objective on the CompTIA A+ 220-801 exam. In the table that follows, list the top five exam objectives that you think will challenge you the most as you begin your journey toward CompTIA A+ certification.

Exam	Objective
Example: 220-801	5.3 Given a scenario, demonstrate proper communication and professionalism.

Step 3   If you are taking this course at your high school, career center, or community college, ask your instructor about the most effective ways to learn and study. If you're studying on your own, think about your favorite teachers from the past and list which methods they used that helped you best learn the material.

1. _____

2. _____

3. _____

Step 4   Now that you know which topics are most important to you and how much time you need to devote to studying them, you need to develop your study plan. Take the amount of time you've set aside and determine how many days you have to prepare. Consider work, holidays, weekends, and anything else that will affect your study time.

Ask your instructor when he or she plans to have you take the certification exam. Every school handles the exam differently. It's important that you know how getting certified at your school works so that you'll know what to expect down the road.

If you aren't taking a course, you need to pick a day to take the exam. Keep in mind how much time you'll need to study, but don't put it off so long that you get lazy. Challenge yourself to take the exam as soon as you feel comfortable.

Enter the number of days you have to prepare for the CompTIA A+ 220-801 exam: _____. You now have your deadline—the day you'll say, "I'm ready to take the exam!"

Step 5   You should also investigate how much it will cost you to take the exam. Several vendors sell vouchers that enable you to take the exam at a discounted price. This step introduces you to a few vendors and their pricing options.

a.   Visit the following link to begin searching for pricing information:

www.vue.com/vouchers/pricelist/comptia.asp

b.   In the Pricing section, click the Pricing Spreadsheet link to download a file containing Pearson VUE's voucher pricing information. Open the downloaded file using Microsoft Excel and record the current cost for a single CompTIA A+ exam voucher for your region.

Price: _____

c.   On the same Web site, click the Academic/E2C Member Pricing Spreadsheet link to download another file. Open the file, and then find and record the cost for a single CompTIA A+ exam.

Price: _____

d.   Now visit this Web site:

www.totalsem.com/vouchers/index.php

e.   At the Total Seminars Web site, listed under Step 1, click the CompTIA A+ certification logo. Find and record the price for a CompTIA A+ Exam Voucher.

Price: _____

Some vouchers require you to be a member of an academic or technology organization. Check to see which voucher applies to you. You may be eligible for one, two, or even all three pricing options!

Step 6   Go online and schedule your exam with Pearson VUE (www.vue.com). You'll almost certainly need to make a phone call to do this. Make sure you have both a method of payment (credit cards are preferred) and some form of identification when you call. In the United States you need your Social Security number to schedule CompTIA exams. It's very important that you schedule your exam *now*—setting a test date early in the process will help motivate you to study, and keep you from procrastinating!

✔ Cross-Reference

For details about taking the CompTIA A+ 220-801 exam, go to the CompTIA Web site (www .comptia.org).

60 MINUTES

Lab Exercise 1.02: Considering Other Certifications

CompTIA A+ certification may be your first certification, but it certainly should not be your last! The information technology (IT) industry considers obtaining certifications an ongoing process, one that continues as long as you're working in the IT field. You need to appreciate how the CompTIA A+ certification leads into other certifications.

Learning Objectives

This lab helps you learn about the various IT certifications that are available, and how they fit with both your skills and aptitude.

At the end of this lab, you'll be able to

- Understand some of the more common certifications that follow the CompTIA A+ certification

- Plan in what order you might attain those certifications

Lab Materials and Setup

The materials you need for this lab are

- A PC with Internet access

Getting Down to Business

It's time to jump onto the Internet and do a little research! You'll tour some of the more popular IT certifications and see how CompTIA A+ helps you gain these more advanced certifications.

✔ Cross-Reference

To review the domains of each CompTIA A+ exam, refer to "The Basic Exam Structure" in Chapter 1 of *Mike Meyers' CompTIA A+ Guide to 801: Managing and Troubleshooting PCs.*

Step 1 Fire up a Web browser and go to this Web address:

http://certification.comptia.org/ExploreCareers/careerpaths.aspx

CompTIA offers many other certifications related to the IT field. Research their certification offerings by clicking the Launch IT Certification Roadmap button. From here, list three careers that most interest you.

1. _____

2. _____

3. _____

Of the three career paths you listed, choose the one that appeals to you the most. You can always change your mind later if you don't like it! List three CompTIA certifications you'll need to become an expert in that field.

1. _____

2. _____

3. _____

List three certifications that CompTIA recommends you take that are *not* CompTIA certifications.

1. _____

2. _____

3. _____

Step 2 CompTIA strongly recommends pursuing CompTIA A+ certification as the starting point to your career in information technology. Why do you think they do that?

_____

_____

_____

Step 3 Now that you've seen some common certifications and career paths that follow the CompTIA A+ certification, write a short paragraph explaining why you chose the career path and certifications that you did.

_____

_____

_____

_____

_____

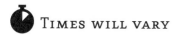 Times will vary

Lab Exercise 1.03: Gathering Equipment

Although it's theoretically possible to obtain CompTIA A+ certification by doing nothing but reading books, you'll be far better prepared for the real world if you can practice with real equipment. You also need some tools so you can take things apart and put them back together. Finally, you need some operating system software, in particular Windows XP, Windows Vista, and Windows 7. If you're taking a course, all of this equipment should be provided to you. If you are not taking a course, you could find yourself spending some serious cash trying to buy everything you need!

Learning Objectives

In this lab, you'll discover some rather interesting ways to get inexpensive or free hardware and software. None of these ideas will work every time, but with a little patience, you'll be amazed how much you can get for very little!

At the end of this lab, you'll be able to

- Acquire inexpensive or free hardware and software

- Acquire a standard PC technician toolkit

Lab Materials and Setup

The materials you need for this lab are

- A phone

- Transportation

- A PC with Internet access

Getting Down to Business

Most of the objectives on the CompTIA A+ 220-801 exam don't require state-of-the-art hardware. If you're willing to use systems that are a few years old, you can get plenty of good hands-on practice with the techniques you need to know to pass the CompTIA A+ 801 exam.

Step 1   Go on a scavenger hunt. Get a list of the smaller "mom and pop" PC repair companies and small PC parts suppliers in your town. Drive to these companies (don't call them) and ask them, "What do you guys do with your broken or obsolete parts?" The vast majority of these stores simply throw the parts away! Ask when they toss stuff and if you can have what they throw away. Most of these companies pay to get rid of equipment and will be glad to give it to you. Oh, and you can forget the big chain stores—they almost never let folks have equipment.

Step 2   Shop the sale bins at the local computer parts stores. You'll always find one or two pieces of equipment at outrageously low prices. Granted, you may end up using a bright pink Barbie keyboard, but if it only costs $3, who cares? Don't forget about rebates—you can often get parts for free after rebate! Really!

Step 3   Tell everyone you know that you're looking for PC hardware. Almost every organization will have occasional in-house sales where they sell older (but still good) PCs, printers, and so on, to employees. If you can get in on some of these sales, you'll have some amazing deals come your way!

✔ **Hint**

You'll often find that older machines still have the Windows 98 or Windows 2000 operating system software installed. If you come across one of these systems, see if you can work with the seller or donor to get the licensed disc. Working with an older operating system (even DOS) will introduce you to the installation and configuration process. Having an operating system installed will also enable you to verify that the hardware is working.

Step 4   Take one weekend to check out local garage sales. People often sell older PCs at a tiny fraction of their original cost. If you're not afraid to barter a bit, you'll get incredible deals—just watch out for equipment that's simply too old to be worthwhile.

✔ **Hint**

I avoid PC flea markets. The problem is that these folks know the value of their computer equipment, so it's often hard to find excellent deals.

Step 5   Locate the local PC user groups in your town—almost every town has at least one. Explain your situation to them; you'll usually find someone who's willing to give you a part or two, and you may also find others who are studying for the CompTIA A+ exams. You may even be able to start or join a study group!

Step 6   Check out the Craigslist page for your area (www.craigslist.org) and look in the For Sale/Computer category. Craigslist is like a big online garage sale, and you can almost always find someone trying to get rid of old PC equipment for next to nothing. Failing that, you can check out their forums, or even place an ad yourself saying that you're looking for old PC parts.

Step 7   Speaking of study groups, try teaming up with as many fellow students as you can to pool cash for parts and to work as a study group. If you're in a course, this is easy—your fellow students are your study group! Have everyone go equipment hunting, using the different methods described to get equipment, and pool the items you find for everyone to use. You might even hold a drawing after you all get certified, to choose who gets to keep the equipment.

Step 8   After searching your area, online and off, for the best deals on tools and equipment, record what you think are the three best deals you found. If you can, find out what the full price is for each product so you can see how much money you saved.

1. _____

2. _____

3. _____

Chapter 2
Operational Procedures

Lab Exercises

Achieving CompTIA A+ certification is a great way to demonstrate to prospective employers that you have the appropriate technical skills to make you a worthy candidate for their workplace. But you have to demonstrate more than just technical skills to get hired by and succeed in an organization. You also need to demonstrate that you have the appropriate interpersonal skills to interact effectively with fellow employees and with clients. CompTIA recognizes the importance of interpersonal skills in the workplace and thus includes related questions on its CompTIA A+ 220-801 exam to make sure you are prepared to show that you have the people skills to work well with others.

Face it: You're great at fixing computers and extremely interested in the latest gadgets, but do you have the people skills to land a job, keep a job, and climb the ladder of success? I've seen many talented young individuals who can fix just about anything, struggle in the area of how to communicate professionally with others; their impressive resume allows them to walk in the front door to a promising future...only to slink out the back door in disappointment after failing due to lack of people skills.

Whether you like it or not, people evaluate you based on how they perceive you. Developing and maintaining personal and professional workplace habits ensures that people perceive you as the IT professional that you are. This set of labs applies the information you learned in Chapter 2 of *Mike Meyers' CompTIA A+ Guide to 801: Managing and Troubleshooting PCs* with a focus on communicating properly, presenting yourself professionally at all times, and demonstrating your technical knowledge regarding safety. These labs will help you not only to pass the CompTIA A+ exam but also to develop skills that will serve you well throughout your career, whether in IT or another field.

The CompTIA objectives challenge you to conduct yourself in a professional manner while on the job. Objective 5.3 goes into detail to clarify how you should act on the job. Let's review some of the major points:

5.3 GIVEN A SCENARIO, DEMONSTRATE PROPER COMMUNICATION AND PROFESSIONALISM

- Use proper language—avoid jargon, acronyms, slang when applicable
- Maintain a positive attitude

- Listen and do not interrupt the customer

- Be culturally sensitive

- Be on time (if late contact the customer)

- Avoid distractions

  - Personal calls

  - Talking to coworkers while interacting with customers

  - Personal interruptions

- Dealing with difficult customer or situation

  - Avoid arguing with customers and/or being defensive

  - Do not minimize customer's problems

  - Avoid being judgmental

  - Clarify customer statements (ask open-ended questions to narrow the scope of the problem, restate the issue or question to verify understanding)

- Set and meet expectations/timeline and communicate status with the customer

  - Offer different repair/replacement options if applicable

  - Provide proper documentation on the services provided

  - Follow up with customer/user at a later date to verify satisfaction

- Deal appropriately with customers' confidential materials

  - Located on a computer, desktop, printer, etc.

Many of the following labs will require you to have a partner, and your instructor will actually lead the classroom through a few of them, so buddy up.

 30 MINUTES

Lab Exercise 2.01: The Rude Computer Technician

Everyone is familiar with the stereotype of the rude technician so wrapped up in technology that he is unable to relate to the people around him. Sneering technobabble, a condescending attitude, and rude remarks have become traits that people expect to find in techs, and, all too often, the techs don't disappoint. In this exercise, you'll work with a partner first to role-play the part of the stereotypical rude tech and then to role-play a professional, well-behaved tech. In this way, you'll learn how you should and should not behave as a technician.

Learning Objectives

The plan is to have a classmate play the role of the client, and to have you play the role of the PC tech. Work through the scenario in a live person-to-person role-playing of the situation, just as if it were real.

At the end of this lab, you'll be able to

- Demonstrate proper communication skills

- Avoid distractions in the workplace

Lab Materials and Setup

The materials you need for this lab are

- Blank drawing paper and pencil

- A clock with a second hand, or a timer

- A space to place chairs so that you can face your partner

- The *Mike Meyers' CompTIA A+ Guide to 801: Managing and Troubleshooting PCs* textbook, for reference

- A PC with Internet access

Getting Down to Business

In this exercise, one person will act as the PC technician while the other acts as a customer sitting in a cubicle. As the PC tech, you will first try to emulate as many bad communication habits as possible while your partner, the customer, identifies and writes down those bad habits. Then, repeat the process, this time using proper communication skills. You will then trade roles and repeat the scenario.

Step 1 Create a scenario in which a customer would ask for technical support. For example, try "My computer is running slowly and all these Web pages keep popping up!"—a classic case of malware infection. The person playing the customer should act as if he or she is not technically savvy and is unable to answer any technical questions or understand any terms outside of what might be considered "common." What is considered "common" is up to the person playing the customer, so have fun!

Step 2 Between 1999 and 2001, the popular television show *Saturday Night Live* put on a series of comedy sketches called "Nick Burns, Your Company's Computer Guy." Many of these sketches are available online. Do a search for and watch a few of these humorous sketches to see actor Jimmy Fallon portray how insensitive a technician can be in his personal communications. Why are these sketches so funny? What does their popularity tell you about how techs are perceived by our society? Use these videos to get an idea of how to behave during the next step, and how never, ever to behave in real life.

Step 3 It's now time for the technician to do his thing in a timed scenario. Pretend the customer is sitting in a cubicle. Every computer has an "asset tag number," and the tech must confirm that number to make sure he is working on the right computer. After that, it's up to the tech! Be as rude as possible (but not so rude that a person normally would get fired), concentrating on the issues listed in Step 1 of this lab. Your goal is to try to get started working on the PC within three minutes.

As the customer, your job is to describe the problem and answer the tech's questions to the best of your ability. You want your computer fixed, but you won't get up until you have confidence in the tech. As the tech talks, jot down how he is rude or inconsiderate to you.

The scenario ends when either the tech is sitting at the customer's computer or three minutes have elapsed, whichever happens first.

Step 4   Discuss the issues that the customer wrote down. After a quick discussion, repeat the process, this time using good communication techniques. In most cases, the customer will quickly relinquish his or her seat and let you get to work.

The scenario ends when the tech is sitting at the customer's computer or three minutes have elapsed, whichever happens first.

Step 5   Repeat the entire process, this time trading roles. The person now playing the tech should attempt to come up with different ways to be inappropriate, within reason.

 15–40 MINUTES DEPENDING ON CLASS SIZE

Lab Exercise 2.02: Communicating Effectively

So, you want to be a successful IT technician but you have trouble communicating? One of the keys to professional communication is being able to listen well as duties are being assigned to you so that you can produce the results expected.

Learning Objectives

At the end of this lab, you'll be able to

- Communicate more effectively

- Help discern when it's best to talk and when it's best to listen

Lab Materials and Setup

The materials you need for this lab are

- Blank drawing paper and pencil

- A clock with a second hand, or a timer

- A sufficient number of folding chairs for all the students involved in the exercise

- The *Mike Meyers' CompTIA A+ Guide to 801: Managing and Troubleshooting PCs* textbook, for reference

For the setup, arrange the chairs back to back in pairs around the room, with about five feet between each set of chairs.

Getting Down to Business

In this exercise, you'll listen as your partner speaks to you and you'll write down whatever he or she tells you under a tight timeline. The goal is to help you work under pressure while remaining professional at all times.

Step 1   Students should pair up. Each pair of students should designate one person to be the PC tech and the other to be the customer and then write their respective titles on the top of their papers.

Step 2   The instructor should start the timer and ask the designated customers to say the first five technology-related problems that come to mind; they have 20 seconds to do this. As the customers speak, their respective partner techs should write down what they say in the order stated. *An example might be "system fails to boot, no wireless connection, printer not printing properly, no picture on the monitor," and so on.*

   Stop the timer at 20 seconds.

Step 3   The PC techs write a brief solution to the five problems just mentioned by the customers. They have three minutes to complete this and must address the problems in the order received.

   Stop the timer at three minutes.

Step 4   The PC tech and customer groups face each other for one minute and share their information. Then, each pair presents their problems and solutions to the class, in turn. They have two minutes to present their solutions. The other groups should sit quietly and listen. After all groups finish, the instructor will give feedback to each group as to how they could communicate better. Students should be allowed to participate in the feedback as well.

 30 MINUTES

Lab Exercise 2.03: Integrating Safety into the Workplace

Demonstrating safety precautions at all times is one of the most important things you can do to protect yourself and your customers...and impress your employer. This mostly involves using common sense, but you should also make sure to carefully read and put into practice the safety guidelines provided in Chapter 2 of *Mike Meyers' CompTIA A+ Guide to 801: Managing and Troubleshooting PCs.*

Many techs go into the field with the mind-set that safety is not that important, but it can save your life and the lives of others. The U.S. Department of Labor Occupational Safety and Health Administration's Web site at www.osha.gov is loaded with information for employers and employees to help them understand the importance of safety. It offers guidelines for electronics and computers/peripherals that we'll explore in this lab exercise.

Learning Objectives

In this lab, you will identify the safety hazards in the workplace and become more aware of guidelines that are useful in a PC environment.

At the end of this lab, you will be able to

- Explain ESD

- Explain MSDSs and various hazards

- Explain proper equipment disposal procedures

Lab Materials and Setup

The materials you need for this lab are

- A PC with Internet access

- A notepad

- Presentation software, if possible, to present your findings

Getting Down to Business

In Chapter 2 of *Mike Meyers' CompTIA A+ Guide to 801: Managing and Troubleshooting PCs*, you read that electrostatic discharge (ESD) can cause permanent damage to some components and erase data on some storage devices. If you take this to heart and practice ESD safety measures as a PC tech early on, you will gain respect in the workplace and demonstrate that you care about your employer's investment.

Step 1 Research ESD, material safety data sheets (MSDSs), and how to dispose of old computer equipment properly, while typing results. You can use the Internet, magazines, tech articles, manuals, and so forth, but make sure you properly document where you find your information.

Step 2 Compile the data into a presentation. Include the following:

1. Pages that describe and define ESD, MSDSs, and proper disposal

2. Pictures of the following:

   a. Various anti-static devices

   b. Samples of MSDSs

   c. Disposing of old, outdated computer devices

3. A short video clip of either:

    a. A student wearing an anti-static wrist strap and installing components into a PC

    b. How to fill out an MSDS

    c. How to properly dispose of computer components

4. A bibliography page listing the sources used for your research

Step 3 (If Time Permits)   Students take turns presenting their report to the class to demonstrate their knowledge.

 30 MINUTES

Lab Exercise 2.04: Safeguarding Your IT Future—Becoming a Professional

To safeguard your IT future, it is extremely important that you know how to carry yourself as a professional and keep your customers satisfied. As discussed in *Mike Meyers' CompTIA A+ Guide to 801: Managing and Troubleshooting PCs*, good techs demonstrate professionalism in the workplace at all times.

Learning Objectives

In this lab, you will learn the proper way to dress and present yourself in the workplace.

After completing this lab, you'll be able to

- Properly dress and present yourself on the job
- Understand the do's and don'ts about cell phone usage on the job

Lab Materials and Setup

- A PC with Internet access

Getting Down to Business

Choosing the proper way to dress and present yourself is extremely important in securing and maintaining a good job. Did you know that within the first 15 seconds of meeting someone, they form opinions of you based entirely on your appearance—your body language, your demeanor, your mannerisms, and how you are dressed? Once you have made that first impression, it is virtually irreversible, so you must be aware at all times how you are being perceived and maintain a positive and clean self-image.

Step 1   Based on your current knowledge of what it means to be a professional in the workplace, list three characteristics that show these qualities.

1. _____

2. _____

3. _____

Step 2   Go to www.mindtools.com/CommSkll/FirstImpressions.htm and read the article "Making a Great First Impression." Notice some of the characteristics you might have missed in Step 1. List three of them.

1. _____

2. _____

3. _____

Step 3   Read the article "Top 6 Rules for Using Cell Phones at Work," by Dawn Rosenberg McKay, at http://careerplanning.about.com/od/workplacesurvival/tp/cell_phone.htm. Then, read the following scenarios and write a short explanation of what you would do next.

A.   Your boss has specifically stated that you cannot use your cell phone on the job unless you are on break (away from your work space) or at lunch. You found out before you left for work that your father will be having outpatient surgery today, and you want to be informed right away about his status. What should you do?

_____

_____

_____

B.   You're on the company phone with a client, attempting to walk her through various troubleshooting steps so that you don't have to travel to the client's location to fix the problem. Your personal cell phone suddenly rings (because you forgot to turn it off) and you can see on the caller ID that it's an old friend you have not talked to in a while. What should you do?

_____

_____

_____

C. Your boss just came in the office from a meeting with his boss and is extremely frustrated about issues that do not involve you. He speaks to you rather harshly and then abruptly leaves. The moment he leaves, you receive a phone call from a client who demands that you return his PC to him today and a text message you've been waiting for about a part for the client's computer that's due in. How should you react?

_____

_____

_____

Lab Analysis Test

1. Your coworker Sara constantly takes personal calls on her cell phone even though she knows your employer has a rule banning personal use of the cell phone while in the workplace. Whenever she's on her cell phone, she does not answer her regular work phone, thus adding more work for you and others. How do you think you should handle this situation?

2. You just got a phone call from a PC repair company that wants to interview you today. It is dress-down day at your workplace, so you're wearing jeans and a T-shirt. Should you accept the offer to interview today or decline? Explain your answer.

3. You're the lead PC technician for a company and have been put in charge of two inexperienced technicians who know nothing about ESD and MSDSs. What steps will you take to educate them to ensure they use anti-static devices and dispose of hazardous materials properly?

4. What is EMI and which components are particularly susceptible to it?

5. What is RFI? Write down three examples of RFI.

Key Term Quiz

Use the following terms to complete the following sentences. Not all terms will be used.

cell phones

electromagnetic interference (EMI)

electrostatic discharge (ESD)

honesty

integrity

professional

radio frequency interference (RFI)

responsibility

1. A(n) _____ technician is one who not only possesses great technical expertise but also has good communication and people skills.

2. Interference produced by microwaves and cell phones is an example of _____.

3. Anti-static wrist straps prevent _____.

4. When on the job, it is your _____ to follow the rules and guidelines set by the company regarding the use of _____.

5. _____ can disrupt wireless network communication.

Chapter 3
The Visible PC

Lab Exercises

Every competent tech knows the PC inside and out. Nothing destroys your credibility in the eyes of a client as quickly as not knowing the basics, like the difference between a graceful shutdown and a forced power down. The word "Oops!" doesn't go over well in the real world! In this chapter, you'll be poking and prodding a real PC. You'll begin by exploring the functions of a PC: input, processing, output, and storage. Then you'll examine the typical user-accessible components—for example, what happens when you press the power button? The final lab takes you on a tour of common connectors.

 30 MINUTES

Lab Exercise 3.01: Exploring the Functions and Components of a PC

Everything a computer does falls into one of four categories: input, processing, output, and storage. To troubleshoot PC problems successfully, you need a good understanding of these four processes and the components that are involved with each one.

Learning Objectives

At the end of this lab, you'll be able to

- Define the four functions of computer systems

- Detail common components involved in each of these four functions

Lab Materials and Setup

The materials you need for this lab are

- A notepad and pencil, to draw a four-column table

- Optional: Access to a working computer with a word processing or spreadsheet application installed to aid in drawing the table

- The *Mike Meyers' CompTIA A+ Guide to 801: Managing and Troubleshooting PCs* textbook, for reference

✔ **Hint**

Get used to taking notes and drawing pictures. Even after many years of repairing computers, from mainframes to PCs, I still use a notepad to keep track of what I see and what I change. I recommend that you save your drawings and notes, as you'll find them useful in subsequent labs.

Getting Down to Business

In this exercise, you'll review, list, and define the various components involved in the PC's vital functions.

Step 1   Reread the "How the PC Works" section in Chapter 3 of *Mike Meyers' CompTIA A+ Guide to 801: Managing and Troubleshooting PCs*, paying particular attention to the sections on input, processing, output, and storage.

Step 2   For each of the following functions, write a definition and give a brief example:

Input:

_____

_____

Processing:

_____

_____

Output:

_____

_____

Storage:

_____

_____

Step 3   Using the following table, list the components that operate in each of the four functional categories. Try to include as many components as you can; you might take a peek at some of the later chapters in the textbook to see if you can add any other components. Think about how each of the components contributes to the overall workings of the PC, and include as much detail about the component as possible.

Input	Processing	Output	Storage

Step 4   If you completed the table right here in the lab book, you can review it later while finishing the rest of the lessons. If you made a table in your notebook or created an electronic version, make sure you keep it nearby. As you work on later chapters, you'll want to update the table with additional components and extra details. The information in the table (and in your head) will expand as you develop a better understanding of how the components relate to the PC's "big picture."

 30 MINUTES

Lab Exercise 3.02: Examining User-Accessible Components

It's been one of those days. You walked into what should have been a simple job interview only to meet a very frantic IT manager dealing with a crisis of epic proportions. She doesn't even bother to interview you. Instead, she shuttles you out of her office, points down the hall, and says, "Go check Jane's PC—fourth cubicle on the left. Her PC's locked up and rebooting itself! I told her to turn it off until you get there. Don't change anything, and don't open it up. Find out if it will shut down, boot properly, and access the drives." Then the IT manager leaves to deal with her crisis, and you're on the spot.

This exercise looks at the many PC components that you can access without removing the case. Scanning the outside of your PC can help you track down any basic issues. Take your time, and jot down notes when you feel the need. Practice each step until you're confident you can do it on the job as a PC tech.

Learning Objectives

In this lab exercise, you will locate and describe the various user controls and built-in user-accessible devices of a PC system. You *will not* be opening the system case during this lab.

At the end of this lab, you'll be able to

- Recognize and manipulate user controls

- Describe the use of built-in user-accessible devices

Lab Materials and Setup

The materials you need for this lab are

- One fully functioning desktop computer system unit, with monitor

- A working *optical drive* (any drive that reads or records CD, DVD, or Blu-ray Discs)

- One readable data CD with files

- One keyboard

- One mouse

- A paper clip

Getting Down to Business

As a technician, you need to know how everything works on a PC. Let's start with the externally accessible functions. Make sure the computer is turned off.

Step 1   Before you can do much work with a PC, you need a functioning output device, such as a monitor. Check the monitor to see if it has power. If the monitor is not on, find the power button on the monitor and press it. You'll notice a small *light-emitting diode* (LED) on or near the monitor's power button. Record the color of the LED when the PC is turned off.

Color of the LED when the system is off: _____

Later in this exercise, we'll check the color of the LED when the PC is turned on. Stay tuned!

Step 2   Look at the front of your system unit. Locate the power button. Compare your button to the one shown in Figure 3-1.

Figure 3-1 Recognizing the power and reset buttons on the front of a PC.

Once you have located the power button on your system, make a note of its appearance. Is it in plain sight, or hidden behind a door or lid? Is it round, square, or some odd shape? Pressing the power button to start a PC when the electricity is off is known as a *cold boot* or sometimes a *hard boot*. Many systems also have a reset button, which you can use to restart a PC that is already on. This is also called a *warm boot*.

Describe your power and reset buttons here:

_____

_____

Sometimes software will lock up your system, in which case the only way to shut the system down is to force a *power down*. This requires that you press and hold the power button for four to six seconds.

Notice the two LEDs on the front panel near the power button. These LEDs will become important later in this exercise.

✔ **Hint**

Most systems have a power switch located on the back of the case that controls the flow of electricity to the power supply, and a power button on the front that boots and shuts down the PC.

Step 3   Locate the floppy drive. You can recognize it by its 3½-inch horizontal slot. How many visible 3½-inch slots does your PC have?

a.   _____

Do you see the eject button below the slot on the right side of the drive? Below the slot on the left side is an LED that lights up when the drive is actively reading or writing information on a floppy diskette.

✔ **Hint**

Because floppy disks can store only a relatively tiny amount of data, floppy drives are disappearing from PCs. In fact, most new computer systems ship without floppy drives. As a computer tech, however, you will most likely still have to deal with floppy drives for a few more years. If your system doesn't have a floppy drive, you may want to explore an older machine to see one in action. Just remember to clear the dust and cobwebs out of the way first.

On the front of your system, you should also see the external face of your system's optical drive. It fits comfortably inside an available 5¼-inch slot (or drive bay). How many 5¼-inch drive bays does your PC have?

b.   _____

You'll see either the front edge of the tray that opens to accept an optical disc, or a small door that protects the tray when it's retracted. Once you've located this drive, notice that it also has a button in the lower-right corner. When the system is on, you can press that button to open the tray door (if there is one) and slide the tray out to receive your disc (see Figure 3-2). Pressing the button while the tray is out retracts the tray so that the drive can read the disc.

Don't be tempted to force the disc tray to close by pushing it in. Always press the button on the front of the drive to close the tray or to eject a disc. Forcing the tray to close can cause the gears inside to become misaligned, so that the tray no longer closes properly.

Your system may have other devices installed, such as a USB flash drive, a tape drive, a Blu-ray Disc drive, or a Secure Digital (SD) memory card slot. Each of these uses removable media; take care when inserting or removing the media.

→ **Note**

With USB flash drives—or *thumb drives*, as they're often called—the drive *is* the removable media.

Figure 3-2 Can you locate the floppy drive and optical drive on this system unit?

Step 4   Now it's time to prepare your system for the scenario outlined in the opening text.

Earlier, this exercise mentioned many different kinds of LEDs. It referred to the monitor and floppy drive LEDs, as well as to the two LEDs next to your power button. Now, let's watch them in action. Turn on your PC.

a.   Color of monitor LED: _____

b.   Color of floppy drive LED: _____

c.   What is the status of the green LED next to the power button? Is it steady, flashing, or intermittent?

_____

d.   What is the status of the red (or amber) LED next to the power button? Is it steady, flashing, or intermittent?

_____

→   **Note**

The power LED generally lights up green to indicate that the power is on, and the hard drive LED lights up red when the internal hard drive is active.

e.   Press the eject button on the front of the optical drive. When the tray opens, carefully insert a disc. Press the eject button again to close the tray. If you haven't done this a lot, practice inserting and removing a disc until you feel comfortable with the process. When the optical drive closes, what is the status of its LED? Is it steady, flashing, or intermittent?

_____

✖ Warning

Don't start any applications yet! Close any open applications or open windows before performing Step 5. You're going to force a "power down," and you do not want to damage any of the software or data.

Step 5   Now you're going to simulate a PC that has become nonresponsive and "locked up." Perform a forced power down as follows:

a.   Press *and hold* the power button.

b.   While continuing to hold the power button in, count out loud (one–one thousand, two–one thousand, three–one thousand...) until the system powers down and the screen goes blank.

   According to your count, how many seconds did it take for the screen to go blank?

_____

Step 6   After the system has been powered down for approximately one minute, do the following:

a.   Press the power button and allow the system to boot.

b.   Log on in a normal fashion so that you are viewing the operating system desktop.

c.   Select Start | My Computer or Computer and double-click the icon that represents the optical drive. This should enable you to view the contents of the disc that was inserted prior to the forced power down.

   List some of the contents of the disc:

_____

_____

_____

d.   Select Start | Shut Down. If you're using Windows Vista or 7, it goes straight to a shutdown routine. Windows XP opens the Shut Down Windows dialog box, in which you select Shut Down from the drop-down list. This performs a graceful shutdown of the system.

✔ Hint

If all the actions in Step 6 were successful, the system likely is stable and you can report to the IT manager that Jane's machine is back up and running. If any of the actions failed, you should select Start | Restart in Windows Vista/7 or Start | Shut Down in Windows XP. In the Shut Down Windows dialog box, select Restart from the drop-down list. After the system reboots, complete substeps b, c, and d once more. Sometimes, the forced power down leaves some of the files in a state of flux; restarting shuts the computer down "gracefully," properly closing all open files before powering down. This should clear everything up and enable the computer to function properly.

Step 7   While the computer is turned off, take a paper clip and straighten it out, giving yourself a small handle to hold. Find the small hole on the front of your optical drive and insert the end of your paper clip. What happens?

---

 30 MINUTES

Lab Exercise 3.03: Recognizing External Connections

Just as you finish working with Jane's PC, her intercom buzzes. It's the head of IT, and she has a new assignment for you: The new satellite office in Albuquerque has received a delivery of new PCs, but the machines are all in boxes and none of the salespeople there knows a mouse from a monkey wrench. Your job is to call him up and walk him through the process of connecting a PC, describing each cable and connector, and explaining how they connect to the PC.

Learning Objectives

In this lab, you will identify, describe, and explain the function of the external connections on a standard PC.

At the end of this lab, you will be able to

- Identify the external connectors on a PC and the related cables

- Explain the function of each external connection

Lab Materials and Setup

The materials you need for this lab are

- At least one fully functioning PC that's less than two years old (two or more systems is ideal, with one older than and one newer than two years old)

✔ **Cross-Reference**

Before you begin this lab, read the sections "External Connections" and "Devices and Their Connectors" in Chapter 3 of *Mike Meyers' CompTIA A+ Guide to 801: Managing and Troubleshooting PCs*.

Getting Down to Business

Now it's time to learn about all the external things that can be attached to a PC. This lab exercise steps you through identifying and understanding the function of the various connectors.

✖ **Warning**

Shut off the power to your system and *unplug your PC* from the wall socket before you start the following exercise.

Step 1 Look at all those wires coming from the back of your PC! There's a power cable, a telephone or network cable, a keyboard cable, a mouse cable, and maybe a few others, depending on your system. Looking at the back of my current system (the one I'm using to write this manual), I count 15 cables coming out the back. Yowza!

The great thing about PCs is that it's difficult to connect the cables incorrectly. Each one has a unique connector; some are male (connectors with pins), and some are female (connectors with holes). Each connector has a particular shape and a specific number of pins or holes that match those of a specific device connected to the system unit.

✔ **Hint**

Cables have conductors. A *conductor* is a wire that can carry electrical signals. You may see a cable described by the number of conductors it has; for example, a telephone cable can be a two- or four-conductor cable. A power cable is a three-conductor cable. A network cable is an eight-conductor cable.

Step 2 Unplug each of your PC's cables one at a time and practice plugging them back in until you get a feel for how each fits. You should not have to force any of the cables, though they may be firm. How is each cable held in place and prevented from coming loose? Is there a screw, clip, or some other fastener that holds the cable connector tight to the system? Is the connector keyed? What does it connect to? What is the shape of the connector on each end? Is it round, rectangular, D-shaped? How many pins or holes does it have? How many rows of pins or holes?

Step 3 Is it possible to plug any cable into the wrong connector? If so, which one(s)? What do you think would happen if you plugged something into the wrong connector?

_____

_____

Step 4 Disconnect the following cables from the back of your PC and record some information about each in the following table. Keep in mind that the table was created for average PCs. I threw in three additional blank spaces for any custom devices in your system. If you don't have a particular connector, don't feel bad. Just write "N/A."

	Number of Conductors/Pins	Cable Gender	Name of the Port	Port Gender	Port Color
Mouse					
Keyboard					
Monitor					
Printer					
Network					
Modem/phone					
Speaker					
Power					

Once you complete this table, know it, live it, and love it. Every great technician should be able to identify these connectors at a glance.

Step 5 If you're working with someone else, play "Flash Cords." Have your partner hold up various cables, and try to guess what they connect to by looking at the connectors on the ends. Then switch roles and quiz your partner. Another really good way to learn the connector names is to have your partner sit behind the computer, while you reach around from the front, feel the various ports with your fingers, and call them out by name. Switch back and forth with each other until you both can easily identify all the ports by touch.

Step 6   Properly reconnect all the cables that you removed and prepare to turn on the system. If you have an On/Off button on the back of the system, be sure it is set to the On position. Make sure the monitor is turned on as well.

Step 7   Identify the connectors pictured next. What is the name of each connector and what does it connect to?

A. _____

B. _____

C. _____

D. _____

E. _____

F. _____

G. _____

H. _____

I. _____

Use the following list of connector names to correctly identify the ports. You will not use every name listed.

PS/2	Parallel	USB	Serial	FireWire	eSATA
RJ-45	RJ-11	1/8-inch audio	DVI	VGA	S/PDIF

Lab Analysis Test

1. Joe has just moved his PC to his new office. After hooking up all the cables, he turns on the system, and when it asks for his password, the keyboard will not respond. What could possibly be wrong?

2. Theresa has just finished the production of a PowerPoint presentation detailing the design of a new office building. She has included some cool 3-D animations in the presentation to show off the design. When she attempts to save the presentation to a floppy disk, an error occurs. What might have caused the error? Do you have any suggestions that may solve the problem?

3. Cal has purchased a new set of speakers for his PC. The old ones worked just fine, but he wanted more power and a subwoofer. When he plugged in the new speakers, they would not work. Power is on to the speakers. What is the first thing you would check?

4. John had a new modem installed in his computer at a local computer shop where he watched as the system successfully connected to his AOL account. When he got home and tried, however, he couldn't get a dial tone. He calls you to ask for help. What should you suggest that he check first?

5. Audrey has just returned to her desk after taking a break. She was only gone a few minutes, so she kept her PC on. Now the monitor is blank and the monitor LED is blinking a different color than usual. What might have happened?

Key Term Quiz

Use the following terms to complete the following sentences. Not all of the terms will be used.

cold boot

data cable

female connector

FireWire

hard boot

light-emitting diode (LED)

male connector

optical drive

parallel port

power cable

power down

thumb drive

USB flash drive

1. Before USB was a common connector standard, printers used the _____ to connect to PCs.

2. A(n) _____ is a visible indicator to tell you that your PC is on or that your hard drive is active.

3. Remember to use the eject button on your _____ when closing the tray so you don't damage anything.

4. A USB flash drive (also known as a(n) _____) is a form of removable storage that plugs directly into a USB port.

5. When the computer is off, pressing the power button begins a(n) _____ (also known as a(n) _____).

Chapter 4
Visible Networks

Lab Exercises

There's no doubt about it—a PC technician *will* have networking issues to work through at some point. Whether it's a three-computer, home-based local area network (LAN), a public Wi-Fi access point, a large company with thousands of connected devices, or the Web itself, networks have become as common as PCs. The main consideration is no longer whether you're going to network your computers—it's now what method you're going to use to network your computers.

A competent PC technician is called upon to be a network guru, answering connectivity questions and making recommendations on the best price/performance considerations for homes and businesses. This happens frequently, especially in smaller companies that can't afford to hire multiple people to support both the network *and* the PCs. The CompTIA A+ 220-801 exam reflects these changing roles of the PC technician and include many questions related to computer networking.

In this chapter's lab exercises, you'll imagine that you've been hired to work for a small company that has made the decision to upgrade the network in their office. You'll need to have a working understanding of network hardware and network operating system issues.

 30 MINUTES

Lab Exercise 4.01: Understanding Network Topologies

Networks don't spontaneously come into being—they must be designed and laid out. Choosing the proper layout, or *topology*, is an important decision because each topology has its own advantages and disadvantages. Knowing how a network is put together and organized is an important part of setting one up.

Learning Objectives

In this lab, you'll learn about network topologies.

At the end of this lab, you'll be able to

- Identify different network topologies
- Understand the benefits and drawbacks of each topology

Lab Materials and Setup

The materials you need for this lab are

- A group of four people

- Any small object

Getting Down to Business

This is a group activity that works best in a classroom. If you are working alone or want more practice, you can achieve the same goals with a few more objects—instead of people, use cups or bowls to represent each device and a ball to represent the data going back and forth. For each demonstration, keep in mind the real-world components that would be involved. How many cables would it use? What special devices do you need? What if a component was broken?

Step 1   First, you'll look at the star topology. A star topology has multiple computers connecting to a single, central wiring point (a switch). This is probably the one you are most familiar with, since most home networks are set up this way.

Have your group stand up and form a circle. Designate someone to stand in the middle and be the "switch." Someone else should then begin by taking an object (the data) and passing it to the switch. The switch then passes the object to someone else, who must first pass it back to the switch before it can move anywhere else—remember that the object cannot pass directly from one computer to the next. It must first move through the switch.

Write down your observations about this topology, including its advantages and disadvantages.

_____

_____

_____

_____

Step 2   Next, you'll look at the ring topology. In this topology, each device attaches to a central ring of cable to form a network. Have your group stand in a circle again. Begin passing the object clockwise around the circle. Remember that it cannot skip any person in the circle, nor can it cross to the other side.

Now have one person leave the circle, breaking the chain. The object cannot pass to the next person if the circle is broken, so the network becomes nonfunctional.

Write down your observations about this topology, including its advantages and disadvantages.

_____

_____

_____

_____

Step 3   Now you'll look at a bus topology, where each device attaches to a single network cable. Instead of a circle, stand in a line with everyone facing the same direction. Have each person pass the object to the next person in the line, and when the object reaches the last person, pass the object back in the other direction.

Have one person step out of the line. The object cannot skip that person's place, so the object now has to bounce back and forth between the people on one side of the missing person.

Write down your observations about this topology, including its advantages and disadvantages.

_____

_____

_____

_____

Step 4   Finally, you'll look at a mesh topology. This topology connects every computer to every other computer, without the use of a bus or switch. Have everyone in the group stand in a circle again, and now pass the object to whomever you wish. Continue to do so, feeling free to pass it to the person next to you or across from you.

Write down your observations about this topology, including its advantages and disadvantages.

_____

_____

_____

_____

 30 MINUTES

Lab Exercise 4.02: Identifying Local Area Network Hardware

Your boss has decided to upgrade the network in your office, which is about five years old. With the changes in networking technology, he wants your ideas about purchasing the right equipment for the upgrade. Your company is a small one, so the task is quite doable, but you need to make sure you know what you're talking about before you give your report.

Learning Objectives

In this lab, you'll familiarize yourself with networking hardware.

At the end of this lab, you'll be able to

- Identify different kinds of network cabling

- Identify different network interface cards (NICs)

- Identify different types of network hubs and switches

- Identify different wireless networking devices

Lab Materials and Setup

The materials you need for this lab are

- Access to a PC running Windows

- Access to a working LAN and the Internet (you may have demonstration devices provided by your instructor)

Getting Down to Business

One of the best ways to find out what a network is made of is to physically look at all of its pieces. Even then, however, it may be necessary to access a manufacturer's Web site to see, for instance, if the "hub" you're using is really a hub or a switch.

Step 1   If you have access to a LAN (the classroom computer lab network, a friend's home network, or your company's network), spend some time exploring the physical hardware connections and devices. If possible, acquire the diagram of the physical layout of the network, or create a simple diagram of the layout to familiarize yourself with the various devices and connections associated with the network you're analyzing.

✖ Warning

Don't disconnect anything, and be careful while probing around. One small mistake, like removing a cable or turning off the wrong device, can disrupt the entire network. If you're using the classroom network, ask the instructor what you can and can't remove while you make closer inspections of the cables and devices.

✔ Cross-Reference

Be sure to check out Chapter 4 of *Mike Meyers' CompTIA A+ Guide to 801: Managing and Troubleshooting PCs* for help identifying network cables and connectors. It's a good idea to have the textbook handy while you progress through this lab.

What sort of cabling does the network use, or is it wireless? Is it twisted-pair cable or older coaxial cable? Are the cable ends RJ-45 connectors? Describe the physical layout of the LAN here.

_____

_____

_____

What sort of NICs do the machines have? Describe the back of the card. Does it have a single connector or a combination of connectors (see Figure 4-1)? Does it have an antenna? Is there a link and/or activity LED? Which of the LEDs is on steady? Which is flashing? Describe the NIC here.

_____

_____

_____

✔ Hint

It is very important to understand the difference between the link light and the activity light. First, these "lights" are really light-emitting diodes (LEDs) and will usually appear in some form of yellow, orange, or green color, depending on the NIC manufacturer. Second, the link light indicates that the NIC and the cable have a valid electrical connection between the PC and the network device, usually a switch. This does not guarantee connectivity—it just means that the electrical connection is intact. The activity light is a better indicator of whether or not the NIC, cable, and hubs or switches are working. When the activity light blinks, it is indicating that data is being transferred between the networking devices. It does not guarantee that the data is usable—it just means that data is making the trip from the NIC to the hub or switch, or from the hub or switch to the NIC. If you are having trouble connecting to a network or communicating to other machines on the network, the link and activity lights are a good place to start your troubleshooting.

Step 2 Switches (and hubs, to an extent) are a part of the majority of networks. (Remember that modern networks almost exclusively use switches.)

Are the PCs connected with a single cable (crossover cable limited to two PCs), or are they connected to a hub/switch (see Figure 4-2)? Is part of the network wireless? What is the model number

FIGURE 4-1 A network interface card (NIC)

FIGURE 4-2 A LAN hub with multiple cables/devices attached

of the network hub/switch? Who manufactures the hub/switch? How many devices can be attached? Record your findings here.

_____

_____

_____

Is the hub or switch a standard single-speed (10BaseT, for instance) device, or can it handle multiple speeds (10/100/1000 Mbps)? Does it have wireless capabilities? Record your findings here. If this information isn't apparent or printed on the device, ask the instructor or the network administrator.

_____

_____

_____

Step 3   Are you going to have a wireless network or wireless devices in your network? Do you plan on installing a wireless network sometime in the near future? In the current world of networking, the terms _hub_, _switch_, and _router_ are often used interchangeably, but they really are very different devices with very different functions. Conduct an Internet search on the definition of each device.

Compare and contrast each type of device. How do they achieve their functionality? Where or for what purpose does it makes sense to use each device?

Hub _____

_____

Switch _____

_____

Router _____

_____

Lab Analysis Test

1. Jodie wants her Windows 7 computer to join a domain. How does she accomplish this?

2. Sam is having a difficult time describing the difference between a switch and a router to a customer. Help him describe the difference between the two devices.

3. You have six computers that need to be networked. Take a moment to draw out how the six computers would look arranged in the four different topologies.

Key Term Quiz

Use the following terms to complete the following sentences. Not all terms will be used.

bus

client

hub

LED

MAC

mesh

NIC

protocol

ring

RJ-45

router

server

star

switch

topology

1. A(n) _____ can effectively place a device on its own collision domain, thereby increasing network bandwidth.

2. A(n) _____ topology is where all the nodes are connected to a central device.

3. Twisted-pair network cabling uses a(n) _____ connector.

4. A set of rules that governs communication on a network is known as a(n) _____.

5. A(n) _____ is a device or computer that requests data from a _____, which holds all of the information.

Chapter 5

Microprocessors

Lab Exercises

Many PC users can perform simple installation and upgrade tasks, such as adding RAM or installing a new sound card. When it comes to the more complicated tasks, however, such as installing or replacing a central processing unit (CPU), wise users turn to the experts—this means you!

As a tech, you will install plenty of CPUs. Whether you're building a new system from scratch or replacing the CPU on an existing computer, it's your job to know the important characteristics of the CPU, match the CPU to compatible motherboards, and confirm that the CPU in the PC is running properly.

In this set of lab exercises, you'll identify current CPU types, form factors, and sockets. You'll then explore the specifications of the microprocessor with a freeware program known as CPU-Z. Finally, you'll learn how to remove and install a CPU.

It's time to find your anti-static wrist strap and get started with your exploration of CPUs!

 30 MINUTES

Lab Exercise 5.01: Identifying CPU Characteristics

There you are, innocently strolling down the hall at work, following the smell of freshly brewed coffee, when you're ambushed by Joe the accountant, brandishing a CPU/fan unit. He wants to replace the CPU in his machine with this new one he bought on eBay, and he wants you to help him. When you're the resident computer tech geek, your coworkers will expect you to be able to deal competently with a situation like Joe's.

Staying on top of the many developments in CPU technology can be challenging, but it's also a necessary part of your job as a PC technician. By this point, you know that you can't just plug any CPU into any motherboard and expect it to work—you have to match the right CPU to the right motherboard. To accomplish this, you need to identify important CPU characteristics such as form factor, clock speed, and bus speed, as well as things like voltage settings, clock multiplier configurations, and cooling requirements.

Learning Objectives

In this lab, you'll practice identifying CPUs and CPU fan components.

At the end of this lab, you'll be able to

- Recognize the different kinds of CPUs

- Recognize different CPU fan attachments

- Identify the basic specifications of different classes of CPUs

Lab Materials and Setup

The materials you need for this lab are

- A notepad and pencil to document the specifications

- Optional: Access to a working computer with a word processing or spreadsheet application installed and access to the Internet, to facilitate research and documentation of the CPU specifications

Getting Down to Business

In the following steps, you'll review your knowledge of CPU specifications, and then examine the CPU and fan attachment on a PC.

✔ **Cross-Reference**

Use Chapter 5 of *Mike Meyers' CompTIA A+ Guide to 801: Managing and Troubleshooting PCs* to help fill in the specifications for each CPU in the following charts.

Step 1 A good tech not only will learn the specifications of different CPU chips, but also will master the use of reference tools such as the Internet, manufacturers' Web sites, product documentation, and reference books. A quick search of the Web or your motherboard manual will generally yield a full list of specs for a given CPU.

See how many CPU chip features you can fill in given the maker and CPU type:

➜ **Note**

CPUs have very short production lives. If some of these CPUs have become obsolete, use the extra rows provided to add more modern processors to the assignment.

Maker	CPU Type	Package	Clock Speed (GHz)	Wattage Consumption	L2 Cache	L3 Cache	Number of Cores
Intel	Core 2 Quad Q9650						
AMD	Phenom II X3 710						
AMD	FX-8150						
Intel	Core i5-2500K						
AMD	Athlon X2 7550 Black Edition						
Intel	Pentium 4 650						
Intel	Core i7-3960X						

Maker	CPU Type	Package	Clock Speed (GHz)	Wattage Consumption	L2 Cache	L3 Cache	Number of Cores
AMD	A8-3850						
Intel	Core i7-960						

Step 2   Look at the CPUs pictured in Figure 5-1, making note of the differences you see. In particular, do the following:

    a.   Distinguish between pin grid array (PGA) and land grid array (LGA) packages by writing LGA or PGA on top of the processor's picture.

    b.   Circle the orientation guides in the corner of each CPU.

FIGURE 5-1 Exploring different CPUs

Step 3   Many users argue that Intel is better than AMD or vice versa. What do you think? Do some research and prepare a recommendation for selecting either an Intel processor or an AMD processor. Check multiple Web sites, read different articles online, and then write a short comparison/contrast essay on which CPU manufacturer you think is better. Be sure to cite your sources!

_____

_____

_____

_____

_____

_____

_____

_____

 30 MINUTES

Lab Exercise 5.02: Recognizing CPU Sockets

Now that you've identified Joe's purchase, you explain to him that you can't be sure it will work in his PC until you see his motherboard. CPU compatibility is determined by what the motherboard can support. Most motherboards enable you to upgrade the PC by replacing the existing CPU with a faster model of the same type. As a technician, your job is to make sure that the newer CPU has the same pin configuration as the motherboard. If you do not know where to begin, perform an online search for the maker of the motherboard. In many cases, you must replace the entire motherboard if you want to move up to a faster microprocessor.

Learning Objectives

In this lab, you'll identify various CPU sockets.

At the end of this lab, you'll be able to

- Recognize different kinds of CPU sockets

- Know which CPUs require which sockets

Lab Materials and Setup

The materials you need for this lab are

- A notepad and pencil to document the specifications

- Optional: Access to a working computer with a word processing or spreadsheet application installed and access to the Internet to facilitate research and documentation of the CPU socket specifications

This lab is more effective if you have access to different types of motherboards with different types of CPU sockets.

Getting Down to Business

In the following steps, you'll review your knowledge of CPU socket types.

Step 1   Identify the different socket types in Figure 5-2 by matching the letter with the corresponding socket name.

Socket 1366 _____   Socket AM2 _____

Socket AM3 _____   Socket 775 _____

Socket FM1 _____   Socket 1155 _____

Step 2   Draw a line connecting each CPU to its corresponding socket type. Choose the *best* match.

CPU	Socket Type
Intel Core i5-2500K	Socket 775
AMD Phenom II X3 710	Socket FM1
Intel Pentium 4 661	Socket AM2+
AMD A8-3850	Socket 1366
Intel Core i7-960	Socket AM3
AMD Athlon X2 7550 Black Edition	Socket 1155

FIGURE 5-2 Identifying sockets

Step 3   Using the Internet as your guide, find and list three processor models that fit in the following sockets.

Socket AM3:   _____

_____

_____

Socket 1155:   _____

_____

_____

_____

Step 4   Read the following statements and determine if each is true or false. (Assume that all of the motherboards have the appropriate BIOS flash update.) Circle T or F for each.

a.   Leonard can install his new Intel Core i7-2700K into his socket 1366 motherboard. (T/F)

b.   Rajesh just upgraded his socket AM2 processor to an AM3 processor but retained his socket AM2+ motherboard. After installing the processor and turning the PC on, everything worked fine. (T/F)

c.   Sheldon can upgrade his Pentium 4 631 to a Core 2 Duo 6600 without any issues. (T/F)

d.   Howard's Phenom II X6 1075T running on a socket AM3 motherboard just bit the dust because of an overheating issue. He wants to play *Star Wars: The Old Republic* with his friends, though. He'll have no problem throwing in a replacement Phenom X4 9600 into his machine. (T/F)

e.   Penny just purchased a used AMD Opteron 250 because she heard it was designed for very powerful server computers. She'll have no problem installing it on her socket FM1 motherboard. (T/F)

 30 MINUTES

Lab Exercise 5.03: Cooling Your CPU

Now that Joe has his processor, he needs to keep it cool, and since you've done everything else for him so far, you might as well make sure it's properly cooled, too! Someone new to the CPU cooling business might be tempted to think that CPUs come from the factory with a defined operating temperature. This isn't the case. The operating temperature depends tremendously on the way you cool the CPU. A far more reliable measurement is *power consumption*, the amount of power a CPU needs. CPU power consumption is measured in watts (W), with most desktop CPUs consuming in excess of 100 W. If you've ever tried to touch a 100-W light bulb, you can appreciate that this level of power consumption generates a tremendous amount of heat.

If this heat isn't taken away from the CPU by some form of cooling, the CPU will begin to overheat. If the CPU gets too hot, it will automatically shut itself down to prevent permanent damage. You need to provide Joe's CPU with some form of cooling device.

Learning Objectives

In this lab, you'll identify the strengths and weaknesses of three CPU cooling options: OEM fan assemblies, third-party fan assemblies, and liquid cooling.

At the end of this lab, you'll be able to

- Determine the cooling needs of your CPU

- Decide on which form of cooling to use for your needs

Lab Materials and Setup

The materials you need for this lab are

- Access to a working computer with Internet access

- A notepad and pencil to document the specifications

Getting Down to Business

The three most common types of CPU cooling are original equipment manufacturer (OEM) fans, third-party fans, and liquid cooling. Each of the following steps gives you an opportunity to investigate each of these options for a particular CPU.

Step 1   For the purposes of this exercise, pick out any single modern CPU as a sample CPU—you'll use this to find the proper cooling devices. Any CPU will work, but you'll find more options if you choose one that's readily available on popular online stores. If you're not sure which online store to use, check out www.newegg.com.

Individual CPUs are most commonly sold in what's known as a "retail box." This includes both the CPU and an OEM fan assembly.

Step 2   Many different types of fan assemblies can be attached to CPUs in many different ways. Describe the characteristics of the types of fans shown in Figure 5-3.

a. _____

b. _____

c. _____

A

B

C

Figure 5-3 Comparing different CPU fans

Step 3   Look online for third-party fan assembly solutions for the CPU you've chosen. Look for the following popular brand names and see what third-party fans each of these manufacturers offers for your CPU:

Antec, Arctic Cooling, Cooler Master, Thermaltake, Zalman

Document the name, model number, and price for one of them and list some of the benefits it offers:

Manufacturer _____

Model Number _____

Price _____

Benefits _____

Step 4   Do some research on liquid cooling. What equipment would you need to liquid-cool your PC? (Water doesn't count!)

_____

_____

Why would anyone want to use liquid cooling?

_____

_____

Step 5   Using the same manufacturers listed in Step 3, try to find liquid-cooling options for your chosen CPU. Most liquid-cooling options are either bolt-on (they can be added to an existing case) or case-integrated (they are built into a system case).

Manufacturer _____

Model Number _____

Price _____

Bolt-on or case-integrated? _____

30 MINUTES

Lab Exercise 5.04: Exploring CPU Specifications with CPU-Z

Joe is very impressed with your knowledge and expertise—and he's relieved that the CPU he purchased on eBay happened to work out. You explain that not only did it work out, but he has really improved the performance of his system with the upgraded CPU. In fact, to further display the characteristics of the CPU Joe has just purchased, you download and run a utility known as CPU-Z from www.cpuid.com. This utility reads the specifications of different PC components from information embedded in those components. You launch the utility to display the parameters of the new CPU for Joe.

Learning Objectives

In this lab, you'll identify various CPU specifications.

At the end of this lab, you'll be able to

- Run the CPU-Z utility

- Recognize key characteristics of CPUs

Lab Materials and Setup

The materials you need for this lab are

- Access to a working computer with Internet access to facilitate downloading and running the CPU-Z utility

- A notepad and pencil to document the specifications

- Optional: A word processor or spreadsheet application to facilitate the documentation

This lab is more informative if you have access to different types of systems with different classifications of CPUs.

Getting Down to Business

In the following steps, you'll download a reference utility known as CPU-Z and use it to further explore the characteristics of the CPU.

Step 1   Log on to a computer with Internet access and point your browser to the following Web site: www.cpuid.com. Follow the directions to download the current version of CPU-Z (the current version at this writing is 1.60). Unzip the file and launch CPU-Z.

Step 2   The CPU-Z utility displays a number of tabs across the top of the window (see Figure 5-4). At this time, you are only concerned with the CPU and Caches tabs.

Using the data gathered by CPU-Z, record some of the pertinent information here:

Name _____

Code Name _____

Package _____

Core Speed _____

Multiplier _____

Bus Speed _____

L2 Cache _____

L3 Cache _____

➔ **Note**

The code name is used by the manufactures to refer to different revisions of a chip. For instance, the Core 2 Duo line of CPUs has three main revisions: Conroe, Allendale, and Wolfdale. Core 2 quad-core CPUs include Kentsfield and Yorkfield.

FIGURE 5-4 The CPU-Z utility

✔ Hint

> Because of variations in CPUs, chipsets, BIOS, and motherboards, CPU-Z may not be able to display all of the information about your CPU. In some cases, the information may actually be erroneous. The CPUID Web site has good documentation on some of the common incompatibilities.

Step 3 If possible, launch CPU-Z on various machines to compare the characteristics of different CPUs. Save the utility for use in future lab exercises.

  30 MINUTES

Lab Exercise 5.05: Removing and Installing a CPU

Luckily for Joe, his motherboard is compatible with his new CPU. Now he expects you to play your "computer expert" role and install the new CPU in his PC. As a PC tech, you must be comfortable with such basic tasks. In this exercise, you'll familiarize yourself with the procedure; using your disassembled PC, you'll practice removing and reinstalling the CPU and fan assembly.

Learning Objectives

In this lab, you'll practice removing and installing a CPU and CPU fan assembly.

At the end of this lab, you'll be able to

- Remove and install a CPU safely and correctly

- Remove and install a CPU fan assembly safely and correctly

Lab Materials and Setup

The materials you need for this lab are

- An anti-static mat, or other static-safe material on which to place the CPU following removal

- An anti-static wrist strap

- Thermal paste

- A small flat-head screwdriver

Getting Down to Business

Time to get your hands dirty! Removing and installing CPUs is one of the most nerve-wracking tasks that new PC techs undertake, but there's no need to panic. You'll be fine as long as you take the proper precautions to prevent ESD damage, and handle the CPU and fan assembly with care.

✖ Warning

Be careful not to touch any of the exposed metal contacts on either the CPU or the CPU socket.

Step 1   Open your PC's case. If you've never done this before, you might feel a little nervous. That's okay. As long as you don't go unplugging things at random and breaking off bits of the motherboard, you shouldn't have a problem.

Each PC case is built differently, so each will be opened in its own way. Some use screws, and others use latches. Almost all cases have a removable panel on one side that you'll need to take off. Refer to the documentation that came with your PC or case for more information.

How do you open your particular case?

_____

_____

Step 2   Find your motherboard, the largest circuit board in your PC. Everything else should be connected to it. Somewhere in that mess of cables, cards, and drives is your CPU.

Determine whether the process of reinstalling and removing the CPU and fan assembly will be easier with the motherboard on an anti-static mat or installed in its case. You may find that it is easier to work with the stubborn fan assembly clamp if the motherboard is secured in the case. The case may even have a removable motherboard tray to ease the installation process.

Step 3   In most cases, you'll have to remove the heat-sink and fan assembly before you can remove the CPU. (You may also need to unplug any cables in your way.) Screw-down fans are easier to remove than clip fans. Screw-down fans require only that you unscrew the securing hardware. Clip fans, found on many types of CPUs, require you to apply pressure on the clip to release it from the fan mount. Use a small slotted screwdriver to do this, as shown in Figure 5-5. Use caution when prying the clip open, and don't forget to unplug the CPU fan!

✔ Hint

You'll discover that releasing a fan clip takes way more force than you want to apply to anything so near a delicate CPU chip. Realizing this in advance, you can be sure to brace yourself and position the screwdriver carefully, to minimize the possibility of it slipping off and gouging something. Always use two hands when attempting this procedure.

Figure 5-5 Using a screwdriver to remove a clip-type CPU fan from its mount

The CPU and fan assembly will have thermal paste residue on the surfaces that were previously touching. You cannot reuse thermal paste, so you'll need to apply a fresh layer when you reinstall the CPU fan. Using a clean, lint-free cloth, carefully wipe the thermal paste residue from the CPU and fan assembly, and then place the fan assembly on an anti-static surface.

Step 4   Before proceeding, notice the CPU's orientation notches. All CPUs have some form of orientation notch (or notches). Remove the CPU. Start by moving the end of the zero insertion force (ZIF) lever a little outward to clear the safety latch; then raise the lever to a vertical position. Next, grasp the chip carefully by its edges and lift it straight up and out of the socket. Be careful not to lift the CPU at an angle—if it's a PGA CPU, you'll bend its tiny pins. LGA CPUs don't have pins, but you can damage the pins on the motherboard, so still be careful! As you lift out the CPU, make sure that the ZIF lever stays in an upright position. Record your socket type in the space provided.

Step 5   Now that you have the CPU chip out, examine it closely. The manufacturer usually prints the chip's brand and type directly on the chip, providing you with some important facts about the chip's design and performance capabilities. Note any markings that denote the processor manufacturer, model, speed, and so forth.

What is the CPU information printed on the chip package?

✖ Warning

Always handle a CPU chip like a fragile old photograph: very gently, holding it only by the edges. Make sure you take *complete* ESD avoidance precautions, because even a tiny amount of static electricity can harm a CPU!

Step 6   Reinsert the CPU with the correct orientation, lock down the ZIF lever, and reattach the fan. Now remove the fan assembly and the CPU again. Practice this a few times to become comfortable with the process. When you're finished practicing, reinsert the CPU for the last time. Be sure to apply a thin film of fresh thermal paste onto the square in the center of the top of the CPU before you place the fan. Now reattach the fan assembly. Don't forget to plug the fan back in!

Step 7   You may leave your CPU/fan assembly installed on the motherboard and place the motherboard on your anti-static mat. Optionally, if you reinstalled the motherboard in the case, you may leave it assembled.

Lab Analysis Test

1. James has an AMD Phenom CPU installed on his motherboard and has just bought a faster Intel Core i7 from an eBay auction. He asks you to install the new CPU. What is your first reaction?

2. Joanna called you to say that ever since you installed her new CPU, the PC experiences intermittent problems when it runs. Sometimes it just quits or freezes up. What could possibly be wrong?

3. Theresa has an LGA 775 motherboard with an Intel Core 2 Quad 2.83-GHz processor and would like to put in a faster CPU. Can she install an Intel Core i7 2.93-GHz processor? Why or why not?

4. Lindsey runs CPU-Z on her system and notices that the processor's core speed is 2191.2 and the displayed multiplier is ×22. What is the speed of the system clock in Lindsey machine? How would the industry display this system clock speed?

5. David has been reading the trade magazines and keeps seeing all the hype over "quad-core" processors. David decides, since he is a power gamer, that he will upgrade to a quad-core CPU to improve the performance of his system when playing his favorite game. Will a quad-core processor improve the performance in this scenario? Explain.

Key Term Quiz

Use the following terms to complete the following sentences. Not all terms will be used.

code name

CPU

fan assembly

land grid array (LGA)

multicore

package

pin grid array (PGA)

screw-down connector

water block

zero-insertion force (ZIF)

1. The Intel Core 2 Duo CPU uses a package known as a _____.

2. Both Intel and AMD have adopted the use of a _____ to distinguish among revisions of their CPUs.

3. You often need to remove the _____ to get to a system's CPU.

4. To remove a CPU, you'll need to disengage the _____ lever.

5. A _____ is placed directly over the CPU in a liquid-cooled system.

Chapter 6

RAM

Lab Exercises

One of the easiest and most cost-effective upgrades you can make to a PC is to add more memory. As such, you'll perform many RAM installations as a PC tech—get used to it.

RAM installation tasks include determining how much RAM the PC has installed, determining how much RAM the PC can support, determining what type of RAM it uses, and then physically installing the RAM on the motherboard. The following labs are designed to help you practice working with RAM by using visual recognition of the different types and packages and by walking you through the steps of installing RAM.

 15 MINUTES

Lab Exercise 6.01: Determining the Amount of RAM in a PC

While pummeling your fellow PC techs in *Team Fortress 2* over lunch, a coworker named Holly appears, clutching a stick of RAM she got from a guy on the fourth floor. She wants you to install it in her system. You tell her you have to check on some things first, including how much RAM her system can handle and how much it already has, before you can help her.

✔ **Hint**

High-end PCs usually come straight from the factory equipped with hefty amounts of RAM. Lower-cost PCs sometimes cut corners by skimping on RAM.

Before installing any RAM, you'll need to determine how much RAM is already installed in Holly's PC and then consult the motherboard book to determine how much RAM the system supports.

Learning Objectives

In this lab exercise, you'll use various methods to determine how much memory is currently installed in your system, and how much it is capable of holding.

At the end of this lab, you'll be able to

- Find RAM measurements
- Identify how much RAM is installed in a system
- Determine how much RAM a particular motherboard supports

Lab Materials and Setup

The materials you need for this lab are

- A working Windows PC

- A notepad

Getting Down to Business

There are several ways to determine how much RAM is installed in a PC. First, you can check the RAM count during the boot process (some newer machines hide the RAM count, even if it's enabled in the BIOS). This tells you how much RAM the system BIOS recognizes during its check of the system. Second, you can check the amount of RAM that Windows recognizes from within the OS. And third, you can remove the PC case cover and physically examine the RAM sticks installed on the motherboard.

Step 1   Turn on your PC, and watch the display as the system goes through its startup routine, otherwise known as a power-on self test (POST). Typically, the RAM count runs near the top-left side of the screen. Figure 6-1 shows an example of a typical RAM count.

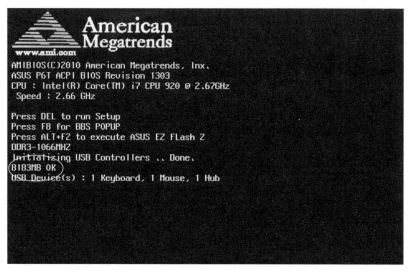

FIGURE 6-1 Viewing a typical RAM count during boot-up

Many systems run through the startup routine quickly, so the RAM count might appear on the screen for only a few seconds. Press the PAUSE/BREAK key to pause the boot process so you have time to write down the number accurately. When you want the boot process to resume, press the ENTER key.

What is the RAM count number displayed on your monitor? _____

✔ **Hint**

If you're starting the PC for the first time that day, the startup routine may run through the RAM count before the monitor has a chance to warm up. If this happens, just reboot the PC and try again.

Step 2   Use the following methods to determine the amount of RAM in a system from within any version of Windows.

   a.   In Windows XP, right-click the My Computer icon and select Properties to see the amount of RAM in your system. In Windows Vista and Windows 7, open the Start menu, right-click Computer, and select Properties. The RAM count is under the System area (see Figure 6-2). You can also see other useful information here, like the processor type, Windows edition, the product ID, and more.

Another way to see the amount of memory installed is to follow this procedure:

   b.   Click Start | All Programs | Accessories | System Tools | System Information. In the System Summary, look for a value called Installed Physical Memory (see Figure 6-3).

   c.   The amount of RAM will be listed in the displayed information.

How much memory is in your system? _____

Does this number agree with what you found in Step 1? _____

Does the amount of RAM shown during the startup routine and that reported by Windows match?

Entry-level PCs and laptops often have onboard display adapters (the display adapter is built into the motherboard). Manufacturers include little to no video RAM on the motherboard, so the display adapter must "steal" some portion of the system RAM to be able to handle today's intense graphic applications.

If the amounts do not add up, and you see a number such as 448 MB or 992 MB, then your system has probably allocated some of the system memory to handle your display adapter's needs.

FIGURE 6-2 Viewing the RAM count in Windows 7 via Computer

FIGURE 6-3 The System Information dialog box showing Installed Physical Memory

Step 3   We'll save the last method for determining how much RAM is installed (looking inside your PC) for the next exercise in this lab. For the moment, let's talk about how to determine the maximum amount of RAM a system can support.

The amount of RAM you can install on a modern system depends on the limitations of the motherboard hardware. All new CPUs are capable of 64-bit processing, so new chipsets support very large amounts of RAM. How much RAM does your motherboard support?

Neither the CMOS setup utility nor the OS can help you determine how much RAM a motherboard can handle. You can usually find this information in the system's motherboard book, if you have it, or on the PC maker's or motherboard manufacturer's Web site.

Examine the documentation that came with your PC, or visit the manufacturer's Web site, to determine how much RAM you can install on the system.

What is the maximum amount of RAM that your system can support?

_____

 30 MINUTES

Lab Exercise 6.02: Identifying Types of RAM

Once you determine how much RAM is installed on Holly's PC, and how much her motherboard can handle, you conclude that there's room for more. But, you explain to Holly, this doesn't mean you can add that RAM stick she got because not all RAM is the same. Having looked at the specs for her system, you know it takes 240-pin DDR2 SDRAM sticks. Holly thinks the stick she got is the right size, but you know it's 240-pin DDR3 RAM, so it won't fit. This is why they pay you the big bucks.

RAM comes in several standardized form factors, each compatible with specific types of systems. Modern desktop systems use full-sized dual inline memory modules (DIMMs) of various pin configurations (168, 184, and 240). Laptop computers use scaled-down sticks called small outline-DIMMs, or SO-DIMMs.

✔ **Cross-Reference**

For details on the various types of RAM found in modern systems, refer to the "DDR SDRAM," "DDR2," and "DDR3" sections in Chapter 6 of *Mike Meyers' CompTIA A+ Guide to 801: Managing and Troubleshooting PCs.*

The steps for identifying the different types of RAM are presented in this lab exercise.

Learning Objectives

In this lab, you'll examine and compare different RAM packages.

At the end of this lab, you'll be able to

- Recognize and differentiate between different kinds of RAM packages

Lab Materials and Setup

The materials you need for this lab are

- Demonstration units of various RAM packages (optional)

✔ Hint

It is helpful to examine the RAM configurations in multiple PCs if you have them available. Having a laptop with removable RAM is a plus.

Getting Down to Business

Let's do a quick review of the types of RAM packages you'll see in modern PCs. Then you'll check your PC or motherboard documentation to determine the type of RAM it uses.

All modern PCs use some form of DDR memory for their system RAM. As was discussed in the textbook, DDR stands for *double data rate*, which means that for every tick of the clock, two chunks of data are sent across the memory bus. This has the effect of giving you twice the performance without increasing the clock rate.

Step 1 Another performance trick modern systems use to increase memory speed is dual- and triple-channel architectures. This enables the memory controller to access more than one stick of RAM at a time, thus increasing performance. In effect, the 64-bit bus acts like a 128-bit bus (for dual channel) or a 192-bit bus (for triple channel). To use these multichannel architectures, you must install memory in identical pairs or triplets. Check your motherboard manual. Does your system support dual- or triple-channel memory?

_____

What colors represent the different channels?

_____

Step 2 There are many different types of RAM. It's important for you to be able to distinguish the difference between all of them by knowing what they physically look like and what their defining characteristics are. For each of the following descriptions, identify the type of RAM described by entering its name on the blank line preceding the definition.

    a. _____ This type of RAM comes in 168-pin packages. It uses two notches to help guide the installation of the module: one near the center, and the other near an end. It was the first type of DIMM technology commercially available for PCs and usually had a speed rating of PC100 or PC133.

    b. _____ The Rambus Corporation developed this type of RAM. It's usually found on a Pentium 4 motherboard. It is a proprietary stick of memory and uses 184 pins. It has two notches in it, both very near each other toward the middle of the stick.

If you are using a typical desktop system and it is relatively new (less than two years old), the motherboard will most likely support one of the following three types of RAM packages:

    c. _____ This type of RAM doubled the speed by transferring data on both the rising and falling edges of the clock cycle. It uses a 184-pin package and is completely incompatible with the memory developed by Rambus. This style has one notch in it.

    d. _____ Like its predecessor, it too transfers data on both the rising and falling edges of the clock cycle, but takes it one step further by doubling the clock speed twice. It uses a 240-pin package and has a single notch.

    e. _____ Well, if doubling the clock speed twice wasn't enough, this type of RAM doubles it three times. Not only is it extremely fast and, as of 2012, the predominant style of RAM, it also uses a 240-pin package. But don't let that fool you: it is completely incompatible with all other types of RAM. Not only is it different electronically, but the notch is in a different place.

Step 3 In your PC or motherboard documentation, or on the manufacturer's Web site, locate the section listing the type of RAM your system uses.

    a. What type of RAM does your system use? _____

    b. What speed of RAM does your system need? _____

Step 4 Open your system case and make note of the following:

    a. How many RAM slots does your motherboard have? _____

    b. How many RAM slots are filled with RAM sticks? _____

    c. Is your system set up to use single-channel, dual-channel, or triple-channel RAM? How could you find out?

    _____

30 MINUTES

Lab Exercise 6.03: Removing and Installing RAM

You've found a stick of RAM for Holly that works with her system, and now you have to install it.

Although RAM installation is one of the simpler PC hardware upgrades, it's still important that you follow the correct steps and take all appropriate safety precautions.

Learning Objectives

In this lab, you'll practice removing and installing RAM.

At the end of this lab, you'll be able to

- Remove RAM safely and correctly

- Install RAM safely and correctly

Lab Materials and Setup

The materials you need for this lab are

- An anti-static mat or other static-safe material on which to place the RAM

- An anti-static wrist strap

- A notepad

✔ **Hint**

If you're in a computer lab or you have access to multiple PCs, you should practice on a variety of systems.

Getting Down to Business

Removal and installation procedures vary depending on the type of RAM your system uses. DIMMs and RIMMs snap into the RAM slots vertically. The following steps describe the removal and installation procedures for DIMMs.

✖ **Warning**

Regardless of the type of RAM in your system, be certain to take measures to prevent ESD damage. Shut down and unplug the PC and place it on an anti-static mat. Strap on an anti-static bracelet and ground yourself. If necessary, remove any cables or components that block access to the system RAM before you begin.

Step 1   Open the PC case. Use whatever methods the case requires: some use screws, some use latches. Once the case is open, look for the RAM sticks on the motherboard. Locate the retention clips on either end of the RAM modules.

Step 2   Press outward on the clips to disengage them from the retention slots on the sides of the RAM sticks (see Figure 6-4).

Step 3   Press down on the clips firmly and evenly. The retention clips act as levers to lift the DIMM sticks up and slightly out of the RAM slots.

Step 4   Remove the DIMM sticks and place them on the anti-static mat, or in an anti-static bag.

Step 5   Make note of the following:

   a.   How many pins does the RAM have? _____

   b.   Where are the guide notches located? _____

   c.   What information is on the RAM's label? _____

Step 6   While you have your system RAM out, this is a good time to check the condition of the metal contacts on both the RAM sticks and the motherboard RAM sockets. Dirty contacts are fairly rare. If you see this problem, use contact cleaner, available at any electronics store.

   Are the contacts free of dirt and corrosion? _____

   After you've examined your system RAM and inspected the motherboard RAM sockets, reinstall the RAM as described next.

FIGURE 6-4 Removing a 184-pin DIMM (DDR SDRAM)

To install a DIMM or RIMM:

Step 1   Orient the DIMM or RIMM so that the guide notches on the RAM module match up to the guide ridges on the RAM socket.

Step 2   Press the RAM stick firmly and evenly straight down into the socket until the retention clips engage the retention notches on the ends of the RAM stick.

Step 3   Snap the retention clips firmly into place.

Step 4   Repeat these steps to install other RAM modules as appropriate. If you're using RIMM RAM, don't forget to install the continuity RIMM (CRIMM) sticks into any empty RAM slots.

To finish a RAM installation professionally, specifically if you are on a production-level machine, follow these steps:

Step 1   Once the system RAM is in place, reattach any cables that you may have had to move, and plug in the system power cable. Do not reinstall the PC case cover until after you've confirmed that RAM installation was successful.

Step 2   Boot the system and watch the RAM count to confirm that you correctly installed the RAM.

✔ **Hint**

If the system has any problems when you reboot, remember that you must turn off the power and unplug the computer again before reseating the RAM.

 30 MINUTES

Lab Exercise 6.04: Exploring RAM Specifications with CPU-Z

Now that you have Holly's system up and running with double the memory it had before, you can take a moment to analyze the memory. You've already downloaded the utility CPU-Z from the Internet in Lab Exercise 5.04; now you'll need to launch CPU-Z and examine the information on the Memory and SPD tabs.

Learning Objectives

In this lab, you'll identify various RAM specifications.

At the end of this lab, you'll be able to

- Recognize key characteristics of RAM

Lab Materials and Setup

The materials you need for this lab are

- Access to a working computer with the utility CPU-Z installed

- A notepad and pencil to document the specifications

This lab is more informative if you have access to different types of systems with different types of RAM.

Getting Down to Business

In the following steps, you'll explore the different characteristics of RAM.

Step 1   Launch the CPU-Z application.

Step 2   Navigate to the Memory tab. The CPU-Z utility displays the current statistics of the RAM installed, as shown in Figure 6-5.

Figure 6-5 CPU-Z showing RAM information

Using the data gathered by CPU-Z, record the following information:

Type _____

Size _____

CAS# Latency (CL) _____

RAS# to CAS# Delay (tRCD) _____

RAS# Precharge (tRP) _____

Step 3   Click the SPD tab in CPU-Z.

Step 4   The SPD tab, shown in Figure 6-6, lists a number of technical bits of information about a particular stick of RAM. This information is contained on every RAM stick in a chip called the serial presence detect (SPD) chip.

Using the data gathered by CPU-Z, record the following information for each of the system's RAM modules:

	Module 1	**Module 2**	**Module 3**	**Module 4**
Slot #				
Module size				
Maximum bandwidth				
Manufacturer				

FIGURE 6-6 CPU-Z showing SPD information

✔ **Cross-Reference**

To review how the SPD chip works with the system, refer to the "Serial Presence Detect (SPD)" section in Chapter 6 of *Mike Meyers' CompTIA A+ Guide to 801: Managing and Troubleshooting PCs*.

Step 5 If possible, launch CPU-Z on various machines to compare the characteristics of different types of RAM. Save the utility for use in future lab exercises.

→ **Try This: PC Wizard**

On a computer with Internet access, point your browser to the following Web site: www.cpuid.com. Follow the onscreen directions and download a copy of PC Wizard.

Extract the files into a folder and launch the PC Wizard application. Once PC Wizard is running, find and click the Mainboard icon in the Hardware area. This brings up a list of components in the right pane of the application window. Click the Physical Memory item and then browse through the information displayed in the lower portion of the window.

Using this information, can you determine the maximum size for individual RAM modules allowed on this system, and the maximum amount of total memory that it supports? Does this correspond to the information you found earlier in the PC or motherboard documentation?

Note that because of variations in chipsets, BIOS, and motherboards, PC Wizard may or may not provide detailed information on the RAM. In some cases, the information may actually be erroneous. The CPUID Web site has good documentation on some of the common incompatibilities.

Lab Analysis Test

1. Jarel wants to upgrade his memory and calls you for help. He knows that he's using DDR RAM and that his system clock is 133 MHz, but he isn't sure what type of DDR SDRAM sticks he should purchase. What DDR RAM would you recommend that he use?

2. Theresa's Windows XP Professional system has 512 MB of RAM. She adds another stick with 512 MB of RAM, but the RAM count still only shows 512 MB. What could be causing this?

3. John's system has 1 GB of PC4200 DDR2 SDRAM. He recently installed an additional 1 GB of DDR2 SDRAM that a coworker gave him. He tells you that his system now boots up correctly and shows the correct amount of RAM, but then it freezes after several minutes. He notes that if he removes the new RAM, the system runs fine. What could be a possible reason for this?

4. Kyle has a system that supports dual-channel architecture (there are two blue DIMM slots on the motherboard). The motherboard has space for three sticks of RAM, so Kyle installs three 2-GB RAM sticks. What will be the result?

5. Joe has recently purchased a pair of 1-GB DDR3 RAM sticks. He's replacing an older pair of DDR2 RAM but can't afford to replace the motherboard. Why won't this work?

Key Term Quiz

Use the following terms to complete the following sentences. Not all terms will be used.

168-pin DIMM

184-pin DIMM

240-pin DIMM

CRIMM

DDR RAM

DDR2 RAM

DDR3 RAM

DIMM

dual channel

megabytes (MB)

RIMM

SDRAM

SO-DIMM

SPD

1. Today's PCs use DDR3 RAM, which comes in a(n) _____ package.

2. A RAM module used in a laptop is called a(n) _____.

3. A component known as a(n) _____ chip provides additional information about an SDRAM module.

4. A stick of _____ looks a lot like a 168-pin DIMM, but it has 184 pins.

5. The technology that uses two sticks of RAM together to increase throughput is known as _____ architecture.

6. When purchasing _____, you must realize that it is not backward compatible with _____ and new hardware must be considered.

Chapter 7

BIOS

Lab Exercises

Basic input/output services (BIOS) provide the primary interface between the operating system's device drivers and most of its hardware. Although a modern BIOS is automated and tolerant of misconfiguration, a good PC technician must be comfortable with situations in which the BIOS may need some maintenance or repair.

A PC needs the BIOS to tell it how each basic component is supposed to communicate with the system. At the beginning of the PC revolution, many different manufacturers developed BIOS for PCs, but over the years the BIOS business has consolidated primarily to only two brands: AMI (American Megatrends, Inc.) and Phoenix Technologies (which absorbed the former third brand, Award Software). Both of these manufacturers provide a utility called the CMOS setup program (CMOS stands for *complementary metal-oxide semiconductor*, which is why everyone says "CMOS") that enables you to reconfigure BIOS settings for boot device order, amount of memory, hard disk drive configuration, and so on. Most of these configurations are automated, but as a PC tech, you're the one who people will call when "automatic" stops working!

As an example for the lab exercises in this chapter, suppose that the company you're working for is planning a mass upgrade from its current OS, Windows Vista, to Windows 7. You've tested the upgrade process on a few lab machines and have found that systems with an out-of-date BIOS are having problems upgrading successfully. In preparation for the Windows 7 installation, besides upgrading any older BIOS versions you find, you'll disable any BIOS-level antivirus functions. You're also aware that the prior IT manager did not use consistent CMOS passwords, so you may need to reset the passwords on a few machines.

The lab exercises in this chapter will teach you to identify, access, and configure system BIOS.

→ **Note**

> You might have heard about a replacement for BIOS called the Unified Extensible Firmware Interface (UEFI). Since 2010, the BIOS firmware of PCs started to be replaced by UEFI. Think of UEFI as a super-BIOS, doing the same job as BIOS, but in a 64-bit environment with a lot of added functionality. While UEFI was introduced years ago, you still won't find it on every PC. Because of this, plus the fact that most UEFI setup screens work just like their BIOS counterparts, this chapter only specifically covers BIOS. If you have a UEFI system, you should still be able to complete the lab exercises.

10 MINUTES

Lab Exercise 7.01: Identifying BIOS ROM

Having received your orders to do the big OS upgrade, your first task is to check the BIOS types and versions on every machine in your office, and then visit each BIOS maker's Web site to determine whether more recent versions are available.

The system BIOS is stored on nonvolatile memory called BIOS ROM. BIOS makers often (but not always) label their BIOS ROM chips prominently on the motherboard. In this exercise, you'll look at two different ways to identify your BIOS ROM chip.

✔ **Cross-Reference**

For details on the two big companies that manufacture BIOS on modern systems, refer to the "Modify CMOS: The Setup Program" section in Chapter 7 of *Mike Meyers' CompTIA A+ Guide to 801: Managing and Troubleshooting PCs*.

Learning Objectives

In this lab, you'll learn two ways to identify your BIOS.

At the end of this lab, you'll be able to

- Locate the BIOS ROM chip on the motherboard
- Identify the BIOS manufacturer
- Determine the BIOS creation date and version

Lab Materials and Setup

The materials you need for this lab are

- A working PC
- An anti-static mat
- A notepad

Getting Down to Business

The first thing you'll do is remove your PC case cover and locate the BIOS ROM chip. Next, you'll make note of the BIOS information displayed during system startup.

✖ Warning

Any time you take the cover off your PC, remember to follow all proper safety and ESD avoidance precautions.

Step 1   Remove the case from your PC and locate the system BIOS ROM chip. Some motherboards label their chip with the name of the BIOS manufacturer. Compare your system BIOS ROM chip to the one in Figure 7-1.

Read the manufacturer's label *if you can*, and answer the following questions:

Who made the BIOS? _____

What year was the BIOS written? _____

Are there any other numbers on the label? Record them. _____

Does it look like you could easily remove the system BIOS chip, or does it look soldered to the motherboard? _____

Step 2   Replace the PC case cover and start the system. Be sure the monitor is turned on. When the first data appears on the screen, press the PAUSE/BREAK key on the keyboard. This suspends further operation until you press ENTER. Newer systems actually have instructions somewhere on the screen that indicate which key or keys to press to get into boot options, CMOS setup, and so forth.

FIGURE 7-1 A typical system BIOS ROM chip

Figure 7-2 shows an example of what you may see. At the top of the screen is the BIOS manufacturer's name and version number. At the bottom of the screen is the date of manufacture and the product identification number.

Make note of the following information:

Who made the BIOS? _____

What version is the BIOS? _____

What year was the BIOS written? _____

✔ **Hint**

Not all BIOS display the same type of information. Some BIOS makers modify the BIOS to show nothing more than their logos during the boot process.

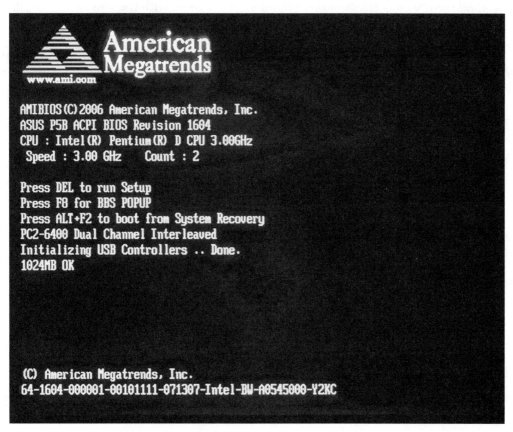

FIGURE 7-2 A typical boot screen

Step 3   Press ENTER on the keyboard to continue booting. Once the system is up and running, go online and find out whether a more recent version of the BIOS is available. Your first stop should be the PC maker's Web site. If it does not have this information available, try the motherboard manufacturer's Web site or the BIOS maker's Web site.

✖ **Warning**

Do *not* "flash" your system BIOS at this time!

 15 MINUTES

Lab Exercise 7.02: Accessing BIOS via the CMOS Setup Program

Once you've assessed the BIOS on each machine, but before you proceed with the Windows 7 installation, make sure the BIOS is properly configured using the special program for this purpose.

You don't access the hundreds of individual programs contained in the system BIOS directly, or from anywhere within the Windows OS. Instead, you use a utility that interfaces with the BIOS programs to enable you to reconfigure settings. This utility is the CMOS setup program.

Learning Objectives

In this lab, you'll go into CMOS and explore your BIOS configuration settings.

At the end of this lab, you'll be able to

- Enter the CMOS setup program
- Navigate the display screens of the system setup utility

Lab Materials and Setup

The materials you need for this lab are

- A working PC whose BIOS settings you have permission to change

Getting Down to Business

In the following steps, you'll reboot your PC and access the boot options or CMOS setup program. Each BIOS maker has its own special way to do this, so how you go about it depends on which BIOS your system has installed. Common methods include the following:

- Press DELETE during the boot process.
- Press F1, F2, F10, or F12 during the boot process.

- Press CTRL-ALT-INSERT during the boot process.

- Press CTRL-A during the boot process.

- Press CTRL-FI during the boot process.

There are four ways for you to determine which method works for your BIOS:

- Check your motherboard or PC documentation.

- Visit your motherboard or PC maker's Web site.

- Watch the screen display after booting your PC. Most BIOS direct you to press a specific key to enter CMOS.

- Use the trial-and-error method! Boot your system and go down the preceding list, trying each key or key combination until one works. You won't hurt anything if you get it wrong, but if you hold the wrong key down for too long, you may get a keyboard error message. If this happens, just reboot and try again.

Step 1   Determine which method you need to use to enter the CMOS setup program. Then reboot your system and use that method to enter CMOS. Which key or key combination did you use to enter your CMOS setup program?

_____

Step 2   Once you've entered the CMOS setup program, look at the screen and compare it to Figures 7-3 and 7-4. The Phoenix BIOS shown in Figure 7-3 opens up to an initial menu, whereas the Phoenix-Award BIOS in Figure 7-4 opens immediately into the Main screen. Although the screens for different CMOS setup programs may look different, they all contain basically the same functions.

```
        CMOS Setup Utility - Copyright (C) 1984-2009 Award Software
  ┌──────────────────────────────────────────────────────────────────┐
  │  ▶ MB Intelligent Tweaker(M.I.T.)    Load Fail-Safe Defaults       │
  │                                                                    │
  │  ▶ Standard CMOS Features            Load Optimized Defaults       │
  │                                                                    │
  │  ▶ Advanced BIOS Features            Set Supervisor Password       │
  │                                                                    │
  │  ▶ Advanced Chipset Features         Set User Password             │
  │                                                                    │
  │  ▶ Integrated Peripherals            Save & Exit Setup             │
  │                                                                    │
  │  ▶ Power Management Setup            Exit Without Saving           │
  │                                                                    │
  │  ▶ PC Health Status                                                │
  ├──────────────────────────────────────────────────────────────────┤
  │ Esc : Quit          ↑↓→←: Select Item      F11 : Save CMOS to BIOS │
  │ F8  : Q-Flash        F10 : Save & Exit Setup  F12 : Load CMOS from BIOS│
  ├──────────────────────────────────────────────────────────────────┤
  │              Change CPU's Clock & Voltage                          │
  └──────────────────────────────────────────────────────────────────┘
```

FIGURE 7-3 Award CMOS Main screen

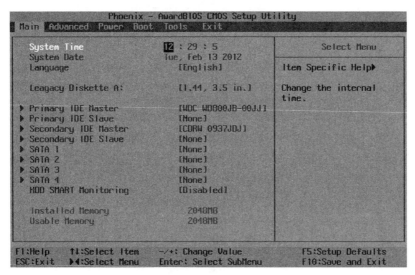

FIGURE 7-4 Phoenix-Award BIOS opening screen

✖ **Warning**

Do not make any changes in BIOS settings during this lab exercise. You'll make changes in the next two lab exercises.

The CMOS setup program controls the "changeable" BIOS settings. Many settings depend on what hardware you add to the system. The following are some sample entries on your system that you can change or update (there are more, the specifics of which depend on your BIOS):

- Date
- Time
- Hard drive configuration
- Boot sequence
- RAM
- Serial and parallel port assignments
- Enable/disable onboard controllers
- Enable/disable supervisor and user passwords

Step 3   Explore each screen and make notes about what each setting does. Navigation, like the method to enter the CMOS setup program, varies from maker to maker. Most programs are navigable by keyboard only, but some (AMI, for instance) support a mouse. Look at the bottom of the CMOS setup program screen to see how to navigate in your particular CMOS utility.

> Usually the arrow keys and the PAGE UP and PAGE DOWN keys will select and change settings. Sometimes the + and – keys or the SPACEBAR will toggle settings. The CMOS setup program screen usually provides a key to the navigation and selection keys; refer to it as well.

While navigating through the different setup screens, pay particular attention to any password or security menu that enables you to configure administrator/supervisor passwords and user passwords. Do not make any changes at this time; just make a note of where you configure these passwords.

Step 4 Following is a list of common settings found in the CMOS. Know that each BIOS arranges its settings differently. View every screen of your CMOS setup program to locate and record these settings and their location:

- **Drives** Depending on your motherboard configuration, you will either set a primary master/slave drive or, if using SATA, see a list of the different drives attached and their name/type.

  _____

- **Onboard Devices** These settings enable you to configure onboard devices such as your USB ports.

  _____

- **Performance** Only common on better motherboards, this area enables you to tweak system timings for improved performance (also known as overclocking).

  _____

- **Security** This section enables you to set administrator or system passwords.

  _____

- **Boot Sequence** This setting enables you to define the order in which your system looks for boot devices.

  _____

- **Power Management** This section defines when devices shut down and how they awaken.

  _____

Once you're done exploring, press ESC a couple of times until you get the message "Quit Without Saving (Y/N)?" Press Y, and then press ENTER. The system will boot into your operating system.

30 MINUTES

Lab Exercise 7.03: Configuring BIOS Settings

If you find any issues when you examine the BIOS settings using the CMOS setup program, you'll need to reconfigure the settings. Remember also that you're preparing the PC for an upgrade to Windows 7. BIOS-level virus checking is known to cause problems with the Windows XP/Vista/7 installation process, so Microsoft advises that you disable it.

Many BIOS functions are unchangeable—such as keyboard and floppy drive recognition—and are therefore inaccessible via the CMOS setup program. Other functions are under your control. These include the boot sequence order and the date/time setting, as mentioned previously, but also some potentially hazardous settings such as BIOS shadowing and memory timing.

✔ Hint

If you're not absolutely certain what a particular setting does, the best course of action is to leave it alone! If you have any doubts, you can always exit the CMOS setup program without saving.

Learning Objectives

In this exercise, you'll access the CMOS setup program, navigate to find the various BIOS settings you would commonly need to modify, and practice disabling BIOS-level virus checking.

At the end of this lab, you'll be able to

- Modify the settings in BIOS

Lab Materials and Setup

The materials you need for this lab are

- A working PC whose BIOS settings you have permission to change

- If possible, a BIOS that includes virus checking

Getting Down to Business

In the following steps, you'll learn how to navigate to the CMOS setup program configuration screen that includes the virus-checking option. This example uses the Phoenix-Award BIOS CMOS setup program. Your CMOS setup program may vary, but many BIOS makers and versions should offer the same option.

✔ **Cross-Reference**

For more details about the features of CMOS setup programs, refer to the section "A Quick Tour Through a Typical CMOS Setup Program" in Chapter 7 of *Mike Meyers' CompTIA A+ Guide to 801: Managing and Troubleshooting PCs.*

Step 1 Enter your CMOS setup program using the steps you learned in Lab Exercise 7.02.

Step 2 Check your notes and navigate to the configuration screen that has the BIOS-level virus-checking option. It's not always obvious where to find this option. For example, the Phoenix BIOS CMOS setup program screen shown in Figure 7-3 doesn't give any hints about where to find the correct screen. As Figure 7-5 shows, virus checking can be disabled in this BIOS from the Advanced BIOS Features screen. Don't hesitate to explore.

Step 3 Follow the screen prompts to navigate to the correct configuration screen and find the virus-checking setting. Highlight the option and change it from Enabled to Disabled. Once again, your CMOS setup program's wording or appearance may be different, but the option to control BIOS-level virus checking should be common to most modern types of BIOS.

Step 4 Save and exit the CMOS setup program. After you exit, the system will reboot automatically. You have just made a change to BIOS.

FIGURE 7-5 Disabling BIOS-level virus checking

The process you just followed is the same process you'll use for any changes you make to BIOS. Be sure to save the settings before exiting the CMOS setup program.

Step 5 Have your instructor (or a friendly neighborhood technician) check your work to ensure that the settings have been saved correctly.

Lab Analysis Test

1. What can you do in a pinch to clear the CMOS settings if you are unable to find the CMOS-clear jumper?

2. After running Windows XP for a few years, Chris has decided to perform a clean install of Windows Vista. After backing up his important files, he places the Windows Vista DVD in the optical drive and reboots his machine—but it just boots into Windows XP like normal. What setting will he most likely need to configure in the BIOS to correct this situation?

3. Arnold has just installed a new sound card. He boots his system to install the drivers, but his system does not recognize the new card. What BIOS settings might he change using CMOS setup?

4. Alex has just finished making changes to the BIOS-level virus checking and would now like to save these changes. Name two ways to save BIOS settings after making changes in the CMOS setup program.

5. Ryan is working on an older Core 2 Duo system. What key or keys should he press to enter the CMOS setup program?

Key Term Quiz

Use the following terms to complete the following sentences. Not all terms will be used.

AMI

Award Software

BIOS (basic input/output services)

BIOS ROM

CMOS (complementary metal-oxide semiconductor)

CMOS setup program

DELETE key

PAUSE/BREAK key

Phoenix Technologies

1. The system BIOS is stored on nonvolatile memory called _____.

2. Technicians configure the BIOS using the _____.

3. Press the _____ to suspend operation of the POST.

4. _____ provides the primary interface between the operating system's device drivers and most of the system's hardware.

5. A common way to enter CMOS setup is to press the _____ during startup.

Chapter 8

Motherboards

Lab Exercises

While the CPU, system RAM, power supply, hard disk drive, and all the other miscellaneous pieces of a typical PC are important, it is the motherboard that brings them together into a working whole. Every bit and byte of data that moves between devices passes through its sockets and traces. Every component plugs into it, either directly or indirectly—a PC wouldn't be much of a PC without it. Replacing a motherboard is one of the most challenging tasks a PC tech will face.

Luckily, only a couple of circumstances require you to undertake this chore. The first is when the motherboard malfunctions or is damaged; modern motherboards aren't made to be repaired, so when they go bad, they must be replaced as a whole unit. The other is when you want to upgrade the PC to a more powerful CPU than its current motherboard supports. In either of these cases, you've got a bit of work ahead of you! Installing a motherboard requires more effort than any other type of installation—more preparation, more time performing the installation, and more cleanup afterward. Still, you shouldn't be intimidated by the prospect of replacing a motherboard—it's a common and necessary part of PC repair. In this chapter, you'll go through the process from start to finish.

In the following lab exercises, you'll research new motherboards, remove the motherboard from a working PC, and explore the motherboard's features. You'll then install the motherboard again and use CPU-Z to discover all sorts of details. The last three labs of the chapter deal with identifying expansion slots, installing expansion cards, and managing hardware with Device Manager.

 15 MINUTES

Lab Exercise 8.01: Researching New Motherboards

While the motherboard may be the backbone of a PC, all good upgrade efforts should begin with the CPU. Trying to pick out a motherboard and *then* a processor that goes with it is a little like choosing a paint color before you've seen the walls—it can be done, but your walls might end up puce when they should be aquamarine. In other words, it's much less painful to work from CPU to motherboard, especially when your goal is to increase performance. Don't tie yourself down by doing it backward.

You need to make several choices when searching for a new CPU and motherboard. Ensuring compatibility is key. Once you've picked the latest and greatest processor from Intel or AMD, you need to find a motherboard that plays nicely with it: Match the socket type of the processor to the socket type of the motherboard. Make sure the motherboard's form factor fits inside your case. And even after you've narrowed it down to that, you still need to pick a manufacturer and choose which features you want the motherboard to have.

Learning Objectives

In this lab, you'll become familiar with different motherboards and their compatibility with various processors and cases.

At the end of this lab, you'll be able to

- Recognize different motherboard form factors

- Understand considerations for upgrading a system with a newer motherboard

Lab Materials and Setup

The materials you need for this lab are

- A PC with Internet access

✔ Hint

As usual, if you have access to multiple systems, take advantage of it. It's most useful to have a variety of motherboards to study.

Getting Down to Business

The following steps will lead you through the process of determining which motherboard you need to obtain to update your client's systems. You'll also see that a motherboard is not an island unto itself, but one piece of the PC archipelago.

Step 1   Go to www.newegg.com (or another online PC component store) and search for a newer, faster processor. When selecting a new processor, be sure to keep track of important specifications so that you can refer to them when you need to pick out a motherboard. Record the following information:

Manufacturer _____

Series _____

CPU socket type _____

Step 2   Search the online PC component store for a new motherboard. Keep in mind that the CPU's socket type must match the motherboard's socket type, otherwise they will be incompatible. You'll find more than one that are compatible, but for now, pick one and record the following information:

Manufacturer _____

CPU socket type _____

Form factor _____

Expansion slots _____

Step 3   The next step to finding a new and compatible motherboard is to make sure that it will work with the form factor of your client's system cases.

Current PC motherboards come in a few different styles, or *form factors*: ATX (Advanced Technology Extended), microATX and FlexATX, ITX, and proprietary form factors from companies such as Dell and Sony. Each motherboard form factor has a corresponding case it is compatible with, but some motherboards will fit in a case with a different form factor. ATX motherboards are what you find in most PCs on the market.

Your client's cases are all ATX. Is the motherboard you picked compatible? _____

Step 4   Look at a few different (but still compatible) motherboards. Compare their features. What makes them different? Does one have more expansion slots than the other? Does one have fewer RAM slots? Are there other features, such as support for NVIDIA's SLI or ATI's CrossFire dual-graphics card technology, that would influence your choice? Using the motherboard you already selected, record the following information:

Number of memory slots _____

Maximum memory supported _____

SATA ports _____

Onboard video chipset _____

Other features _____

 15 minutes

Lab Exercise 8.02: Identifying Motherboard Features

At a glance, one motherboard pretty much looks like any other. Of course, as a PC tech, you know that many differences may exist: Two identical-looking motherboards can have completely different feature sets. Chipsets, bus speed, CPU socket type, and clock speed are just some of the important features that separate one motherboard from another. These differences aren't always obvious, but you can turn to your motherboard book to identify your motherboard's features, as described in the following steps.

Learning Objectives

In this lab, you'll become familiar with different motherboard features.

At the end of this lab, you'll be able to

- Recognize different motherboard features

- Identify the location of motherboard features

Lab Materials and Setup

The materials you need for this lab are

- A motherboard

- The motherboard book or online documentation for that motherboard

Getting Down to Business

In the following steps, you'll identify the location of key features on your motherboard.

✔ **Hint**

If you're using an old motherboard, take this opportunity to clean any dust off of it, using canned air, before you begin.

Step 1   Note the location of the make and model information on the motherboards in Figure 8-1. Compare this to your motherboard and locate the manufacturer name and model number.

✔ **Cross-Reference**

For details on chipsets, refer to the "Chipset" section of Chapter 8 of *Mike Meyers' CompTIA A+ Guide to 801: Managing and Troubleshooting PCs.*

Figure 8-1 Two examples of model number information printed on motherboards

What is the name of your motherboard manufacturer? _____

What is the model number of your motherboard? _____

What CPU socket do you have on your motherboard? _____

What type of chipset do you have on your motherboard? _____

Keep this information handy! Having the make and model of your motherboard readily available makes it easy to search the Web for drivers and updated BIOS.

Step 2   Look for any charts or numbers printed on the surface of the motherboard.

Are there any jumper blocks? _____

What are some of the settings that can be configured using jumpers?

_____

_____

_____

Step 3   Find the following on your motherboard and note their locations:

- System clock battery _____

- BIOS _____

- RAM slots (What type? Dual-channel or triple-channel support?) _____

- SATA or RAID (if present) _____

- Graphics adapter support (onboard, PCI, AGP, PCIe?) _____

 30 MINUTES

Lab Exercise 8.03: Exploring Motherboard Features with CPU-Z

Now that you've completed the analysis and upgrade of your client's systems with new motherboards and CPUs where needed, you can verify some of the characteristics and features the motherboard manufacturer has promoted. You already downloaded the CPU-Z utility, so you can launch that to examine the information on the Mainboard tab.

✔ **Hint**

Over the years, motherboards have been called many names—and not just the bad names you might use when one doesn't work properly! Early motherboards were sometimes called the *planar board*. A motherboard can be referred to as the *system board*, *mainboard*, and sometimes just *board* or *mobo*. Regardless of the name, these terms refer to the large printed circuit board (PCB) used to connect all the components in a computer system.

Learning Objectives

In this lab, you'll identify various motherboard features.

At the end of this lab, you'll be able to

- Verify motherboard features

Lab Materials and Setup

The materials you need for this lab are

- Access to a working computer with the CPU-Z utility installed

- A notepad and pencil to document the specifications

- Optional: A word processor or spreadsheet application to facilitate the documentation

✔ **Hint**

This lab is more informative if you have access to different systems using various motherboards.

Getting Down to Business

In the following steps, you'll verify the features of your motherboard.

Step 1   Launch CPU-Z and navigate to the Mainboard tab. CPU-Z displays some of the key features of your motherboard, as shown in Figure 8-2.

Step 2   Using the data gathered by CPU-Z, record as much pertinent information as possible:

Manufacturer _____

Model _____

FIGURE 8-2 CPU-Z displaying motherboard information

Chipset _____

Southbridge _____

BIOS brand _____

Graphic interface version _____

Step 3   If possible, launch CPU-Z on various machines to compare the features of different motherboards.

→ **Try This: PC Wizard**

Go to http://www.cpuid.com/softwares/pc-wizard.html and download and install PC Wizard.
After you've installed it, launch the PC Wizard application. Once PC Wizard is running, click
the Mainboard icon. This brings up a number of items (components) in the top-right pane of the
window. Click the Mainboard item to display detailed information in the lower-right pane of the
window, as shown here:

Using this information, can you determine the integrated devices supported by your motherboard? Does this correspond to the information in the PC or motherboard documentation?

30 MINUTES

Lab Exercise 8.04: Identifying Internal Expansion Slots

Unless you've got X-ray vision, the best way to examine expansion slots is to remove the PC case cover. In this exercise, you'll identify the type of expansion slots on your motherboard. Does your system use a PCIe, AGP, or PCI graphics card, or does it use onboard video? Check to see how many other expansion slots are available for adding a sound card and (if required) upgrading the graphics adapter.

✖ Warning

Remember to use proper safety and electrostatic discharge (ESD) avoidance procedures when working inside the PC case.

Learning Objectives

In this exercise, you'll properly identify expansion slots and the basic features of each type of expansion technology.

At the end of this lab, you'll be able to

- Identify PCI expansion bus slots and component cards

- Identify the AGP expansion bus slot and video card

- Identify PCIe ×1 and PCIe ×16 expansion bus slots and component cards

Lab Materials and Setup

The materials you need for this lab are

- A non-production, disassembled PC

- A working PC (or more than one if possible)

- An anti-static mat

- A notepad

- Optional: Some sample motherboards

Getting Down to Business

Shut down your PC and unplug it from the wall. Place it on your anti-static mat, remove the PC case cover, and take a good look inside. Your aim is to determine what type of expansion slots your motherboard has, and what peripheral card components are currently installed.

Step 1 Here are the physical characteristics of PCI expansion slots:

- About 3 inches long

- Usually white in color (modern motherboards may use bright colors like yellow or green to enhance the visual appeal of the motherboard)

- Offset from the edge of the motherboard by about 1 inch

Figure 8-3 shows PCI slots on a modern motherboard.

Record the following information:

How many PCI slots are on your motherboard? _____

What PCI devices are installed on your system? _____

How many PCI slots are empty? _____

Step 2 See if you can locate a 32-bit AGP slot. As the name suggests, the AGP slot is designed to be used with one type of component only—a graphics adapter. Here are the physical characteristics of the AGP slot:

- One slot per motherboard

- A little less than 3 inches long

- Usually brown in color

- Offset from the edge of the motherboard by about 2 inches

FIGURE 8-3 A group of PCI slots

Figure 8-4 shows an AGP slot in its natural habitat. While popular on older motherboards, AGP slots have been all but ousted by PCIe, so your motherboard may not have one.

Record the following information:

Is there an AGP video card slot on your motherboard? _____

What can you tell about the installed video card without removing it?

Step 3   Take a look at your motherboard and see if there are any PCIe slot connectors. PCIe is very interesting, offering a theoretical throughput of 2.5 Gbps per lane and supporting from 1 to 32 lanes. The first devices to take advantage of PCIe were graphics cards using the 16-lane configuration. The physical characteristics of the PCIe expansion slots depend on the number of lanes.

PCIe ×1 slots have the following characteristics:

- About 1 inch long

- Often brightly colored (blue and white being fairly common)

- Offset from the edge of the motherboard by about 1.25 inches

FIGURE 8-4 An AGP slot

PCIe ×16 slots have the following characteristics:

- About 3.5 inches long

- Often brightly colored (blue and white being fairly common)

- Offset from the edge of the motherboard by about 1.25 inches

Figure 8-5 shows PCIe slots on a modern motherboard.

Record the following information:

Are there any PCIe slots on your motherboard? _____

If yes, how many PCIe ×1 slots are there? _____

How many PCIe ×16 slots are there? _____

Are there any PCIe cards installed in the system? _____

✔ **Cross-Reference**

For more detail about the PCI, AGP, and PCIe buses, refer to the "Expansion Bus" section in Chapter 8 of *Mike Meyers' CompTIA A+ Guide to 801: Managing and Troubleshooting PCs.*

After you've completed your inventory of installed expansion bus devices, put the case cover back on your PC, plug it back in, and turn on the power of the system.

FIGURE 8-5 A motherboard with both PCIe ×1 and PCIe ×16 expansion slots

30 MINUTES

Lab Exercise 8.05: Installing Expansion Cards

There are four steps to installing any expansion card device properly:

1. Arm yourself with knowledge of the device before you install it. Is the device certified to run on the Windows OS that you're running? Is it compatible with your motherboard and other hardware? If you are running Windows 7, a good place to start is the Windows Compatibility Center Web site, found at www.microsoft.com/windows/compatibility/windows-7/en-us/default.aspx.

2. Remove the cover from your PC case and install the device. As always, follow all ESD and safety precautions and handle the card with care.

3. Install device drivers for the component. Windows comes with a large device drivers catalog, so it may try to help you by installing the driver that it thinks the device needs. In most cases, you should visit the card manufacturer's Web site, download the latest drivers for the card and your operating system, and then install the updated drivers. You can also install the card and then use Microsoft/Windows Update, which may find and download a copy of the latest driver from the manufacturer.

4. Verify that the device is functional.

The following exercise is a somewhat abridged version of this procedure; instead of installing a new device, you'll remove and reinstall devices that are already on your system.

✔ **Cross-Reference**

To review the details of device installation, refer to the "Installing Expansion Cards" section in Chapter 8 of *Mike Meyers' CompTIA A+ Guide to 801: Managing and Troubleshooting PCs.*

Learning Objectives

In this lab, you'll practice removing and installing internal expansion cards.

At the end of this lab, you'll be able to

-   Remove and install expansion cards in a system correctly and safely

Lab Materials and Setup

The materials you need for this lab are

- At least one working Windows computer with expansion cards installed
- A Phillips-head screwdriver
- An anti-static mat and wrist strap
- Anti-static storage bags
- A notepad

Getting Down to Business

In this exercise, you'll physically remove expansion card devices from your PC. You'll then make note of any important information you can find on the device's label: device maker, version, and so on. Finally, you'll reassemble and restart the system. In Lab Exercise 8.06, you'll use Device Manager to make sure everything is working properly.

Shut down the system and unplug the power cable, placing it on your anti-static mat. Once you remove the PC case cover and strap on your anti-static wrist strap, you're ready to start.

Step 1 Make a list of the expansion cards installed in your motherboard and note which slot each one uses. You'll want to know this for when you put the cards back in at the end of the lab exercise.

Step 2 Remove the cards one at a time from your system. For each card, follow these procedures:

a. Remove the retaining screw and store it safely. Check for any latches on the expansion slot (see Figure 8-6) and release them when removing the video card.

✔ **Hint**

You'll see two main types of screws used in PCs. At first glance, they may look all the same, but while these screws are the same overall size, they have different sizes of threads. Screws with the larger threads, commonly called *coarse-threaded* screws, are generally used to secure expansion cards, hard drives, power supplies, and case covers. Screws with the smaller threads, commonly called *fine-threaded* screws, are typically used to secure storage devices such as floppy disk drives and optical drives into their respective bays.

---

b. Taking hold of the card by its edges, carefully and firmly pull it straight up and out of its slot.

FIGURE 8-6 Releasing a latch holding in the video card

✔ **Hint**

These cards can be difficult to remove. If a card seems stuck, try rocking it back and forth (from front to back in the direction of the slot, not side to side).

c.   Holding the card only by the edges and the metal flange, place it in an anti-static bag for safekeeping.

Step 3   Examine each of the cards you removed from your system and record the pertinent information.

Do any of the cards have writing or labels on them? If so, what information do these labels provide?

_____

_____

_____

Can you identify the manufacturers of the cards? If so, list each card and its manufacturer.

_____

_____

_____

Are there any version numbers or codes on the cards? If so, list this information for each card.

_____

_____

_____

What kind of interface does each card use? List whether it is PCI, AGP, or PCIe (or something else).

_____

_____

_____

Step 4 Reinstall into your system the expansion cards you removed. For each card, follow these procedures:

    a. Check your notes to confirm where to reinstall the card.

    b. Align the card over its motherboard slot, making sure that the metal flange is aligned properly with the case slot. Holding the flange with one hand, place the heel of your hand on the top edge of the card and push the card firmly into the expansion slot.

    c. Once the card is in the slot and the flange is flush with the case, replace the screw that holds the card in place. Don't be tempted to skip the screw! It keeps the card from working loose over time.

> **✖ Warning**
>
> After you have reinstalled all the expansion cards, take a look at the back of your system (where you can see input/output connections for the cards). Are there any holes where no cards are installed and a slot cover has not been used? It's very important to install slot covers wherever an expansion card is not installed. This ensures that air will flow properly through the computer case, keeping your critical components cool.

 30 MINUTES

Lab Exercise 8.06: Managing Hardware with Device Manager

Windows is capable of utilizing a universe of peripherals and expansion cards—everything from modems to TV tuners. Management of this massive collection of hardware in Windows is handled by Device Manager.

Device Manager provides a centralized location for dealing with all aspects of a computer's hardware. This includes a simple inventory of all installed devices, notification of malfunctioning devices, and the capability to install and update drivers.

This exercise will cover some of the more useful features of Device Manager.

Learning Objectives

In this lab, you'll use Device Manager to examine and update a system.

At the end of this lab, you'll be able to

- Use Device Manager to examine devices on your system, check for problems, and update drivers

Lab Materials and Setup

The materials you need for this lab are

- A working computer running Windows
- Access to the Internet

✔ **Hint**

As usual, if you have access to more than one system, take advantage of it.

Getting Down to Business

In this exercise, you'll use Device Manager to view the system resource settings on your PC.

Step 1 Open the Windows Control Panel. In Windows XP, click the icon for the System applet. Select the Hardware tab and then click the Device Manager button; this brings up Device Manager in a separate window. In Windows Vista, select System and Maintenance, and then choose Device Manager. In Windows 7, select System and Security, then click on Device Manager under System to open Device Manager in a separate window (see Figure 8-7). Note that you can also access Device Manager from the System applet. In Windows Vista and Windows 7, press the WINDOWS KEY and the PAUSE/BREAK key at the same time to open the System applet, then click on Device Manager. (In Windows XP, you'll first need to select the Hardware tab.)

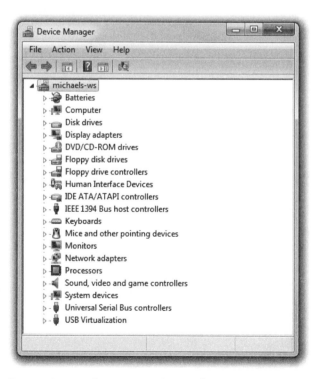

FIGURE 8-7 Device Manager in Windows 7

Step 2   Check for any missing devices, or devices marked with error icons:

- A device marked with a black "!" on a yellow circle (Windows XP) or triangle (Windows Vista/7) means that the device is missing, Windows does not recognize it, or there is a driver issue.

- In Windows XP, a device marked with a red "X" means the device is disabled. In Windows Vista/7, it is marked with a black downward-pointing arrow.

Step 3   Download and install the latest device drivers for each of your expansion cards. There are many methods you can use to accomplish this task, but the two that follow are the most common.

- If your working PC is connected to the Internet, you can use the Update Driver Wizard from the device's Driver tab in Device Manager to connect to Windows Update. Open Device Manager and select *View device by type*. Locate your expansion cards and right-click one and select Properties. Select the Driver tab, shown in Figure 8-8, and then click Update Driver. This opens a wizard that helps you find new drivers, as shown in Figure 8-9; from here you can manually browse for drivers on your computer or have Windows search for drivers both on your computer and online.

FIGURE 8-8 The Driver tab of the device's Properties dialog box in Windows

Figure 8-9 Updating drivers

- If your working PC is not connected to the Internet, or the device does not have a signed driver available through Windows Update, you will have to follow these instructions before clicking Update Driver. Using a computer with Internet access, find and connect to the manufacturer's Web site. Using the model number of the device, locate and download the correct driver for the operating system on the PC where the device is installed. Save the driver to a USB thumb drive, remove the thumb drive from that system, and insert it into your working PC. Open Device Manager and select *View device by type*. Locate the device that matches the expansion card you have installed, and open its properties. Select the Driver tab, and then click Update Driver. When prompted to connect to the Internet, choose *No, not this time*, and follow the directions to locate and load the new device driver (see Figure 8-10).

✔ **Hint**

Many manufacturers include installation wizards for their devices, so that is yet another method that you can use to update device drivers. Many times, the manufacturer will include related applications along with the drivers to enhance the performance of the device. A good example of this is an inkjet printer that includes the driver and utilities for adjusting print quality, performing printer maintenance, and so on.

FIGURE 8-10 Manually browsing for new drivers

Lab Analysis Test

1. Jonathan is building a system using an Intel Core i3 processor, and he's purchased a new motherboard from ASUS. He would like to use an old (but working!) ATX power supply he has laying around to power the system. Why might this *not* be a good idea?

2. John has a system that runs at 3.2 GHz and uses a 128-MB AGP video card. He uses Windows XP Professional and wants to try its multiple-monitor support feature. Can he add another AGP video card? Why or why not?

3. Dianne is trying to install an ATX motherboard in a new, empty ATX case. She tries to set it down in the bottom of the case, but it won't fit—the ports on the side are too low to poke out the back of the case, and she can't make the screws work at all. What has she forgotten?

4. After Erik reassembled his PC and turned it on, he noticed that the green LED and the disk active LED never light up, but everything seems to work okay. What is the problem?

5. You've installed an NIC and a PCI FireWire controller card on Susan's Windows Vista Professional system. The system starts up fine, but when you check Device Manager, you see a yellow triangle with a black exclamation mark beside the NIC icon. What is the problem?

Key Term Quiz

Use the following terms to complete the following sentences. Not all terms will be used.

AGP

ATX

device drivers

expansion card

FlexATX

ITX

microATX

motherboard book

PCI

PCIe

sockets or slots

1. Once a standard graphics expansion slot, _____ has been replaced in favor of PCIe video cards.

2. To check the technical specifications of a motherboard, consult its _____.

3. The _____ bus provides for ×1, ×2, ×4, ×8, ×16, and ×32 lanes of bidirectional communication.

4. _____ are the areas where CPUs are installed on motherboards.

5. One motherboard design, known for its lower power-consumption characteristics and small size, is called _____.

Chapter 9

Power Supplies

Lab Exercises

The term "power supply" is somewhat misleading. After all, the power supply in a PC does not actually *supply* power; it just takes the alternating current (AC) supplied by the power company and converts it to the direct current (DC) used by your computer. Local power companies supply AC to the outlet in your home or office, and some conversion must take place to supply the lower operating voltages and DC power required for the PC to function.

As a PC technician, you need to understand the difference between AC and DC power. You should be able to measure the AC power at the wall outlet and determine whether the hot, neutral, and ground wires are properly connected. You must also measure the DC output of the power supply inside the PC case to determine whether the power supply is providing the correct DC voltage.

The power supply in a PC is an electronic device that converts the higher voltage—120 volts of alternating current (VAC) in the United States or 240 VAC outside the United States—into the 12, 5, and 3.3 volts of direct current (VDC) used in today's PC systems. The 12-volt level is traditionally used for devices that have motors to spin, such as hard drives, floppy drives, optical drives, and cooling fans. The 5-volt and 3.3-volt power usually supports all of the onboard electronics. Modern CPUs often use less than 3.3 volts, so there are further step-down regulators and filters to provide core voltages as low as 1.4 volts.

ATX power supplies are, by far, the most common power supplies you will see on desktop PCs. These include ATX (with a 20-pin P1 power connector), ATX 12V 1.3 (which added the AUX 4-pin connector commonly referred to as P4), and the ATX 12V 2.0 (which swapped out the 20-pin P1 connector for a 24-pin P1 connector). Higher-end computers such as servers and gaming systems with multiple high-powered video cards often require much more current, so you may start to see the Server System Infrastructure (SSI)–developed, non-ATX-standard motherboard with a power supply named EPS 12V; it uses a 24-pin P1 connector, a 4-pin P4 connector, and a unique 8-pin connector.

Suppose a client calls you saying that her PC keeps locking up. After walking her through a few simple troubleshooting steps, you rule out a virus or a misbehaving application. This leaves hardware as the likely culprit, and in all likelihood, it's the power supply. In these lab exercises, you'll practice the procedures for measuring power going to the PC, testing the PC's power supply, and replacing a PC power supply.

✔ Hint

The CompTIA A+ certification exams show their American roots in the area of electrical power. Watch for power questions that discuss American power standards—especially ones related to household voltage and outlet plug design. The exams will also typically refer to the power supply using the abbreviation PSU (power supply unit) or the acronym FRU (field replaceable unit). FRU can describe any component that would be replaced in the field by a technician.

 30 MINUTES

Lab Exercise 9.01: Electricity

Troubleshooting power-related problems is one of the trickier tasks you'll undertake as a PC tech. Your first step is to go right to the source, so to speak, and make certain that the power being supplied to the PC from the electrical outlet is good.

✔ Cross-Reference

For details on AC power from the power company, refer to the "Supplying AC" section in Chapter 9 of *Mike Meyers' CompTIA A+ Guide to 801: Managing and Troubleshooting PCs*.

Learning Objectives

At the end of this lab, you'll be able to

- Determine if the AC wiring is correct at a wall outlet
- Determine if the AC voltages are correct at a wall outlet

Lab Materials and Setup

The materials you need for this lab are

- An AC electrical outlet tester
- A multimeter

Getting Down to Business

Measuring the voltage coming from an AC outlet is a nerve-wracking task even for experienced techs! Sticking objects into a live power outlet goes against everything you've been taught since infancy, but when done properly, it's completely safe.

Use common sense and appropriate safety procedures. If you're not familiar with using a multimeter, please review the "Supplying AC" section in Chapter 9 of *Mike Meyers' CompTIA A+ Guide to 801: Managing and Troubleshooting PCs*, or ask your instructor for a demonstration.

✔ **Hint**

If a PC experiences unexplained errors and you suspect the power supply, don't be too hasty in replacing it. First check the wall outlet. In some buildings, especially older ones, the wiring can be improperly connected or otherwise provide poor power.

Step 1   Look at Figure 9-1, and compare it to your electrical outlet.

A typical electrical socket has three openings: hot, neutral, and ground. The hot wire delivers the juice. The neutral wire acts as a drain and returns electricity to the local source (the breaker panel). The semi-rounded ground socket returns excess electricity to the ground. If your outlet doesn't have a ground socket—and outlets in many older buildings don't—then don't use it! Ungrounded outlets aren't appropriate for PCs.

FIGURE 9-1 A typical AC electrical outlet

✖ **Warning**

Take all appropriate safety precautions before measuring live electrical outlets. In a classroom, you have the benefit of an instructor to show you how to do these exercises the first time. If you're doing these on your own with no experience, seek the advice of a trained technician or instructor.

Step 2   Determine whether or not your electrical socket is "live." Do this with your electrical outlet tester. Plug your outlet tester (see Figure 9-2) into the electrical outlet or power strip where you plug in the PC. Look at the LED indicators. Are they showing good power?

Step 3   Now measure the voltage between the hot and neutral openings of the outlet. Start by setting your multimeter to AC voltage; do not proceed until you're sure you have done this correctly! If you aren't sure, ask your instructor for guidance. Referring to Figure 9-3, take the black probe and place it in the neutral opening of the wall socket. Make sure you have good contact inside the outlet. The metal probe tip must contact the metal connector inside the outlet.

Next, place the red probe inside the hot opening. Again, you must make good metal-to-metal contact. You may have to reposition the probes to get a good connection and proper reading for the AC circuit. Your reading should be somewhere between 110 and 120 V.

What is your reading? _____

Figure 9-2 A circuit tester for AC electrical outlets

Figure 9-3 Multimeter probe locations when testing an AC outlet's hot-to-neutral circuit

Step 4 Measure the voltage in the hot-to-ground circuit. Place the black probe into the ground opening of the outlet, as shown in Figure 9-4. Make sure you have good contact. Then place the red probe into the hot opening. Move the probes around until you get a good reading for the AC voltage. Again, your reading should be in the 110- to 120-V range.

What is your reading? _____

Step 5 The last measurement you need to take is the voltage in the neutral-to-ground safety circuit. When the neutral wire is broken or missing, the ground wire is the only way for wayward electrons to depart safely. Any electricity on both the neutral and ground wires should have a direct path back to earth, so there should be no voltage between these wires.

Place the black probe into the ground opening of the outlet. Make sure you have good contact. Place the red probe into the neutral opening (refer to Figure 9-5). Move the probes around until you get a good reading for the AC voltage. You should get a reading of 0 V.

What is your reading? _____

Step 6 Measure another outlet in the same building, and repeat the previous steps. Are the readings similar? If the readings from your electrical outlets are outside of the ranges described, it's time to call an electrician. Assuming your reading is showing good power, go to the next exercise.

FIGURE 9-4 Multimeter probe locations when testing an AC outlet's hot-to-ground circuit

FIGURE 9-5 Multimeter probe locations when testing an AC outlet's neutral-to-ground circuit

30 MINUTES

Lab Exercise 9.02: Power Supply Output

Once you've determined that the AC power going to your client's PC is good, you need to test whether the DC power traveling from the power supply to the rest of her system is good.

Learning Objectives

At the end of this lab, you'll be able to

- Identify the connectors of a PC power supply

- Measure the output of a PC power supply

Lab Materials and Setup

The materials you need for this lab are

- An ATX power supply

- A multimeter

- A PC power supply tester

- Optional: A working PC with an ATX power supply

Getting Down to Business

There are two ways to determine whether a power supply is providing the proper voltages to the components of the computer. One is the traditional method, using a multimeter to measure the actual voltages. Another method growing in popularity is the use of a PC power supply tester.

✔ Cross-Reference

For details on DC power from the power supply, refer to the "Supplying DC" section in Chapter 9 of *Mike Meyers' CompTIA A+ Guide to 801: Managing and Troubleshooting PCs*.

In the following steps, you'll measure DC voltage coming from the PC power supply. The three places to measure power supply output are at the Molex power connectors, the SATA power connectors, and the motherboard power connectors. Molex power connectors plug into devices that need 5 or 12 volts of power. These include PATA hard drives and PATA optical drives. SATA power connectors connect to SATA hard drives and optical drives. On most recent systems, the power supply will provide two motherboard power connectors: the 20- or 24-pin P1 and the smaller P4 (see Figure 9-6). Both of these power connectors are used on motherboards requiring an additional 12-V power supply.

FIGURE 9-6 Motherboard power connectors: P1 (left) and P4 (right)

You'll then plug the P1 power connector into a PC power supply tester and verify that the readings you measured with the multimeter are within tolerance. The power supply tester has LEDs that will glow green for each of the voltages that it passes.

✖ Warning

Although the power coming out of the PC power supply is considerably less lethal than that coming directly out of the electrical outlet, you should still take all appropriate safety precautions before taking measurements.

Step 1   Set the multimeter to read DC voltage. Find a Molex connector that's not being used for a device. If no Molex connectors are unused, turn the system off and disconnect the one from the optical drive, and then turn the PC back on.

Do you have a free Molex connector? _____

If not, which device did you unplug? _____

Step 2   Referring to Figure 9-7, place the black probe into either one of the holes on the Molex connector that is aligned with a black wire. Now place the red probe into each of the other three holes of the Molex connector in turn, first the other black wire, then the red, then yellow, and record your findings.

Black wire to black wire: _____ V

Black wire to red wire: _____ V

Black wire to yellow wire: _____ V

FIGURE 9-7   Measuring the voltage in a Molex connector

Step 3   Measuring the voltage from the motherboard connector is a little trickier. Leave the power connector plugged into the motherboard and push the probes into the end of the connector that the wires run into. You must push the probe deep enough to touch the metal contact pins, but be careful not to push too deeply or you might push the pin out of the connector.

Push the black probe into the motherboard connector alongside any black wire, and leave it there. Insert the red probe into each of the other wires, and record your findings. Depending on your motherboard connector, you may not have all of these wires.

Black wire to red wire: _____ V

Black wire to yellow wire: _____ V

Black wire to purple wire: _____ V

Black wire to white wire: _____ V

Black wire to black wire: _____ V

Black wire to blue wire: _____ V

Black wire to green wire: _____ V

The voltages generated by the power supply must be within a tolerance (range) level; readings outside these ranges mean the power supply should be replaced. The 5-V connections have a tolerance of ±2 percent (4.9 to 5.1 V is okay), and 12-V connections have a tolerance of ±6 percent (11.25 to 12.75 V is okay).

✔ Hint

A single reading from a power supply may not be enough to pinpoint a power-related problem. Sometimes a power problem becomes evident only when the power supply is placed under a heavier-than-normal load, such as burning a CD or DVD. Also, some RAM-related errors mimic a failing power supply.

The other method to verify that the power supply is operating properly and supplying all the voltages within tolerance is to use a power supply tester. There are many styles of PSU testers on the market, so make sure you follow the specific directions included with your tester as you complete the steps.

Step 1   Starting with the P1 connector, follow the directions for connecting it to your specific PSU tester. Verify that all of the voltages provided through the P1 connector are acceptable (usually an LED will light to verify voltage present and within tolerance).

Did it light up or display an acceptable voltage? _____

✔ Hint

When connecting and disconnecting the power supply connectors, always take care to insert the connector with the proper orientation. Most power connectors are keyed to make it difficult to install the connector backward, but if you use excessive force, you may be able to insert the connector improperly. This applies to powering the motherboard, plugging in devices, and even using the PSU tester.

Step 2   Now, depending on your tester and power supply, plug either the 4-pin, 6-pin, or 8-pin auxiliary connector into the appropriate socket on the PSU tester and verify the voltages provided through this connector. Once they are verified, remove the connector from the socket.

Did it light up or display an acceptable voltage? _____

Step 3   Plug the Molex connector into the PSU tester and verify the voltages provided through this connector. Once they are verified, remove the connector from the socket.

Did it light up or display an acceptable voltage? _____

Step 4   Plug the SATA HDD power connector into the appropriate socket and verify the voltages provided through this connector. Once they are verified, remove the connector from the socket.

Did it light up or display an acceptable voltage? _____

Step 5 Finally, plug the mini floppy drive power connector into the PSU tester and verify the voltages provided through this connector. Once they are verified, remove the connector from the socket and remove the P1 from the socket.

Did it light up or display an acceptable voltage? _____

 30 MINUTES

Lab Exercise 9.03: Power Protection

You've successfully fixed your client's power-problem-plagued PC (say that five times fast), but now you've noted that she has nothing in the way of power protection for her system, nor do any of her coworkers. None!

When you mention this to her, she tells you that her boss never really saw the point of spending money on surge protectors, uninterruptible power supplies, or any of "that stuff." With a straight face, she asks, "Do those things really do any good?"

Now it's your task to sell the boss on the idea of power protection. To do this, you must explain the types of power problems that lurk in the bushes just waiting to pounce on unwary users without power protection, and suggest precautions that they can take to prevent power-related damage.

Learning Objectives

At the end of this lab, you'll be able to

- Explain the need for power protection
- Explain the types of power protection available for a PC

✔ **Cross-Reference**

For details on power protection, refer to the "Protecting the PC from Spikes and Sags in AC Power" section in Chapter 9 of *Mike Meyers' CompTIA A+ Guide to 801: Managing and Troubleshooting PCs*.

Lab Materials and Setup

The materials you need for this lab are

- A working PC

Getting Down to Business

Too often, PC users take for granted the electricity that powers their system. After all, there's not much you can do about the electricity, is there? Not so! Armed with the knowledge of the types of power conditions that can affect your PC, you can best determine what precautions to take.

Step 1   Describe the following types of power conditions and the types of damage they can cause.

Power spike: _____

_____

Brownout: _____

_____

Blackout: _____

_____

Step 2   Describe the following types of power protection equipment.

Surge suppressor: _____

_____

Online uninterruptible power supply (UPS): _____

_____

Standby UPS: _____

_____

Lab Analysis Test

1.   Your client calls you and says that her PC is unusually quiet and keeps rebooting for no apparent reason. What should you ask her to check?

2.   Athena lives in an area where the power is often interrupted. She bought a good surge protector strip, but that does not seem to help. What does she need to prevent her system from shutting down unexpectedly?

3.   Your assistant technician calls you and says he suspects a bad power supply in one of your client's systems. He said the multimeter readings are 12.65 volts and 4.15 volts. What should he do?

4.   One of your clients has an older Pentium 4 system with a single IDE hard drive and 512 MB of RAM. He had been using this PC as his main workstation, but he's recently purchased a newer system and now wants to redeploy the older system as a file server on his network. He has ordered a PCI SCSI controller board and three SCSI hard drives, so that he can configure a RAID array, and an additional 2 GB of RAM. He also ordered two Y adapters for the power supply connectors. He asks for your advice about any additional hardware he should order. What do you tell him?

5. Approximately how many watts would the power supply for this system need?

- AMD Athlon 64 X2 CPU and 512 MB RAM

- Two SATA hard drives and one floppy drive

- One CD-RW drive and one DVD-ROM drive

- PCIe video

- PCI sound card

- NIC

Key Term Quiz

Use the following terms to complete the following sentences. Not all terms will be used.

3.3 V

5 V

12 V

20-pin P1

24-pin P1

Molex connector

P4

P8/P9

power sags

power spikes

power supply

UPS

1. The ATX 12V 2.0 power supply plugs into the motherboard using the _____ connector(s).

2. PC devices with motors, such as hard drives and optical drives, usually require _____ of DC electricity from the power supply.

3. PATA hard drives and optical drives connect to the power supply with a _____.

4. A surge protector prevents damage from _____ in the voltage.

5. For the best protection against power problems, connect your PC to a _____.

Chapter 10
Hard Drive Technologies

Lab Exercises

As the primary storage area for the operating system, applications, and vital data, the hard drive takes on a level of importance to PC users that borders on reverence. Considering the fact that the death of a drive can mean many hours or days of tediously rebuilding your OS install, reloading applications, and re-creating data, such strong feelings make sense. And that reverence can turn quickly to agony if the user hasn't backed up his or her data in awhile when the hard drive dies!

Every tech must know how to connect, configure, maintain, and troubleshoot hard drives of all types. A fully operational drive requires proper hardware setup and installation, CMOS configuration, and software setup (usually performed by tools that come with the operating system). The first few labs in this chapter cover physical installation and CMOS configuration of the mainstream hard drive technology, namely Integrated Drive Electronics (IDE), in both parallel and serial flavors, and solid-state drives (SSDs). You will then conduct research on the developments of Small Computer Systems Interface (SCSI), primarily used for large, fault-tolerant data storage in network server environments.

 60 MINUTES

Lab Exercise 10.01: Installing Parallel ATA Hard Drives

The local nonprofit organization where you volunteer has received a donation of 10 used PCs. Most of them have tiny hard drives, so they need an upgrade before you can distribute them to the various workers at the agency. All of the motherboards have built-in parallel ATA (PATA) controllers. Your boss breaks out a stack of donated hard drives and tells you to get to work!

Installing a PATA hard drive successfully requires little more than connecting data and power cables to the drive and plugging the other end of the data cable into the motherboard. Sounds simple enough on the surface, but because all PATA drives give you options to install two on each motherboard controller, unwary techs get tripped up here. This lab walks you through the physical installation of the hard drive.

✔ **Hint**

As you know from Chapter 10 of your textbook, IDE drives have several names that techs use pretty much interchangeably: IDE, EIDE, and ATA. You'll see all three terms in this lab manual and on the CompTIA A+ 220-801 exam. Except for discussions of very old technology, the terms describe the same type of hard drive today.

Learning Objectives

In this lab exercise, you'll identify the different components of PATA hard drives and cables and learn installation procedures.

At the end of this lab, you'll be able to

- Remove a hard drive safely and correctly

- Describe PATA cables and connectors

- Describe jumper settings

- Identify the major parts of a hard drive

- Install a hard drive safely and correctly

Lab Materials and Setup

The materials you need for this lab are

- A working PC with a PATA hard drive installed

- The Windows operating system installed on the PC

- Optional: Access to one or more broken hard drives that have the covers removed for observation of the internal parts

Getting Down to Business

Grab your handy screwdriver and anti-static wrist strap; it's time to remove a hard drive! Make sure you're using a hard drive that doesn't have any mission-critical data on it, just in case.

Step 1 Shut down your system and remove the system cover, following proper electrostatic discharge (ESD) avoidance procedures.

Step 2 Disconnect all the ribbon cables from the hard drives, but first note which device is connected to which cable and where the orientation stripe is located on each device. Be careful but firm. Grasp the cable as closely as possible to the connector on the drive and pull, rocking the connector gently from side to side.

Examine the connector on the end of the ribbon cable. Use Figure 10-1 to help you.

How many holes does your connector have for pins? _____

Are any of the holes in your connector filled in? Does your connector have a raised portion on one side so that it only fits one way? In other words, is it keyed? _____

How many connectors are on your ribbon cable? _____

Do you have a 40-wire or 80-wire ribbon cable? _____

Disconnect the power supply from the PATA hard drives by unplugging the Molex connector from each one.

✖ Warning

Molex plugs can be difficult to remove and brutal on the fingers. Little "bumps" on each side of the plug enable you to rock the plug back and forth to remove it.

Step 3   Now look at the motherboard connections and note the orientation of the cable connectors. Disconnect the ribbon cables from the motherboard. Be careful but firm. Grasp the cable as closely as possible to the connector on the motherboard and pull, rocking the connector gently from side to side. Lay the cables aside for later reinstallation.

Step 4   Look at the PATA connections on your motherboard; they may be labeled "IDE" (see Figure 10-2). How many PATA controllers do you see on your motherboard?

_____

Figure 10-1 ATA cables: Comparing 40-wire and 80-wire ribbon cable connectors

FIGURE 10-2 Viewing the PATA connectors on a motherboard

Look closely at your motherboard and see if you can find writing on the board next to the IDE connections. Are the interfaces grouped into pairs? Are any of them dedicated to special configurations such as RAID?

_____

_____

What color are the IDE connections on the motherboard?

_____

Step 5   Remove a hard drive from the system. Be careful to note the type of screws you removed and store them for safekeeping. Also be sure to use proper ESD avoidance procedures when removing the drive from your system.

Because of the variety of cases, caddies, bays, slots, and so on, it's not possible to give detailed instructions on how to remove the drive from your particular system. Look closely for caddy releases or retaining screws. Close inspection and a little logic will usually make it clear how to remove the drive. Make notes of how the drive comes out, as you'll have to reinstall it later.

Step 6 With the hard drive out of the system and on a static-free surface, ground yourself, pick up the drive, and examine it carefully.

Note its dimensions. It should measure about 6" × 3.5" × 1". Some drives are smaller, but those are used mostly in laptops.

Look at the largest surfaces of the drive (the top and bottom). The bottom is where the printed circuit board with a ROM chip is located. This circuitry is the hard drive controller. The top side of the drive normally has a label or another means of listing the specifications for the drive, but this is not always the case.

Write down all the information on the label. Be sure to include the manufacturer and the model number for future reference.

_____

_____

Step 7 Look at the end of the drive where the ribbon cable connects. (Make sure the label is facing up.) Find the markings for where pin 1 of the ribbon cable should go.

a. Is pin 1 on the left side of the connector or the right side? _____

b. Does your hard drive have jumpers like the ones in Figure 10-3? _____

c. Notice that the drive in Figure 10-3 has the jumper set to CS. What does CS stand for?

_____

FIGURE 10-3 Locating the PATA hard drive jumper setting

Each PC system that boots from a PATA hard drive should have the hard drive located on the first PATA interface (IDE1). Normally the jumper must be set to master so that the system can recognize it as the boot drive. A second drive (hard drive or optical drive) can be on the same cable, but must be set to slave.

d.   How are the jumpers set on your hard drive?

_____

e.   How are the jumpers set on your optical drive?

_____

f.   Can you have two master drives in the system? Why or why not?

_____

_____

_____

For the purposes of this exercise, make sure you leave your hard drive jumpered as it was when you removed it.

Step 8   Locate a broken hard drive. If you're in a class, ask your instructor for one. Remove its cover.

✖ Warning

Never remove the cover from a functioning hard drive! Hard drives are extremely sensitive, so merely exposing the inside to the air will cause irreparable damage.

Notice the round polished platters that spin in the middle of the drive. This is where the data is stored magnetically.

The actuator arms that move across the platters have tiny coils of wire attached to their ends. These coils hold the read/write heads.

a.   How many surfaces does your sample drive have (one platter = two surfaces)?

_____

b.   How many physical heads does your sample drive have?

_____

Figure 10-4 The internal parts of a hard drive

Both of the preceding answers are most likely the same because usually there is a read/write head for each surface.

   c.   Look at Figure 10-4 and identify the following parts by number.

      Read/write heads _____

      Platters _____

      Voice coil motor _____

   d.   Now look at Figure 10-5 and match the numbered components.

      EIDE controller _____

      Molex connector _____

      PATA connector _____

      Master/slave jumper _____

Step 9 Insert the drive back into your system, and secure it with the proper screws. Connect all the ribbon cables to all the drives, and pay attention to the proper alignment of the connectors. Connect the Molex power connectors.

Leave the system case off until you verify that everything works properly.

If you used a working machine for the prior steps, you can verify that you've reinstalled the drives correctly by going to the next major step in the process of hard drive installation: CMOS configuration. Lab Exercise 10.03 in this chapter covers the CMOS details, but if you just can't wait, try Step 10. This bonus step should work on newer motherboard models.

FIGURE 10-5 The external parts of a hard drive

Step 10   Turn on the system and wait for it to boot to the desktop. Double-click the My Computer/Computer icon, and confirm that the icons for the reinstalled drives are displayed. The fact that you were able to get to the desktop confirms that you've reinstalled the boot drive correctly, but do the other drives (if you have them) and your optical drive work?

✔ **Hint**

If you cannot boot the system or the optical drive does not work, the first and obvious place to start is to verify all the cable connections. Any kind of disk errors at this time were most likely caused by the technician; after all, it worked before you touched it!

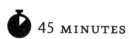 45 MINUTES

Lab Exercise 10.02: Installing Serial ATA Hard Drives

A wealthy donor has just given your nonprofit organization a dozen brand-new desktop machines. Since these are new machines, their motherboards have built-in serial ATA (SATA) controllers, but the SATA hard drives have yet to be installed or configured. You're asked to do the job!

Installing SATA hard drives is a simple matter of plugging in the data and power cables to the drive and attaching the other end of the data cable to the SATA controller card or motherboard connection. You don't even have to shut down Windows. No, really—it's that simple! Let's go through the steps.

Learning Objectives

This lab is designed to introduce you to the three current flavors of SATA and walk you through the straightforward installation.

At the end of this lab, you'll be able to

- Explain key features of SATA 1.0, SATA 2.0, and SATA 3.0
- Install a SATA hard drive

Lab Materials and Setup

The materials you need for this lab are

- A newer PC system with an onboard SATA controller and Windows installed
- At least one additional SATA hard drive
- Optional: A PCI SATA controller may be installed into an older PC system

Getting Down to Business

To start, you'll review the features and specifications of SATA, and then you'll compare and contrast the technology with PATA. Keep that screwdriver handy, because you'll finish with the installation and hot-swap of a SATA drive.

✔ Cross-Reference

To help in answering the following questions, reference the "ATA-7" section in Chapter 10 of *Mike Meyers' CompTIA A+ Guide to 801: Managing and Troubleshooting PCs.*

Step 1   Using your reference materials, review the features and specifications of SATA hard drive technology. Then answer these questions:

a.   What is the speed of data transfer for ATA/133 drives? _____

b.   What is the speed of data transfer for SATA 1.0 drives? _____

c.   What is the speed of data transfer for SATA 2.0 drives? _____

d.   What is the speed of data transfer for SATA 3.0 drives? _____

e.   What is the maximum length of a SATA cable? _____

f.   How many wires are in a SATA cable? _____

g.   What is the maximum length of an 80-wire PATA cable? _____

h.   How many drives can a single SATA cable support? _____

SATA RAID has waltzed into the mainstream today. Motherboards are now being sold with a SATA RAID controller built-in, from Promise or another company, but you can also readily buy a PCIe or PCI SATA RAID controller at your local computer parts store.

Step 2   It's time to get working with some SATA drives. Shut down your system and remove the system cover, following proper ESD avoidance procedures.

Step 3   Disconnect the data cable(s) from the SATA hard drive(s), as shown in Figure 10-6. Grasp the cable as closely as possible to the connector on the drive and pull, rocking the connector gently from side to side.

Disconnect the power supply from the SATA drive(s) by unplugging the SATA connector from each one. Is the power supply a newer model with SATA connectors directly attached, or is there a Molex-to-SATA power adapter like the one shown in Figure 10-7?

Step 4   Now look at the motherboard connections and note the orientation of the connectors. Disconnect the data cables from the motherboard, being careful but firm. Grasp the cable as closely as possible to the connector on the motherboard and pull, rocking the connector gently from side to side.

Lay the cables aside for later reinstallation.

Step 5   Look at the SATA connections on your motherboard (see Figure 10-8).

How many SATA connectors do you see on your motherboard?

_____

Figure 10-6 Removing the SATA data cable

Figure 10-7 Molex-to-SATA power adapter

Figure 10-8 The SATA connectors on a motherboard

Look closely at your motherboard, and see if you can find writing on the board next to the SATA connectors. Are the interfaces grouped into pairs? Are any of them dedicated to special configurations such as RAID?

_____

_____

Step 6   As in the previous exercise, remove the hard drive from the system, note the type of screws you removed, and store the screws for safekeeping. Be sure to use proper ESD procedures when removing the drive from your system.

Because of the variety of cases, caddies, bays, slots, and so on, it's not possible to give detailed instructions on how to remove the drive from your particular system. Look closely for caddy releases or retaining screws. Close inspection and a little logic will usually make it clear how to remove the drive. Make notes of how the drive comes out; you'll have to reinstall it later.

Step 7   With the hard drive out of the system and on a static-free surface, ground yourself, pick up the drive, and examine it carefully.

Note its dimensions; it should measure about 6" × 3.5" × 1", the same as a PATA drive. Here, too, the bottom of the drive boasts the hard drive controller, and the top of the drive is normally labeled with the drive's specifications.

Write down all the information on the label. Be sure to include the manufacturer and the model number for future reference.

_____

_____

_____

Step 8   To demonstrate one of the benefits of SATA—hot-swapping—you will now reinstall all the drives you removed and, if necessary, install an additional SATA drive to be hot-swapped. With the PC still powered down, insert all of the original drives back into your system, and at least one additional SATA drive with no critical data. Secure the drives with the proper screws, connect all the data cables, and connect the SATA power connectors using Molex-to-SATA adapters if required.

Leave the system case off to verify that everything is working properly and to facilitate the last steps.

✔ **Hint**

> If you are performing this lab using a PCIe or PCI SATA controller card, you'll have to install
> the expansion card and load the drivers for the card. If you haven't loaded drivers for the SATA
> controller, you should do so now. Otherwise, this is going to be a very frustrating lab for you!

Power up the PC and boot into Windows. Windows should pick up the drive(s) with no problems at
all. Check My Computer/Computer to verify that the drive is installed and functional. If the drive has
no partition, then of course it won't show up in My Computer/Computer; if this is the case, you can use
the Computer Management console to verify that the drive works.

Step 9   With Windows still running, disconnect the SATA data cable from the additional drive. What
happened?

_____

Step 10   Plug the data cable back in. Does Windows see the drive?

_____

Step 11   Try the same hot-swap test with the SATA power cable—unplug it, then plug it back in. Does
this produce the same effect as the hot-swap with the data cable?

✔ **Cross-Reference**

> Windows won't redetect the SATA drive if AHCI mode is not enabled in CMOS. For more
> information, reference the "AHCI" section in Chapter 10 of *Mike Meyers' CompTIA A+ Guide to 801:
> Managing and Troubleshooting PCs*.

 30 MINUTES

Lab Exercise 10.03: Configuring CMOS Settings

After installing either PATA or SATA devices, the second step you'll want to perform is the configuration
of the BIOS to support these devices. On most motherboards, the BIOS automatically detects devices, so
you will primarily be confirming the detection of all the devices and configuring advanced features such
as RAID, S.M.A.R.T., and boot options. Autodetection does not render CMOS irrelevant, though; you can

do or undo all kinds of problems relating to hard drives using CMOS setup. This lab walks you through the important configuration options.

Learning Objectives

At the end of this lab, you'll be able to

- Configure the CMOS settings for the hard drive
- Confirm that the hard drive is indeed installed properly

Lab Materials and Setup

The materials you need for this lab are

- A fully functioning PC with PATA and/or SATA devices installed
- Optional: A second drive with no important data

Getting Down to Business

There are many possible CMOS settings for the hard drive, depending on the BIOS installed on the motherboard. For example, every motherboard gives you the option to disable the built-in hard drive controllers. Why is this relevant? You can install a drive into a perfectly good system, but it won't work if the controllers are disabled!

Step 1   Turn on your system, and enter the CMOS setup program by pressing the appropriate key(s) while your system is booting.

Select the Integrated Peripherals option from the main menu, or the Drive Configuration option from the Advanced menu (you may have to hunt around for where you enable the PATA/SATA devices in your CMOS setup program), and look for the various controllers. You can enable or disable the controllers here.

✔ **Hint**

This option may look somewhat different depending on the version of CMOS you are using. Look for a menu option such as one of these:

- Onboard Primary PCI IDE
- Onboard Secondary PCI IDE
- PCI Primary and Secondary IDE
- Onboard IDE
- Use Automatic Mode
- SATA Port 0

When the controllers are disabled in CMOS, no device attached to them can be used—not even optical drives. This is why some systems will not let you disable the controllers at all.

If you are performing the labs in sequence, and have arrived at this lab directly from Lab Exercise 10.01 or Lab Exercise 10.02, here's where you find out whether or not you installed and jumpered the drive correctly.

Make sure all controllers are enabled, and then look for the Autodetection option in the CMOS settings. Older systems have a separate category in CMOS, appropriately named Autodetect or something similar; newer systems have it integrated into the main settings screen. Run this utility now. If your hard drive shows up in Autodetect as the drive you thought it would be—primary master, secondary master, SATA Port 0, or what have you—then you installed and (if necessary) jumpered it properly (see Figure 10-9).

Step 2   Save your settings, exit CMOS, and reboot your PC. You should boot into Windows normally. Check My Computer/Computer to verify that you can see and access all drives.

Step 3   Reboot your PC and go into CMOS. Access the settings to enable or disable the various controllers, and disable them all. (This won't affect your data; it will just prevent drive access for the next couple of steps in this lab.)

Step 4   Save your settings, then exit CMOS to reboot the system. Watch the monitor display for messages.

What message is displayed last? _____

With most systems, the PC searches its various storage devices for a way to boot. It looks for a bootable drive (connected to an EIDE, SATA, or SCSI controller), a bootable optical disc, a USB drive, a floppy disk,

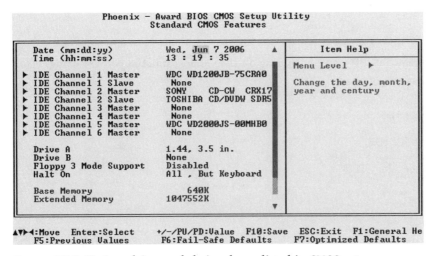

FIGURE 10-9 Various drives and their roles as listed in CMOS setup

or a network connection—not necessarily in that order—and then stops if it cannot find the operating system. It then displays a message indicating "no bootable device" and waits for your instructions to continue.

✖ Warning

If your system is connected to a network and uses the network boot option, disconnect the network cable for this exercise to get the desired results. Be sure to plug the network cable back in when finished.

When the system is not able to find a disk (because you disabled the controller), it will probably hang for a long period of time and then return a Primary Hard Drive Failure code or error message. Some systems try to recognize that you have a hard drive regardless of the disabling of features, but this is rare.

Okay, so the system can't find your hard drive. You obviously know why—you turned off the controller!

Step 5   Reboot your system and enter the CMOS setup program by pressing the appropriate keystroke combination while your system boots. Navigate to the menu where you disabled all of the controllers and reenable them.

Step 6   Now that the controllers are enabled, go back to the autodetection utility and look for any drives connected.

If autodetection still does not see a hard drive, save your settings, reboot your system, and reenter the CMOS setup program. Then try it again.

Do you now see all of the storage devices that are installed in the system?

Step 7   While you're still in CMOS, navigate to the menu where all of the storage devices can be configured. Use this screen (sometimes there are multiple screens) to examine the device settings and answer the following questions:

Are there any devices listed as ATA/IDE devices (Primary Master, Primary Slave, Secondary Master, or Secondary Slave)? _____

Are there any SATA controllers present? If yes, are there any SATA devices installed on the system (SATA Port 0, SATA Port 1, and so on)? _____

Is the motherboard capable of implementing RAID? If yes, how is it currently configured?

_____

Exit CMOS without saving changes and let the PC reboot.

Step 8   At this point, if you did everything as described and if you started with a known good hard drive containing a working operating system, the system will boot back into the operating system. Otherwise, you'll have to wait until you partition and format the drive to see if everything is working as it should (for example, if your instructor gave you, to use, a demo hard drive with nothing on it).

 30 MINUTES

Lab Exercise 10.04: Comparing Solid-State Drives and Magnetic Hard Drives

PATA and SATA hard disk drives store data magnetically and have moving parts, but solid-state drives (SSDs) store data on dynamic RAM (DRAM) or flash memory boards and have no moving parts. In other words, SSDs use *nonvolatile* memory—memory that retains data even when it's not powered on—to store data and emulate a hard drive. Most common uses of SSDs have been in what are called flash drives or thumb drives, but now PC users are installing SSDs as their primary storage in desktops and laptops. SSDs have no moving parts, which makes them tougher, quieter, and oftentimes faster than hard disks.

Learning Objectives

This lab explores the differences between solid-state drives and magnetic hard drives and is designed to help you recommend drives to clients as the need arises.

At the end of this lab, you'll be able to

- Explain solid-state drives

- Explain magnetic hard drives

- Discern which one will be best for your clients

Lab Materials and Setup

The materials you need for this lab are

- Access to a PC system and the Internet

- A solid-state drive and a magnetic hard drive

Getting Down to Business

It's so cool to see how technology has changed over the years and migrated to smaller, less noisy equipment. Heck, I remember when we used to have to park the heads to move a hard drive, and now we just pull them out and put them in our pocket—what will they think of next?

In this scenario, your boss is not convinced that SSDs are all that great, so your job is to explain to him why you think SSDs are better than magnetic hard drives.

Step 1   Search the Internet for "solid-state drives." Use manufacturer and retailer Web sites to find the information listed in the following table. Record your findings.

Maker	Cost	Capacity	Pros	Cons	Unique Features

Step 2   Now do the same thing for "hard drives" and note whether it's a PATA or SATA drive.

Maker	Cost	Capacity	Pros	Cons	Unique Features	PATA or SATA

Step 3   Now that you've compiled some hard facts about SSDs and magnetic hard drives, prepare (electronically) a proposal to your boss explaining why you think SSDs are superior to magnetic hard drives. Be prepared to share your proposal with the class.

 60 MINUTES

Lab Exercise 10.05: Exploring SCSI and RAID

As you inventory the machines that were just donated to your nonprofit organization, you discover two additional machines with small computer system interface (SCSI) controllers. You want to use them in a RAID array, but don't know much about either technology.

Learning Objectives

This lab touches on important tech skills, helping you research hardware so you can provide good information to clients. With the introduction of the SATA interface, the need for SCSI implementation on desktop machines is quickly fading. However, SCSI—which is well over 20 years old—is still used in large-capacity, data server environments.

At the end of this lab, you'll be able to

- Explain key features of SCSI

- Define the levels of RAID

Lab Materials and Setup

The materials you need for this lab are

- Access to a PC system and the Internet

- A trip to the local computer store for research

- A notepad and pen to take notes at the store

Getting Down to Business

Limber up your surfing fingers, as you'll start your search on the Internet. Then you might want to make a visit to the local computer store to explore further how the technologies of SCSI and RAID are being used in today's computing environments.

Step 1   Access the Internet and search for information on parallel SCSI devices, primarily hard drives. Use keywords such as *Ultra320, Ultra640, white paper, controllers,* and *storage solutions.* Then answer the following questions:

a.   What speed of data transfer can be achieved with parallel SCSI?

_____

b.   How many drives can be attached to a single controller?

_____

c.   What is the price range of parallel SCSI drives?

_____

d.   What is a SCSI chain?

_____

✔ **Cross-Reference**

For more information on SCSI, refer to the "SCSI: Still Around" section in Chapter 10 of *Mike Meyers' CompTIA A+ Guide to 801: Managing and Troubleshooting PCs*.

Step 2 As you surfed around to the different sites on SCSI, you probably noticed that many of these drives are implemented in different RAID configurations. With the overall cost of hard drives dropping, many desktop motherboard manufacturers (ASUS, Gigabyte, Intel, and so on) are incorporating RAID controllers into their motherboards. Visit a few of the motherboard manufacturers' Web sites and research their implementation of RAID. Use the following questions to refine your focus.

✔ **Cross-Reference**

For more information on RAID, refer to the "Protecting Data with RAID," "RAID," and "Implementing RAID" sections in Chapter 10 of *Mike Meyers' CompTIA A+ Guide to 801: Managing and Troubleshooting PCs*.

a. What are the most popular implementations of RAID used on desktop machines?

_____

b. How many drives are required to support the various RAID levels?

_____

c. Can you configure desktop RAID using both PATA and SATA drives?

_____

d. What are the two goals when implementing a RAID solution?

_____

_____

Step 3 Gather the information you've found in your Internet research and head to your local computer store. Explore the current trends, based on the systems and components your local supplier is promoting. Write (on a separate sheet of paper) a brief summary of your findings and share it with your instructor and classmates.

Lab Analysis Test

1. Matthew has decided to use the RAID integrated into the SATA controller on his new system. He uses the system for high-end video editing, and would like to improve the performance of the system for this task. What implementation of RAID would you recommend to improve performance?

2. In what situation(s) might it be appropriate to disable the motherboard's hard drive controllers?

3. Sean would like to install four additional hard drives in his system. His motherboard has two IDE controllers and two SATA controllers. There is one SATA drive installed, and the optical drive is an IDE device. How would you configure Sean's system?

Key Term Quiz

Use the following terms to complete the following sentences. Not all terms will be used.

autodetect

cable select

master

PATA

platters

RAID

SATA

sectors

slave

SSD

1. A(n) _____ uses memory chips to store data and has none of the moving parts of traditional hard drives.

2. The data in a traditional hard disk drive is actually stored magnetically on disks called _____.

3. One type of IDE drive transfers data in a parallel fashion. The other type of IDE drive transfers data in a serial fashion. These two types are known as _____ and _____, respectively.

4. To secure data in servers and high-end PCs, use a(n) _____ controller.

5. A great way to determine whether a new drive is installed and configured correctly is to run _____.

Chapter 11
Removable Media

Lab Exercises

Removable media storage is one of the fastest-changing components of the PC, and these days it's also very much in the public eye. With the advent of USB thumb drives, iPods, and digital cameras using CompactFlash and Secure Digital memory cards, all kinds of people—from children to great-grandmothers, from artists to zookeepers—are using removable storage. With the high resolution of today's audio and video files, photographs, and games, the need for portable large-capacity storage is greater than ever.

The lowly floppy drive has the distinction of being the only component of a "modern" PC to employ basically the same technology as the original IBM PC. It's hard to believe, but when the first PCs came out, the entire data storage system consisted of a single floppy drive and multiple floppy disks holding a little more than 300,000 bytes of data each! Floppy drives (and disks) have been around ever since, but with the recent advances in storage technology, the floppy has finally entered its twilight, due mostly to its tiny capacity.

Technicians were the last holdout in keeping floppy drives around. Although hard drives can contain trillions of bytes of data, they can also fail; until recently, techs could still depend on the floppy drive, and a disk that can hold less than 2 MB of data, to boot a failed system and provide troubleshooting utilities that might breathe life back into the PC. While techs still need these tools, they now come in the form of bootable CDs, DVDs, and USB thumb drives.

As a budding tech, you'll work with all types of removable media. The labs in this chapter will introduce you to the installation, configuration, and use of optical drives, burners, and media. You'll work with thumb drives and even learn to install the venerable floppy drive—this is important because the CompTIA A+ 220-801 exam thinks you should still know how to deal with floppy drives. The final lab in the chapter looks at some troubleshooting techniques for removable media.

30 MINUTES

Lab Exercise 11.01: Installing Floppy Drives

Your boss recently approved the purchase of a number of new workstations, all without floppy drives. "Times are changing," he explained, "and floppies just hold too little data. Plus they're slow and cumbersome!" But the employees assigned to the new machines complained so much that the boss has decided to retrofit all the new workstations with 3.5-inch floppy drives. Some manufacturers offer external USB 3.5-inch floppy drives, but you found a supply house closeout on old, internal floppy drives. You've been assigned the task of installing them into each system.

✔ Cross-Reference

To review the details of floppy drive installation, refer to the "Installing Floppy Drives" section in Chapter 11 of *Mike Meyers' CompTIA A+ Guide to 801: Managing and Troubleshooting PCs.*

Learning Objectives

In this lab, you'll practice removing and installing a floppy drive.

At the end of this lab, you'll be able to

- Remove a floppy drive safely and correctly

- Install a floppy drive safely and correctly

Lab Materials and Setup

The materials you need for this lab are

- A working computer system with a floppy drive installed

- A known good floppy disk with data

Getting Down to Business

Although this lab starts with a working floppy drive installed in a PC—a likely scenario in a classroom setting—you would obviously need to install one yourself when building a system.

Step 1   Begin with the PC turned on and the standard Windows desktop displayed. To verify that the floppy drive works, insert a known good floppy disk containing files into the drive, and then view the files on it by following these steps:

    a.   Double-click the My Computer/Computer icon on the desktop.

    b.   Double-click the 3½ Floppy Disk Drive (A:) icon in the window (see Figure 11-1).

    c.   Observe the files and folders displayed.

       Do you see files displayed? _____

✔ **Hint**

If no files are displayed, try another floppy disk. Also, be sure to insert the disk properly. You should hear a ratcheting sound when you double-click the floppy drive icon. This is the sound of the read mechanism opening the metal cover so that it can read the data on the disk.

FIGURE 11-1 Accessing the contents of a floppy disk in Windows Vista

Step 2 Properly shut down the system, unplug the main power cable, and open the case following good ESD procedures.

Step 3 Carefully disconnect the two cables from the back of the floppy drive. One is the four-wire cable from the power supply (with its mini power connector), and the other is the flat ribbon cable that carries the data to and from the drive.

✖ **Warning**

> Be sure to notice the seven-wire twist in the ribbon cable before you disconnect it. Is the twist closer to the drive or to the motherboard? If you put this cable back on incorrectly, the floppy drive will not work. The end with the twist (see Figure 11-2) always goes closest to the floppy drive.

✔ **Hint**

> If your lab uses rounded data cables rather than the traditional flat ribbon cables, you can safely assume that one of the connectors will have a marking for the A: drive.

Now disconnect the other end of the ribbon cable from the motherboard. These cables can be quite firmly attached to the motherboard, so use caution! Grab the connector (or grab as close to the connector as you can) and pull straight up firmly but gently. Sometimes a connector will seem to stick on one side—make sure that you don't pull unevenly, or you may bend the pins on the motherboard.

Floppy B

Floppy A

Floppy Controller Plug

Figure 11-2 The twist in one end of the floppy drive ribbon cable

 a. How many wires make up the ribbon cable? (Go ahead, count 'em!)

_____

 b. Is one of the wires a different color from the rest, and if so, what does that mean?

_____

 c. Look at the motherboard where the cable was attached, and examine the pins. How many pins do you count?

_____

 d. Look at the shape of the connection. Is it symmetrical, meaning you can plug the connector in either direction, or is one side of the connector keyed to prevent you from inserting it backward?

_____

Locate pin 1 (where the colored wire attaches) and pin 34. The thirty-fourth pin is the drive change signal/disk change signal. It indicates when a disk has been physically changed. If this wire is broken or not connected, the system will read the initial disk placed in the floppy drive after power is applied and remember the contents for that disk, no matter how many times you change disks during a session, until you reboot the system.

Compare your motherboard connection for the floppy drive with the one shown in Figure 11-3.

Step 4 Remove the floppy drive from the case. There are so many different ways that floppy drives are held into system cases that it would be impossible to list all of the various carriers, caddies, bays, and so on, that might be used to hold your floppy drive.

Figure 11-3 The orientation of the floppy drive connector on the motherboard

Almost all floppy drives are secured to these carriers, caddies, and bays with fine-threaded screws. The threads on these screws are narrower than those on the screws commonly used to secure expansion cards and the case cover. There should be two screws in each side of the floppy drive for support.

✔ **Hint**

Get in the habit of storing screws safely while you're changing out or inspecting hardware. You can use a small plastic bowl, a coffee cup, or an empty baby food jar or breath mint tin—but if you let those screws roll around loose, you may not have enough of them the next time you need to install a device!

Step 5   Now that you've removed the floppy drive, give it a thorough inspection. Look at the area where the cables connect (see Figure 11-4).

a.   Is this ribbon cable area keyed or notched? _____

b.   Find the indicator for the location of pin 1 on the floppy drive. What and where is it?

_____

c.   On which side of the connector does the red (or other colored) orientation stripe of the cable go—toward the center or toward the outside?

_____

d.   How many physical pins are on your floppy drive? _____

e.   Look at the area where the power is attached. How many pins are there? _____

FIGURE 11-4 Examining the connections for the ribbon cable (top) and power cable (bottom) on the back of a floppy drive

    f.   Take a moment to experiment to see if you can insert the power connector into the floppy drive incorrectly. Be gentle!

    g.   Can you connect it upside down? _____

    h.   Can you connect it without covering every pin? _____

    i.   On which side of the mini connector does the orientation stripe go: toward the center or toward the outside?

_____

✖ Warning

It is possible to force the power connector on incorrectly, which will cause damage to the drive. Practice how it feels to make this connection properly and improperly, so that when you do it from an odd angle (for example, lying on your back under a desk), you know how it should feel.

Step 6   Reinstall the floppy drive by placing it back where you found it in the case. Be sure to use the proper fine-threaded screws to secure the drive.

Now attach a mini connector to the floppy drive to provide power, and attach the 34-pin ribbon cable securely to the drive.

Attach the ribbon cable to the motherboard. Make sure it is secure and all the pins are covered.

    a.   Did you make sure that pin 1 was connected properly at both ends of the ribbon cable?

    _____

    b.   Are the connectors properly aligned so that pin 34 is connected on both ends of the cable?

    _____

Step 7   Once everything is back in place, leave the system cover off so that you can make adjustments if needed. Start the system and watch the green LED on the front of the floppy drive.

If the green LED does not turn on at all during the boot process, then check your power connection.

If the green LED comes on and stays on all the time, then the ribbon cable is not connected properly (it is probably reversed either on the motherboard or on the floppy drive).

Is everything working properly? _____

After you confirm that everything is working, place the cover back onto your system. Start Windows and test your floppy drive as you did in Step 1 of this lab.

30 minutes

Lab Exercise 11.02: Installing Optical Drives

Your supervisor calls you in one day and announces that he wants to simplify the daily database backup procedures for your company. You will still use tape backups for archival backups, but he wants all the CD-R/RW drives on your company's servers replaced with DVD-R/RW drives. The increased storage capacity of this type of drive will enable you to back up onto a single disc most of the critical files that change during the day. To accomplish this task, you must physically uninstall all the existing CD-R/RW drives and replace them with DVD-R/RW equivalents.

You should be comfortable removing and installing optical drives. Many optical drives still use the PATA interface to connect to your system, making the installation process fairly simple. If you are lucky enough to be working with a newer system, you will probably uninstall and install SATA optical drives. The CompTIA A+ 220-801 exam assumes you know how to install both PATA and SATA optical drives!

Learning Objectives

In this lab, you'll remove and inspect an optical drive, and then reinstall the drive.

At the end of this lab, you'll be able to

- Remove and install an optical drive safely and properly

- Identify the physical features of an optical drive

Lab Materials and Setup

The materials you need for this lab are

- A working computer with Windows and an optical drive of some type installed (what type you use doesn't matter, but it's helpful if you have both a PATA and a SATA drive)

Getting Down to Business

Removing an optical drive is almost too easy. The only real secret here is to remember which cable you removed and how the cable ends were oriented—you've got to make sure you can put it back! Also, PATA optical drives use the standard master/slave jumpers—these also need to be inspected to make sure that the drive runs properly on the PATA connection. For a quick look at jumper settings check out the PDF file at www.wdc.com/en/library/eide/2579-001037.pdf.

Step 1   Properly shut down your system. As I've mentioned before, there are so many different ways that drives are held into system cases that it would be impossible to list all of the various carriers, caddies, bays, and so on, that might be used to hold your drive. Using whichever method is appropriate, remove the cover from the PC case so that you can access the screws on both sides of the drive. Using proper ESD procedures, perform the following steps to remove the drive from your system:

a. Unplug the connections. First unplug the Molex or SATA power connection from the back of the drive, and then disconnect the PATA ribbon cable or SATA cable from the drive. Unplug the audio cable coming from the sound card (if present) that plugs into the back of the drive.

b. Using a Philips-head screwdriver, remove the screws holding the drive in place. Notice that the screws are small-threaded screws—the same type you encountered when you removed and installed your floppy drive.

✔ **Hint**

Some optical drives are held in their bays by rails. Simply squeeze the rail toggles (sticking out of the front) and remove the drive by pulling it forward.

Step 2   Inspect the optical drive. Look at the front of the drive. Do you see a tiny hole near the edge of the tray door? Most drives have such a hole. You can take a straightened-out paper clip and push it into this hole to release the tray. This is handy in case you accidentally leave a disc in the drive when you remove it from the system. Go ahead and push a straightened-out paper clip into the hole to eject the tray.

Look at the back of the drive. You should see several areas for connections:

- The Molex or SATA power connection

- The connection for the PATA or SATA cable

- An audio connection for a cable to the sound card (there may be more than one connector because of different styles of cables, but only one cable should be connected)

- Jumper settings: master, slave, and cable select (PATA only)

✔ **Hint**

On PATA drives, look for the orientation of pin 1. It is usually closest to the power connection.

Step 3   Reinstall the optical drive into your system. It can be a master drive or a slave drive, depending on what other PATA devices are installed. Figure 11-5 shows a properly installed drive.

Now answer these questions:

a. Did you fasten the drive using the correct screws? _____

b. Is the master/slave jumper set correctly? _____

c. Is the PATA/SATA cable connected properly? _____

FIGURE 11-5 Viewing a properly installed optical drive

d. Is the power plug fully inserted? _____

e. Is the audio cable connected to the drive? _____

Step 4   Leave the cover off the system and boot the PC to the Windows desktop.

Step 5   Select My Computer/Computer. Notice if the drive's icon is present. If so, all is well. If not, repeat Steps 2 and 3. The most common problem when installing hardware is a loose connection, so recheck your cable ends and try again. Replace the PC cover once the drive is recognized in Windows.

 30 MINUTES

Lab Exercise 11.03: Working with USB Thumb Drives

Your company is finally being forced to provide larger-capacity removable storage for all of the sales organization staff. In the not-so-distant past, PowerPoint presentations were moved from machine to machine via floppy disks, and then via CD-Rs. With the ease of use and convenient size of USB thumb drives, all sales personnel will now be issued 4-GB thumb drives. Your mission (should you choose to accept it) is to teach the field sales personnel how to properly use their new thumb drives.

✔ Cross-Reference

For a primer on USB flash memory drives (often called thumb drives), see the "USB Thumb Drives" section in Chapter 11 of *Mike Meyers' CompTIA A+ Guide to 801: Managing and Troubleshooting PCs*.

Learning Objectives

In this lab, you'll learn to insert, use, and safely remove USB thumb drives.

At the end of this lab, you'll be able to

- Insert and remove USB thumb drives
- Save and transfer data using USB thumb drives

Lab Materials and Setup

The materials you need for this lab are

- A Windows PC
- A USB thumb drive

Getting Down to Business

In Lab Exercise 11.01, you physically removed and reinstalled a floppy drive, but as you are aware, this technology is quickly being retired. This lab exercise uses the newest technology to replace the function and ease of the floppy disk, the USB flash drive (thumb drive). You will use a USB thumb drive to transfer a large file by inserting the drive into a Windows system, copying some data onto it, removing it, and reinserting it into a new system (or the same lab machine) and transferring the data to the new machine.

Step 1   USB thumb drives come in many shapes and colors, as well as many data capacities. An older thumb drive might be as small as 256 MB, while a newer thumb drive might be as large as 256 GB. They are typically a few inches long, and most provide protection for the USB connector using either a cover of some type or a retractable mechanism as shown in Figure 11-6.

Figure 11-6 A USB thumb drive with a retractable connector

a. Boot your lab system and allow it to finish displaying the Windows desktop. Insert the USB thumb drive and note any activity on the screen.

b. Did a window appear asking what you want Windows to do? _____

c. If yes, what were some of the options you could choose?

_____

_____

Close the options window.

Step 2 Open an application on your PC, such as Word or PowerPoint, and select and open a file. If you can find a file larger than 1.44 MB, you can experience firsthand the benefit of USB thumb drives over floppy drives.

Step 3 In the application window, select File | Save As. In Windows XP, click the drop-down arrow for the Save in field. You will see a number of folders and drives where you could choose to save the file. One of these should be the thumb drive, as shown in Figure 11-7. Select the thumb drive and save the file. In Windows Vista/7, click Browse Folders (if necessary). In the list that appears, click Folders. Then scroll until you see the thumb drive. Select it and save the file. Close all open windows.

Figure 11-7 The Windows XP Save As dialog box showing a Lexar Media thumb drive

Step 4   In the system tray, find and click the Safely Remove Hardware icon, which in Windows XP is a green arrow and a gray rectangle, and in Vista/7 is a white checkmark on a green circle in front of a tiny USB symbol. A tiny pop-up message appears adjacent to the icon, listing all removable devices; click the name of the thumb drive. In XP, an information balloon with a *Safe to Remove Hardware* message should notify you that you can now remove the USB mass storage device. In Vista/7, an announcement will appear with the same message.

Remove the thumb drive from the USB port.

✔ Hint

If you forget to close one or more windows with a focus on the thumb drive, you will receive an error message: *The device "Generic Volume" cannot be stopped right now. Try stopping it later.* If you receive this message, just click OK, close all open files and folders on the thumb drive, and try again.

If you have some open files or folders on the thumb drive and you just pull it out of the machine, you may receive an error message such as *Fail Write Delay*. Most of the time the files and folders will remain intact, but this is not the recommended removal method.

Step 5   At this point, if you have a second machine where you can plug in the thumb drive, it will make the lab exercise more realistic. If you don't, you can just use the same system again for this step. Insert the thumb drive into a USB port and again note any activity on the screen. This time, double-click *Open folder to view files using Windows Explorer*.

Step 6   Double-click the file you saved previously; if the file has an associated application, this should launch that application and open the file.

You have now successfully used a USB thumb drive—also referred to as a *jump drive*—to "jump" files from one machine to another.

 30 MINUTES

Lab Exercise 11.04: Configuring Removable Media Drives

A new client has very specific needs for the boot order and access to removable media in his computer center's seven computers. For the two servers, the floppy drive and USB ports will be installed, but the floppy drive will be disabled in CMOS. Three of the five workstations need the optical drive set as the first drive in the boot sequence, but the other two need the USB drive to be first in the boot sequence, with the optical drive second. It's your job to set up these PCs properly, so get to work!

Learning Objectives

In this lab, you'll use the CMOS setup program to configure the settings for the floppy drive, USB devices, optical drive, and boot order.

At the end of this lab, you'll be able to

- Locate the CMOS setup screens for configuring the floppy drives, USB devices, optical drives, and boot order

- Configure various scenarios for the floppy drive, USB devices, optical drive, and boot order

Lab Materials and Setup

The materials you need for this lab are

- A working computer system with a floppy drive, an optical drive, and USB device support

Getting Down to Business

This lab exercise involves the floppy drive controller, optical drive, and USB controller, and shows you how to configure these devices and the boot order of these devices in CMOS.

Depending on your BIOS manufacturer and version, you may or may not be able to perform all of the following steps. Explore the different screens to discover whether you can enable/disable the floppy drive controller (FDC) and the USB controller, and which devices you can put in the boot order (floppy drive, optical drive, hard drive, and USB devices).

Step 1 You will start by disabling the floppy drive. Enter the CMOS setup program by pressing the appropriate key or key combination (which you should remember from Lab Exercise 7.02) while your system is booting.

Having previously browsed through your version of CMOS, you should be able to locate the screen that contains settings for the FDC. If you can't remember which screen deals with the FDC, browse through the CMOS screens until you find it.

a. Do you have an option in CMOS to disable the FDC? _____

b. Under what title heading did you find this option?

_____

c. How do you disable this setting?

_____

Now disable it.

✔ **Hint**

Disabling the FDC is a good way for a network administrator to prevent users from using floppy disks to either take information off the network or introduce viruses into the network.

Step 2   Restart your system and see if you can access the floppy drive. Did the LED on the front of the floppy drive turn on as the system booted up?

_____

Step 3   Re-enter the CMOS setup utility and turn the FDC back on. Reboot the system, and test the floppy drive. Does it function properly?

_____

Step 4   One of the most important aspects of removable media is that you can boot a nonfunctioning system from a device other than the hard drive with the diagnostic and troubleshooting tools included. The next CMOS setting to play with is the boot sequence.

When you boot up a PC, the system needs to know where to get the operating system software to load into memory. The three standard places to store this software are the hard drive, the optical drive, or a USB thumb drive. In some cases, you might boot from a server somewhere on your network.

Using the CMOS setup utility, you can designate the order in which your system will check the devices for the operating system software. Specifying the proper boot sequence—that is, the search order—saves time by telling the system where to look first. After all, if your operating system is on the hard drive, why should your system waste time looking on the optical or USB thumb drive every time you boot?

Enter the CMOS setup utility, and look for a screen that includes a boot sequence setting.

a.   How many different boot sequences can you configure in CMOS? _____

b.   How many different devices can be in the search sequence? _____

Set your system to boot from the optical drive first (see Figure 11-8).

Step 5   Restart your system. Typically, the boot screen will prompt you with the message _Press any key to boot from the CD_. If there is a bootable CD in the drive, the system will boot from that disc. Leave this boot order in place for the next lab exercise, in which you'll learn how to create bootable CDs.

Step 6   Re-enter the CMOS setup utility, and note whether your system will allow you to boot from a USB device, such as a USB thumb drive.

```
                    Phoenix - Award BIOS CMOS Setup Utility
                            Advanced BIOS Features

      Quick Power On Self Test    Enabled             Item Help
   ▶  Hard Disk Boot Priority     Press Enter
      First Boot Device           CDROM          Menu Level    ▶
      Second Boot Device          Hard Disk
      Third Boot Device           Floppy         Allows the system to
      Boot Other Device           Enabled        skip certain tests
      Boot Up Floppy Seek         Disabled       while booting. This
      Boot up NumLock Status      On             will decrease the time
      Security Option             Setup          needed to boot the
      MPS Version Control For OS   1.4           system
      Delay For HDD (Secs)        0
      Full Screen LOGO Show       Disabled





   ▲▼◄:Move  Enter:Select    +/-/PU/PD:Value  F10:Save   ESC:Exit  F1:General Help
      F5:Previous Values          F6:Fail-Safe Defaults   F7:Optimized Defaults
```

FIGURE 11-8 Boot sequence screen from CMOS with the optical drive as first boot device

If your machine is capable, you can substitute a USB thumb drive for the optical drive in the next lab exercise and create a live USB of the GParted partition editor. For now, leave the optical drive as the first device in the boot order and shut down the machine.

 60 MINUTES

Lab Exercise 11.05: Burning Optical Discs

PCs today are used more than ever for storage of digital photographs, music, and video, in addition to more traditional types of data. Even a modest collection of MP3 files, family photos, and home video clips requires many gigabytes of space! Hard drives do have space limits, and at some point they tend to fail, so wise PC users turn to recordable CDs, DVDs, and Blu-ray drives. These discs provide an affordable large-capacity portable storage option; you can put your important data onto a disc, or make multiple copies of that disc to store in two or more secure locations.

This lab will introduce you to the process by which we record, or *burn*, optical discs. Rather than burning a disc full of your favorite tunes or photos, you'll be making the type of disc that a technician would have in his toolkit when troubleshooting a machine that won't boot.

→ **Note**

If your systems have Blu-ray drives, you will be burning your disc the same way. However, be aware that Blu-ray Discs are better armed than current DVDs. They come equipped with a secure encryption system—a unique ID that protects against video piracy and copyright infringement.

> **✔ Cross-Reference**
>
> For additional information on burning optical discs, refer to the "Applications" section in Chapter 11 of *Mike Meyers' CompTIA A+ Guide to 801: Managing and Troubleshooting PCs.*

Learning Objectives

In this lab, you'll use a third-party burning program to create bootable ISO images on recordable optical discs.

At the end of this lab, you'll be able to

- Work with optical discs and burning tools

- Create a bootable optical disc

Lab Materials and Setup

The materials you need for this lab are

- A working computer system with a CD-RW or DVD-RW drive installed

- Internet access (preferably a high-speed connection) for downloading

- An optical disc burning application such as the included tool in Windows 7, ISO Recorder, Nero Burning ROM, or freeware CDBurnerXP

- Blank optical discs (more than one if possible)

Getting Down to Business

If you're at all interested in the world of open-source software, you'll eventually run into the venerable ISO file. ISO files are images of optical discs that are stored on hard drives instead of on optical media. However, it's possible to burn those ISO files to optical media in order to boot from them. In this lab, you will burn the ISO image of the open source, bootable live CD of Gnome Linux and the utility GParted.

Step 1　Ensure that you have optical disc burning software that will enable you to burn ISO images. An ISO image is a complete copy of a disc, including all of the boot information in the boot record. Popular third-party products include the freeware ISO Recorder for Windows XP, Vista, or Windows 7 (http:// isorecorder.alexfeinman.com/isorecorder.htm) and the commercial Nero Burning ROM (www.nero.com). Windows 7, helpfully, includes the ability to burn ISO images without the need for a third-party tool.

You can also try CDBurnerXP, an excellent freeware burning tool that supports the burning of ISO images; it's available at www.cdburnerxp.se. Just go to the CDBurnerXP Web site, follow the instructions, and run the installation. After you've successfully installed the program, you should have all the tools necessary to burn ISO images (see Figure 11-9).

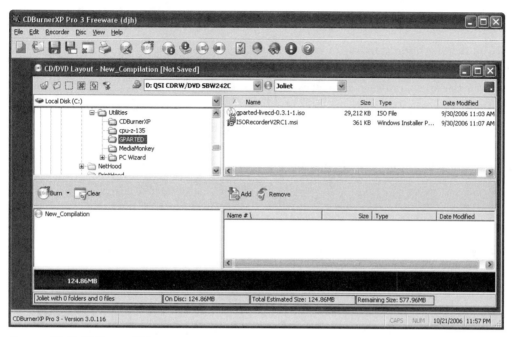

FIGURE 11-9 CDBurnerXP

Step 2   Now visit the GParted Web site at http://gparted.sourceforge.net. Click Downloads and follow the instructions. You can download the full ISO, or download the .zip file to improve transfer times (remember you will have to expand the .zip file after it's on your system).

Step 3   Once you have the ISO image, open the tray on your optical drive and insert a blank optical disc. Close the tray and launch your optical disc burning software. Navigate to the GParted ISO file and follow the instructions to burn the ISO image onto the optical media. Most programs will eject the tray with the disc once the writing process is complete.

Step 4   Place the newly created disc into the optical drive tray, close the tray, and reboot the computer. If all has gone well, GParted will boot, detect your hard drives, and give you the option to partition and format these drives.

✖ Warning

Remember, any time you format a hard disk, you delete the data currently on that disk. Do not run GParted on the disk containing your operating system unless you have been instructed to delete this system's OS.

→ **Try This: Ultimate Boot CD**

Now that you have an understanding of why you might want to boot a machine from removable media—to perform low-level diagnostics, troubleshoot, or just prep the disk before installing an operating system—take a cruise over to www.ultimatebootcd.com.

You can download the ISO image of Ultimate Boot CD (UBCD), which has over 100 different freeware tools, all placed on a live CD. Use the method you learned in this exercise to burn the ISO image to a CD, boot a machine with the UBCD, and explore some of the tools. You might find that using some of the drive manufacturer's low-level formatting tools will bring a dead drive back to life.

Lab Analysis Test

1. Jovan installed an optical drive on the same cable as his primary hard drive, and now the system will not boot. What could be causing this?

2. Mark wants to use optical discs to create backups of his data. He has about 20 GB of documents, movies, photos, and music. Using what you know about optical disc capacities, what would you recommend to him as the best solution for backing up data to optical discs? What, if any, special considerations will Mark need to keep in mind?

3. Cecelia is a freelance Web designer who is delivering some files to a client. She sits down at a Windows XP system in the client's office and plugs in her trusty USB thumb drive, but nothing happens—Windows doesn't acknowledge the device at all. The thumb drive has been working perfectly well, as recently as this morning. What is most likely the reason that the USB thumb drive won't connect with the client PC?

4. When Philip puts his CD-RW disc in the drive and copies files to and from it, he notices that the drive speeds up and slows down. Is this normal? If not, what should he do to fix it?

5. After removing an optical drive for replacement, you remember that you left a disc in the drive. You look for a hole to insert the paper clip into, but there is none. How do you remove the disc?

Key Term Quiz

Use the following terms to complete the following sentences. Not all terms will be used.

Blu-ray

CMOS

disc

DMA

label

optical drive

scratches

spiral

surface

USB 1.0

USB 2.0

USB 3.0

1. An optical drive must be identified in the _____ settings.

2. _____ Discs can hold and play back large quantities of high-definition video and audio, as well as photos, data, and other digital content.

3. Any drive that uses a laser of some sort to read data from a disc is called a(n) _____.

4. The _____ version of thumb drives supports a maximum throughput of 480 Mbps.

5. The reflective aluminum layer of an optical disc can be damaged by _____.

Chapter 12

Input Devices

Lab Exercises

The world of input and output is one full of peripherals. These range from the more obvious (keyboards and mice) to the more specialized (digital cameras, bar code readers, and KVM switches) devices. It is these components that allow you to interact with the computer. Without a keyboard or mouse, you would be sitting in front of a computer all day *waiting* for something to happen spontaneously. While you are most likely familiar with the use of input devices such as keyboards and mice, you may not be as intimately acquainted with their connection method or maintenance.

Most peripherals use a USB connector of one kind or another. While USB is a plug-and-play technology, the device itself still requires a driver, and you need to know where to find that driver and how to install it. Maintaining peripherals is also important. Keyboards, in the wrong hands, can be quite breakable, but even well-kept keyboards can't last forever. Of course, there is more to life than just plain text. With the rise of digital photography and online image-sharing services, more people than ever want to keep their photos on their computers. Two peripherals can help them do just that—scanners and digital cameras. But these devices are not all built the same. Cost and quality can vary dramatically, and even a single device is capable of producing images of different qualities, depending on its settings and how it is used.

 30 MINUTES

Lab Exercise 12.01: Using USB Drivers

USB's incredible ease of use makes it the most popular type of general-purpose connection used on PCs. USB is so popular that every type of peripheral (other than monitors) has someone making a USB version. The downside to this ease of use is that it can be a challenge to deal with USB when it doesn't work as specified.

Learning Objectives

At the end of this lab, you'll be able to

- Diagnose and repair common USB driver failures

- Recognize the limitations of built-in Windows USB device drivers

Lab Materials and Setup

The materials you need for this lab are

- A Windows system using USB

- At least one "human interface" USB device, such as a mouse or keyboard

- At least one mass storage USB device, such as a USB thumb drive

- At least one USB device that is neither a human interface device nor a mass storage device (for example, a wired NIC, Bluetooth hub, or wireless NIC)

- A notepad and pencil

Getting Down to Business

The biggest problems you'll see with USB are the result of improper drivers. If you know how to recognize these problems from error messages or by using third-party tools, you shouldn't have too much trouble fixing them.

Windows comes with very good built-in support for what it calls human interface devices (HIDs), such as keyboards and mice. It also does a good job supporting most USB mass storage devices such as USB thumb drives. Once you move outside these two classes of devices, however, Windows won't work properly (if at all) without the drivers supplied by the manufacturer.

✔ **Cross-Reference**

For more information on setting up USB devices, refer to the "USB Configuration" section in Chapter 12 of *Mike Meyers' CompTIA A+ Guide to 801: Managing and Troubleshooting PCs.*

Step 1 Connect any HID or mass storage USB device to the Windows system *without* first installing the supplied driver. Does the device work as expected? Is it missing any features? Does the device even come with drivers? Write down your conclusions and unplug the device.

_____

_____

_____

Step 2 Check the Web site of the manufacturer of the USB device you just installed to see if a driver exists. If there is a driver, download it and install it into your system. Now connect the device again. Does the device work the same as it did before?

_____

_____

Step 3   Select another USB device—specifically, one that is neither an HID nor a mass storage device—and connect it to the same system *without* first installing the supplied driver. Does the device work as expected? Is it missing any features? Does the device even come with drivers? Write down your conclusions and unplug the device.

_____

_____

_____

Step 4   Check the Web site of the manufacturer of the USB device you just installed to see if a driver exists. If there is a driver, download it and install it into your system. Did the installation work? In many cases installation will fail because Windows may have loaded an improper driver when you first installed the device. Does the device work the same as before? You'll probably find that it doesn't, for the same reason.

_____

Step 5   Go to the manufacturer's Web site and see how to remove the device driver properly. Delete the driver and then remove the device.

✔ Hint

Installing a USB device without first installing the proper driver on a non-HID or mass storage device will almost always require you to uninstall the USB device completely from Device Manager. Even so, you should still check the manufacturer's Web site first!

Step 6   With the previous drivers properly removed, again install the drivers you downloaded earlier. Then insert the USB device. Does the device work as expected? Are there features now that did not appear earlier? What does this tell you about the importance of installing USB device drivers before you install the actual USB device?

_____

_____

_____

Step 7   As time and available hardware allow, practice installing other USB devices and document how they work, both with and without proper drivers.

30 MINUTES

Lab Exercise 12.02: Paging Dr. Keyboard!

Keyboards are plentiful and common, and a new basic keyboard is very inexpensive. Even with cheap keyboards, users tend to get attached to these devices over time—and in the case of an expensive keyboard with lots of extra buttons and features, the user may have both a financial *and* an emotional attachment! For these reasons, it's important that you learn to play "Dr. Keyboard," fixing these devices when they break.

Learning Objectives

At the end of this lab, you'll be able to

- Repair stuck keyboard keys

- Dismantle and clean a keyboard

Lab Materials and Setup

The materials you need for this lab are

- A Windows system

- As many "throw-away" keyboards as possible (functional keyboards that you won't mind throwing away at the end of this lab; connection type is unimportant as long as they're usable by a Windows system)

- A medium-sized flathead screwdriver

- Compressed air

- A lint-free cloth

✔ **Hint**

Try to avoid using older (pre-2004) laptop keyboards, as many older laptop keyboards used a delicate type of scissors key connector that would shatter if pried off.

Getting Down to Business

In this exercise, you'll dismantle one or more keyboards, cleaning up the keyboard components in the process, and then reassemble the device(s) and test for functionality.

Step 1 Disconnect the keyboard from the Windows system. Try prying off two or three keys using the flathead screwdriver (see Figure 12-1). Include more difficult keys such as the SPACEBAR, ENTER/RETURN, and a key from the center of the keyboard such as the letter G. Inspect the bottom of the key and the key post that it sits on—how much dirt is there? Reinsert the keys, making sure they are snapped all the way down.

Step 2 Test the keyboard by installing it into a Windows system. If any of the keys you removed aren't working, double-check that they're properly snapped in. Shut down the system and remove the keyboard. Repeat this process until all keys are working.

→ **Note**

What should you do if you break a key? Well, nobody sells replacement parts for keyboards—they're just too darn cheap to bother! You might be lucky enough to have a nonworking keyboard that's the exact same model, which you can cannibalize; otherwise, just consign the affected keyboard to the scrap heap after you've used it for this lab.

Step 3 Insert the nozzle of the compressed air under a key and start blasting away. If the keyboard is really old or looks dirty, you may want to do this outside! Did you see any dust or crumbs come out?

Step 4 Completely dismantle the keyboard. Most keyboards have a number of screws underneath that you must first remove to begin this process. Inspect the screws—are they different sizes? Keep track of which screw goes into which hole.

Figure 12-1 Removing the CTRL key with a screwdriver

Figure 12-2 Inside a keyboard

Step 5 The inside of the keyboard will have a number of plastic contact templates (see Figure 12-2). Remove these, keeping track of their relation to each other so you can reassemble them. Wipe down each template with the lint-free cloth dampened with water. If you run into serious dirt, add a bit of mild detergent and repeat until the keyboard is clean.

 Hint

All keyboards have small circuit boards inside as well. Don't get them wet!

Step 6 After allowing everything to dry, reassemble the keyboard and test it on a Windows system. If the keyboard is not working properly, dismantle it and try again.

 30 minutes

Lab Exercise 12.03: Exploring Scanners

With the near ubiquity of digital cameras, most people keep the majority of their photographs in digital form, whether on their hard drive or uploaded to a photo-sharing Web site like Flickr.com. But what do you do with all of those photographs from the old days of film cameras? Sadly, you can't just shove them into your hard drive and have them magically appear on your computer. Instead, flatbed scanners are a popular choice for those people who wish to preserve their photographs or just share them online with friends and family. There are several image-editing applications that will interface with your scanner. You can often scan, import, edit, and upload from a single application!

Learning Objectives

At the end of this lab, you'll be able to

- Use and configure a scanner

Lab Materials and Setup

The materials you need for this lab are

- A Windows system

- A scanner with the proper drivers for your operating system

- An image-editing utility, such as Google's Picasa

- A photograph or document to scan

Getting Down to Business

In this exercise, you'll scan various images at different resolutions to see how various settings impact the speed of the scanner and the quality of the images. Make sure that your scanner is hooked up to your system and properly set up with the correct drivers. Also, make sure you have software capable of interfacing with your scanner. This exercise is written for use with Google's Picasa, but you should be able to follow along with any image-editing utility.

Step 1   If you haven't already, download Google's Picasa from http://picasa.google.com, install it, and open it. (Now would be a good time to check and make sure your scanner is turned on!) Meanwhile, find something (preferably flat) that you can scan. The best things to use include old photographs and paper printouts. Newspapers and magazines are good, too, but depending on the resolution used to print them, you may have mixed results. Place the item facing down on the scanner bed.

Step 2   With Picasa open, select File | Import From. At the very top of the screen is a drop-down box. Use it to select your input device (your scanner).

Step 3   When you select your scanner from the list, the configuration utility for your particular scanner should appear. This will be different for every scanner, but it should have some common features. The most important setting is quality, or resolution. The resolution your scanner uses is the number of dots per inch (dpi) used to create the digital image on your computer. You might have settings called Draft, Good, or Best quality, or they may be more specific, such as 150 dpi, 600 dpi, or 2400 dpi. You might even be able to type in any number you want, up to the maximum resolution of the scanner. There are probably other settings available, but you can play with these later. For now, choose the lowest quality setting available, such as Draft, 150 dpi, or what have you.

Step 4   Click the Preview button. This will scan the entire bed of the scanner at a low resolution so you can accurately select where you want to scan the final image. When the preview is complete, use the tool that is (hopefully) provided to select or highlight the photo, document, or whatever you're scanning. Click the Scan button.

Step 5   Your scanner will now begin to hum and buzz and maybe even shake a little—do not be alarmed. This is the part of the process when whatever you put on the scanner bed is actually *scanned*. When finished, you may be able (or asked) to scan another image, but for now, close the scanner utility.

Step 6   Back in Picasa, your image should appear in the Import window. At the bottom of the screen, select Import All. You'll be asked to name the folder that the image is saved to as well as designate where that folder goes. Click Finish, and you'll be returned to Picasa's main gallery.

Step 7   Find and double-click the image you just scanned. Zoom in and out and pan around. At 150 dpi or Draft settings, the picture will be very small, and any attempt to enlarge it will cause severe pixilation and loss of quality.

Step 8   Now that you know how to scan an image, repeat the process, but this time, select Best quality, or the highest resolution available. Preview and scan the image.

Step 9   Notice anything about the humming and buzzing this time around? Unless you have a magic make-believe scanner, it probably took a lot longer to finish scanning the image this time. That's because the scanner needed to create more digital dots per inch, which takes more time. Import the image into Picasa and open it. Zoom in and out and pan around. Compare this second scan to the first one.

Which scanned image is better? Why?

_____

60 MINUTES

Lab Exercise 12.04: Testing Digital Cameras

As much as we would all like to always be working with the latest and greatest equipment and most advanced technology around, there is one limiting factor that always seems to get in the way: cost. Some people firmly believe in the mantra, "You get what you pay for." And they may be right. But with all of the different features and specifications of digital cameras, some of which are nice and some of which are needless, it is very possible to spend way too much on a bad camera. Personally, I like to focus (an unfortunate pun) on the quality of the pictures taken, and *then* look at the available features, because a camera with more features doesn't necessarily take better pictures. It's possible to buy a cheaper camera with fewer features that takes better pictures—the trick is to know how to find it.

Learning Objectives

At the end of this lab, you'll be able to

- Use a digital camera
- Compare digital cameras
- Upload photos to a computer
- Research digital cameras

Lab Materials and Setup

The materials you need for this lab are

- At least two digital cameras, preferably more if possible
- Cables to connect the digital camera to a computer
- A Windows system with access to the Internet
- An image-editing utility, such as Google's Picasa
- Something to photograph

Getting Down to Business

In this lab exercise, you will compare the quality of images taken by multiple digital cameras in order to determine which camera is the best. To facilitate this, try to use as many different digital cameras as possible. If students have access and permission, they could use their own. The school may also have digital cameras available for student use.

Step 1 To ensure proper testing, you'll need to set up a test shot—something that can be photographed by each digital camera but won't move or change. This can be either a single object or an arrangement of several objects. You may even want to put people in the picture, but make sure they don't move! The object or scene should have color, depth (objects in the foreground and background), and contrast. It should also be adequately lit.

Step 2 Using each digital camera, take a picture of the object or scene. For best results, you may wish to mount the digital cameras on a tripod so that the picture is taken from the same spot each time and the images don't turn out blurry.

Step 3 With all of the pictures taken, plug in each digital camera to your computer using the cable that came with the camera. The image-editing utility will often open automatically when the computer detects a camera has been plugged in, but if not, open your image-editing utility. Find the Import feature for your particular program. In Picasa, you'll find it under File | Import From. Select the digital camera and import your images. Make sure to label the images in a way that lets you know which camera was used; the image itself will store this data, but depending on your software, this information could be difficult to find. Repeat this step for each digital camera used.

Step 4   With all of the images imported into your image-editing utility, open each of them and take a good look. Zoom in and out and pan around. Look at colors (are they accurate?), detail (is this image clear or grainy?), and any obvious flaws (artifacting, pixilation, and so forth). Then, using the following chart, rank each camera in each category to determine which is the best.

Camera	Quality/Clarity	Color Accuracy	Absence of Flaws	Overall

Step 5   Now it's time to do some research. Using Google or a digital camera review Web site (Steve's Digicams, CNET.com, and Digital Camera Resource Page are all good sources of information), find the cameras you used, read about them, and fill in the following chart. Try to use the same Web site for each review score to keep it consistent. Then answer the questions following the chart.

Camera	Average Cost	Review Score

Compare the cost of each camera with its review score and your own findings. Is there a connection between the cost of the digital camera and the quality of its output? If so, what is the connection? Do you think this is true of all digital cameras? Why or why not?

_____

_____

_____

_____

Lab Analysis Test

1.   Beth's brand-new USB keyboard has a piece of the packaging stuck under the keyboard in such a way that she simply can't pull it out, even with a pair of needle-nose pliers. What should she do to fix this problem?

2.   Mario recently purchased a used digital camera capable of taking pictures with a resolution of up to 2 megapixels. He wants to eventually make printouts of these images at 8 × 10 inches or larger. Why or why not is this a good idea?

3. Edward is on a trip with his family and has been taking pictures using a traditional film camera. He has had several rolls of film developed and wants to share some pictures online. Fortunately, he has packed his laptop and a portable scanner for the trip. But when he goes to scan the pictures, the scanner doesn't work. He tries again, with the lid of the scanner opened this time, and notices the light of the scanner is on, but won't move. What's wrong?

4. Whitney sits down at her Windows Vista computer one day to do some work, but notices that something is different about her mouse clicks. She finds it difficult to double-click fast enough for anything to open. Describe how to fix this in Windows Vista.

5. Rita has been using two different computers at her desk at work. She has two cases, two monitors, two keyboards, and two mice. What device could she use to simplify this setup, and how would she set it up?

Key Term Quiz

Use the following terms to complete the following sentences. Not all terms will be used.

bar code reader

biometric device

device driver

digital camera

keyboard

KVM switch

optical resolution

scanner

touch screen

USB

webcam

1. An example of a(n) _____ would be a fingerprint scanner.

2. A(n) _____ usually has two types of zoom: optical and digital.

3. The color depth of a(n) _____ is commonly measured in bits, such as 24-bit, 36-bit, and 48-bit.

4. When installing any USB device, make sure you have the appropriate _____.

5. The main interface for most smartphones is a(n) _____.

Chapter 13

Video

Lab Exercises

Few components affect the PC user like the video system, the primary output for the PC. As you know from the textbook, the video system has two main hardware components—monitor and display adapter—that work together to produce the image on your screen. Both components must be installed and configured properly in Windows, or your viewing pleasure will be seriously compromised. Good techs know how to do video right!

In this set of labs, you'll install a display adapter, hook up a monitor, load video drivers, and configure Windows for optimal viewing. You'll then work with the growing practice of using multiple monitors (for example, a projector and a laptop screen) to expand your desktop viewing area. The last lab exercise will run you though some of the typical troubleshooting issues that techs face when dealing with video.

✖ Warning

It is critical to understand that only *trained* monitor technicians should remove the cover of a video monitor (or a television set, for that matter). The inside of a traditional monitor might look similar to the interior of a PC, with printed circuit boards and related components, but there's a big difference: No PC has voltages up to 50,000 volts or more inside, but most CRT monitors *do*. So be sure to get one thing clear—casually opening a monitor and snooping around has the potential to become harmful to you and the monitor—and in cases of extreme carelessness, it can even be deadly! Even when the power is disconnected, certain components (capacitors) still retain substantial levels of voltage for an extended period of time. Capacitors work like batteries. Yes, they can maintain 50,000 volts! If you inadvertently short one of the capacitors, a large discharge will occur into the monitor circuits, destroying them. If you're touching the metal frame, you could fry yourself—to death. Given this risk, certain aspects of monitor repair fall outside the necessary skill set for a standard PC support person, and definitely outside the CompTIA A+ 220-801 exam domain. Make sure you understand the problems you can fix safely and the ones you need to hand over to a qualified electronics repair shop.

---

 30 MINUTES

Lab Exercise 13.01: Installing Video

Your office staff's computers need a serious video upgrade. Some of the PCs have tiny 17-inch LCD monitors that simply have to go, while others have decent 19-inch and 20-inch LCDs that have a year or two of life left in them. Your boss has bought new PCIe video cards and some 24-inch-widescreen LCD monitors. You're tasked with installing the cards, loading drivers, and setting up everything in Windows.

✔ **Cross-Reference**

For the details of CRT versus LCD monitors, refer to the "CRT Monitors" and "LCD Monitors" sections in Chapter 13 of *Mike Meyers' CompTIA A+ Guide to 801: Managing and Troubleshooting PCs.*

Learning Objectives

At the end of this lab, you'll be able to

- Identify the make and model of a video card

- Install a video display adapter card

- Check BIOS for proper video settings

- Adjust the monitor for the proper display

- Optimize the video settings in Windows

Lab Materials and Setup

The materials you need for this lab are

- A working PC with Windows installed

- A working monitor (access to both a CRT and an LCD monitor is recommended)

- A working computer system with access to the Internet

✔ **Hint**

Classrooms that have a variety of different monitor types and video display adapter cards are a plus.

Getting Down to Business

To begin this lab, you'll become familiar with the video components in your system. You'll then step through the proper installation and configuration of a video adapter.

✖ **Warning**

Some versions of Microsoft Windows operating systems have problems when you make changes to the video display adapters, even when you're simply removing and reinstalling the same card into a different slot. If you perform this lab on a test machine, you should have no real problem if things go wrong. If you're using your primary PC to do the lab, however, make certain you have current drivers available for your video card, or a source to get drivers if necessary.

Step 1   Shut down your system properly and unplug the power cable from the system unit and the wall. Remove the cover from the PC to expose the expansion buses.

    a.   Find your video display adapter card (the one to which the monitor is attached). What type of video display adapter is installed: PCIe, AGP, or PCI? _____

✔ **Hint**

Many laptop computers and some low- to mid-level desktop systems include display adapters integrated right into the electronics of the motherboard. On desktop systems with this configuration, the connector will appear in line with the PS/2 and USB ports. If your system uses this type of display adapter, the overall performance of the system may suffer because the display typically "steals" system RAM to serve as video RAM. Laptops are usually designed around this limitation, but if your desktop system is of this type, you can increase the performance (and usually the video quality) by installing a display adapter card and disabling the onboard video in the BIOS.

---

    b.   Detach the monitor's cable from the video card. Using good ESD avoidance procedures, remove the screw that holds the card in place, put it in a secure location, and then remove your video display adapter card (see Figure 13-1). Examine it closely to answer the following questions. Be careful not to touch the expansion slot contacts on the card!

    c.   Look for a name or model number on the adapter's circuit board or chipset.

Who is the manufacturer, or what is the model number? Write it down. (Note that for this lab's scenario, you'd actually be looking up the information for the new video cards, not the ones already installed—*those* will most likely be donated to charity!)

Figure 13-1 This video card has a large cooling fan for the graphics processing unit (GPU) and its onboard RAM chips

Be sure to write down as much information as you can collect from the display adapter for a later assignment.

    d.   Reinsert the video card into the same slot, and make sure it is properly seated. Reattach the monitor cable and test your system with the case still open to see if it works. This could save you the frustration that results when you close the case, fire up the system, and get a video error. (Not that I've ever done that!)

✔ **Hint**

AGP and PCIe cards can be a little tricky. They must be seated perfectly or they will not work. Many of these types of cards use slots with locking levers—if you were observant when you removed the card initially, you'll know what you have to do now for proper physical installation.

    e.   Boot your system and open your favorite browser to search the Web.

        Conduct your search using the information you've gathered about the manufacturer and model number of your card.

        Can you find the specifications for your display adapter? _____

        What is the highest resolution you can achieve with your video adapter according to these specifications? _____

        How much memory is available? _____

        What type of memory is used? _____

        Does the adapter support SLI or CrossFire? _____

        Does the adapter have any other features, such as an HDMI connector?

        _____

        _____

Step 2   Reboot your system and press the proper key sequence to enter the system setup utility. Depending on the BIOS manufacturer and version, there can be as many as five or more video-related settings. My lab system has 10 settings directly related to video or the PCIe slot. Complete each of these questions based on your specific BIOS. Some of the names of the sections will undoubtedly differ from the ones presented here. Search around a bit and you'll find video options in your CMOS.

        On the Standard CMOS Setup or similar screen, how many choices are there for video, and how is your video set? _____

        On the Chipset Features Setup or similar screen, what is the value for your Video RAM Cacheable setting? _____

Are there any PCIe-specific settings? _____

Are there any settings for the amount of RAM the onboard adapter will use? _____
_____

On the Power Management Setup or similar screen, do you have settings to control how the
monitor and video adapter will react when not in use for a period of time? What are your settings?
_____

On the Integrated Peripherals or similar screen, do you have an Init Display First setting?
What are the choices?
_____

What does your setting say?
_____

Know that when this setting is wrong, the display might not work.

Step 3   You'll now examine a monitor and see what external controls it has. If you're not in a
computer lab, you can go to your local computer store and examine a wide variety of monitors.

Figures 13-2 and 13-3 show the control buttons for adjusting the display attributes for an LCD and a
CRT monitor, respectively. Both of these have the controls on the front of the monitor, but some have the
controls behind a door under the front of the monitor screen, and others may have them on the back.

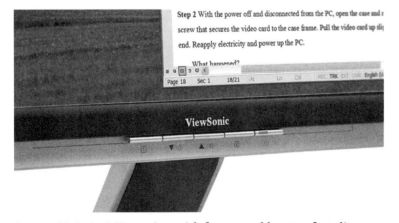

FIGURE 13-2 An LCD monitor with front-panel buttons for adjustments

FIGURE 13-3 Front controls on a CRT monitor

A monitor can have quite a few adjustable features. How many of the following can you adjust on your LCD monitor?

Brightness	
Contrast	
Clock	
H-position	
V-position	
Color temperature	
Auto balance	
Sharpness	
Gamma	
Signal select (for LCDs with both VGA and DVI inputs)	
Full screen	
Language	

How many of these can you adjust on your CRT monitor?

Brightness	
Contrast	
Color saturation	

Vertical size	
Vertical position	
Horizontal size	
Horizontal position	
Pincushioning (for adjusting displays that are narrow in the middle but flare out at the top and bottom)	
Keystoning (for adjusting displays that are narrow at the top but flare out at the bottom)	
Degauss (for adjusting displays that have become fuzzy due to electromagnetic interference)	

Play with the controls of your monitor or a test monitor. If the current settings use percentages, write down the settings before doing any adjustments. Then follow these steps:

a. Change the settings such as color and sizing. Don't be shy!

b. Put the settings back as close as possible to their original positions.

c. Optimize the screen for clarity and position.

Step 4 The hardware is set up properly and the BIOS settings should be correct, so now you need to configure and optimize the Windows settings that determine your video display characteristics. To do this, you need to use the Display applet (or Display Settings applet in Windows Vista).

✔ **Hint**

This lab simulates a working PC that you upgrade with new hardware and drivers. All the steps can work just as well for installing a video card into a new system, although the pace of that installation would differ. In a new system, you would physically install the video card, let Windows use generic VGA drivers until you make sure you can boot properly, and only then install the drivers for the video card. Finally, you'd go to the Display/Display Settings applet and optimize the video card settings. Windows is fairly good at finding a suitable driver the first time around, but you should still understand how to locate and update drivers for your video card.

In Windows XP, navigate to the Display applet and click the Settings tab. In Windows Vista, go to Control Panel | Personalization | Display Settings. In Windows 7, go to the Display Control Panel applet and click on *Change display settings*. This displays the monitor settings, such as those shown in Figure 13-4.

FIGURE 13-4 The Screen Resolution dialog box in the Display applet of Windows 7

✖ **Warning**

You're going to make changes to the look and feel of Windows. Making some of these changes can result in frustrating and time-consuming problems. Use a test machine if you have one available. If you must use your own machine, write down all your display settings before you make any changes.

Each video display adapter manufacturer has different options for its cards. By clicking the Advanced button (Advanced settings in Windows 7), you can access more information about the display adapter. You may see a choice for setting the refresh rate, as well as other features. Look through the settings on the Advanced tab or Properties dialog box, and see what your display adapter manufacturer provides. Remember that the video adapter "pushes" the monitor. If you set the refresh too high, it can cause problems, and, in the case of older CRTs, may even damage your monitor.

Write down your display's current resolution, color depth, and refresh rate. In Windows 7, you may need to look around to find these. Go ahead and explore!

Close the Advanced/Properties dialog box (if you selected it), but leave the Display Properties/Screen Resolution dialog box open.

Make some changes to the background and colors on your screen. In Windows XP, you'll find these options on the Desktop and Appearance tabs, respectively. In Windows Vista/7, you'll find these options in the Personalization applet. Be sure to note the original settings so you can change things back when you're done.

✔ **Hint**

The setting changes suggested in this step are perfectly safe and easy to undo.

Change the desktop background to something you might like better. Then try the following:

- Experiment with color combinations.

- Make some changes to the displayed fonts and menu bars.

- Experiment with changing the colors and resolution of your display.

    Can your machine run in 16-bit color? _____

    How about 24-bit color? _____

    Can you run 800 × 600 resolution? _____

    Can you run 1024 × 768 resolution? _____

    Can you run 1280 × 960 resolution? _____

    Do you have any other options? _____

In Windows XP, click the Advanced button again. In Windows Vista, click Advanced. In Windows 7, click on the Advanced settings link. Open the Monitor tab. Experiment with changing the refresh rate (see Figure 13-5).

✔ **Hint**

Because of the way that LCD monitors work, the refresh rate setting doesn't really apply to them. As a general rule, LCD monitors display a stable, flicker-free image at 60 hertz (Hz). There are no visible differences between 85 Hz and 60 Hz.

FIGURE 13-5 A typical refresh setting on the Monitor tab

Can you make specific numeric changes? _____

Are the Optimal and Adapter Default settings the only choices you have? _____

✔ Hint

The refresh rate is not an option on all video adapters. This setting may be in a different location, or not on your system at all.

Make sure you return all the settings to their original values, and then close the dialog box.

Check the drivers for your video card and monitor. Are they "standard" drivers, or are they specific to your hardware? Follow these steps:

a. Go to Device Manager, locate your display adapter, right-click, and select Properties.

b. Locate your driver information.

c. Can you identify the version number(s) of your video drivers? Write them down.

_____

d. Go online and find the manufacturer's Web site.

e.   Check to see if newer drivers are available. If so, download and install them. (Do this on a test machine first. Get comfortable with the whole process before you do this on your personal computer.)

How did this affect your machine?

_____

✔ Hint

New drivers will sometimes fail to work properly, thereby crippling your PC. Windows XP and higher have the Roll Back Driver feature that enables you to go back to a driver that worked correctly in case this should happen.

Step 5   One more place to look for video settings is the Power Options Control Panel applet. Take a look at any power management settings you may have.

Go to the Control Panel and double-click the Power Options applet.

Read through the list of available power management schemes.

Which one do you have running? _____

How long is the period of inactivity before your monitor shuts off? _____

Close the applet and the Control Panel.

 30 MINUTES

Lab Exercise 13.02: Configuring Multiple Displays

Your consulting firm has just been awarded a contract to perform complete upgrades on the 12 digital audio workstations at a local recording studio. Among the various considerations for this type of application—large data storage, backups, fast processors, and loads of memory—the application also requires high-performance display adapters with multiple monitors for each station. It is not unusual for a recording engineer to have three or four critical windows open simultaneously during a session, so the studio design has included three widescreen monitors for each station.

You jump on the project and immediately stage one of the systems in the shop to run it through its paces. You decide to use one of the new ASUS motherboards with three PCIe slots and three high-performance NVIDIA display adapters. You finish the video configuration and attach three 30-inch widescreen monitors—this system looks impressive!

✔ **Cross-Reference**

For additional information on configuring your multiple displays, refer to the "Installing and Configuring Video" section in Chapter 13 of *Mike Meyers' CompTIA A+ Guide to 801: Managing and Troubleshooting PCs*.

Learning Objectives

At the end of this lab, you'll be able to

- Install an additional video display adapter card

- Configure a system to use multiple displays

- Expand the desktop across two or more displays

Lab Materials and Setup

The materials you need for this lab are

- A working PC with Windows installed

- At least one additional display adapter or a display adapter that supports multiple monitors

- At least one additional working monitor (CRT or LCD)

✔ **Hint**

This lab exercise does not require any of the high-end equipment discussed in the scenario. You should be able to complete the steps to configure multiple monitors using a few video cards and the monitors in your classroom lab. You can even use the integrated display adapter on many motherboards and install one additional video card to complete the lab steps. If time permits, hop on a system with Internet access and explore some of the components discussed in the scenario. Manufacturers such as ASUS, NVIDIA, and NEC are always adding new technology to their product lines.

Getting Down to Business

To explore the system configuration presented in the opening scenario, you will install at least one additional display adapter and monitor on a working system. You will then use the Display applet in Windows to configure the multiple monitors for use as an expanded desktop.

Step 1 Shut down your system properly and unplug the power cable from the system unit and the wall. Remove the cover from the PC to expose the expansion bus slots.

a.   Verify the type (PCI, AGP, or PCIe) and location of the current video display adapter. Using proper ESD avoidance procedures and one of the available expansion slots (depending on the additional video card available to you), install a second video display adapter in your system. Remember that AGP and PCIe cards can be a little finicky during installation, so make sure they are inserted securely.

→ **Note**

You may have a display adapter that already supports multiple monitors and has two display ports on a single card. If this is the case, you don't need to add a second adapter to set up multiple monitors, but it's good to practice, either way.

---

b.   Attach the second monitor cable to the new display adapter, and test your system with the case still open to see if it works.

To verify that the second display adapter and monitor have been installed correctly, are recognized by the system, and have drivers available, open Device Manager and expand the display adapter's icon. View the properties of the newly installed card and select the Drivers tab. Does everything appear to be in order?

c.   If the new display adapter is not working properly, you may need to install specific drivers or updated drivers. Access the Internet to download and install the appropriate drivers for your display adapter.

Step 2   Now that the hardware is set up and functioning properly, you will configure Windows to expand your desktop across two or more displays. To do this, you will again open the Display applet.

In Windows XP, navigate to the Display Properties dialog box's Settings tab. In Windows Vista, go to Control Panel | Personalization | Display Settings. In Windows 7, go to the Display applet and click on *Change display settings*. This shows the monitor settings and should now display two monitor icons, as shown in Figure 13-6.

Now complete the following steps to expand your desktop across the displays you have installed.

a.   Click the drop-down arrow next to the Display field. Are both of your display adapters available?

b.   Select the second monitor icon. In Windows XP, check the *Extend my Windows desktop onto this monitor* box, and click the Apply button. In Windows Vista/7, click on the Multiple displays drop-down box and select *Extend these displays*. Your monitor icons should now look something like Figure 13-7, and the display on your monitors should change accordingly.

c.   Click and drag the dialog box or another open window from one monitor to the other. Notice that the standard setup has the second display as the display to the right, so the expansion should allow you to use the second monitor as the rightmost portion of the desktop. Open a few windows and place them in different locations on the two monitors (see Figure 13-8).

FIGURE 13-6   The Display applet showing two monitors available

FIGURE 13-7   Extending the Windows desktop

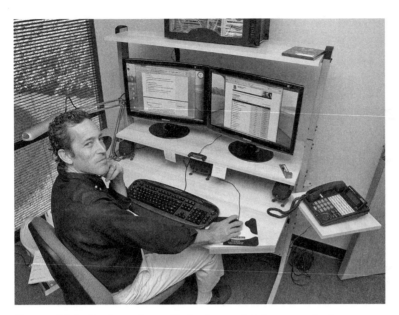

Figure 13-8 Dual monitors displaying multiple open windows

d. Experiment with the "virtual" placement of the monitors by clicking one of the numbered monitors and dragging it around the other monitor(s). Also click and highlight one of the numbered monitors and select it as the primary display.

Can you place the monitors on top of each other (see Figure 13-9)? _____

Can you set the second display as the primary monitor? _____

Right-click one of the displays in the Display Properties dialog box and select Identify. What are the results? _____

Figure 13-9 Configuring monitors to be "virtually" on top of each other

Lab Analysis Test

1. If you remove an AGP video display adapter and replace it with a PCIe video display adapter, what must you do to be sure the Windows desktop will display properly?

2. What can happen if the refresh rate for a CRT is set too high?

3. Taylor installed a new video display adapter, but the best setting he can adjust it to is 800 × 600 resolution with 256 colors. What must he do to make it go higher?

Key Term Quiz

Use the following terms to complete the following sentences. Not all terms will be used.

color depth

Direct3D

DirectX Diagnostic Tool

Display applet

Display Settings

Init Display First

refresh rate

resolution

1. Once software is installed, test your video using Microsoft's _____.

2. Erin's monitor was set to 640 × 480, a very low _____.

3. John complained constantly about getting headaches every day. When you looked at his PC, you noted that the screen flickered. John's monitor had the _____ set too low!

4. The _____ is the one-stop shop in Windows XP and Windows 7 for changing your video settings. In Windows Vista, many of these same settings can be found in _____.

5. You can adjust the number of colors displayed by the monitor by using the _____ option.

Chapter 14
Local Area Networking

Lab Exercises

In Chapter 4, you were introduced to basic networking concepts. You explored network topologies, devices, and settings. Now that you have that introductory knowledge, it's time to move on to tougher topics and more advanced exercises. This chapter is all about building and using a local area network.

In this chapter, you'll first learn how to construct an Ethernet patch cable. While you can easily find patch cables at any electronics store, a tech should be able to make his or her own. Next, you'll verify TCP/IP settings such as your IP address and default gateway using both the Control Panel and the command prompt. The third lab exercise in this chapter explains how you can share resources on your computer with the entire network. Finally, you'll return to the command prompt and work with several commands that enable you to test and troubleshoot your network connection.

 30–60 MINUTES

Lab Exercise 14.01: Building an Ethernet Patch Cable

CAT 5e and CAT 6 UTP cabling are now the dominant cabling media for wired networks. This is due to the fact that Ethernet has become the dominant networking technology, and Ethernet uses UTP cabling to electrically transmit the data frames. To ensure that these data frames are transmitted and received correctly requires that these UTP cables are wired to exacting specifications. The Telecommunications Industry Association/Electronics Industries Alliance (TIA/EIA) defines the industry standards for wiring Ethernet UTP cables.

Typical IT departments will have several lengths of premade patch cables on hand to be used as needed. Nonetheless, a well-versed tech should have a good command of assembling and testing UTP patch cables. Some folks refer to the building of UTP patch cables, which requires stripping the insulation, arranging the wires to meet the TIA/EIA standards, and crimping the RJ-45 connectors onto the ends of the wire, as an "art." You will now practice the art of building UTP patch cables.

Learning Objectives

In this lab, you'll assemble a TIA/EIA 568B patch cable.

At the end of this lab, you will be able to

- Identify proper orientation of RJ-45 connectors

- Identify the wire pairs of a UTP patch cable according to the specifications of the TIA/EIA 568A and 568B standards

- Successfully crimp an RJ-45 connector to the end of a UTP cable

- Verify proper wiring of a completed patch cable using a commercial cable tester

Lab Materials and Setup

The materials you need for this lab are

- A working computer with Internet access

- A length of CAT 5, CAT 5e, or CAT 6 UTP cable

- RJ-45 connectors

- Wire strippers

- Wire snips

- A crimping tool

- TIA/EIA 568B color codes

- A cable tester

→ **Note**

Though CAT 6 UTP cable is the current choice for high performance, it can prove much more difficult to use when making cables. CAT 6 cable has a plastic spine that must be trimmed before inserting it into the RJ-45 connectors. There are many variations on the RJ-45 connectors for CAT 6 cable, and special crimping tools may be required.

Getting Down to Business

The TIA/EIA 568A and 568B standards define the arrangement of four-pair UTP cabling into RJ-45 connectors. When purchasing commercial, premade cables, the emerging default standard to follow is TIA/EIA 568B. For the purposes of this lab, you will adhere to the default industry standard of TIA/EIA 568B.

You'll find that once you develop some technique, you will enjoy making patch cables. As mentioned earlier, in the eyes of some, this is an "art." I want to caution you against spending too much time making cables, however, or spending too much time completing this lab exercise. The skill you develop will not be tested on the CompTIA A+ 220-801 exam, and even in the field, making cables will not be the prime example of your skills as a tech.

That said, you will want to spend enough time to know the basics so that you will not look like a novice when it comes to whipping up a few patch cables.

Step 1   You'll begin with a cut length of UTP cable. Your instructor may define the lengths based on actual implementation. Shorter, 2- to 5-foot cables may be made to patch in a new switch or router, and medium lengths of 15 to 25 feet may be used to connect computers and printers to wall jacks. What lengths of cable will you be using?

_____

Step 2   Using the Internet, conduct a search for TIA/EIA 568A and 568B wiring diagrams. There are many sites that offer color-coded diagrams of the standards for wiring both straight-through and crossover patch cables. I found a nice diagram on the Web site of the Internet Centre, an Alberta, Canada Internet provider, at www.incentre.net/content/view/75/2/. I have also included the wiring diagram from the *Mike Meyers' CompTIA Network+ Guide to Managing and Troubleshooting Networks* textbook (see Figure 14-1).

Using either the diagram shown in Figure 14-1 or a diagram you've found on the Web, record the proper color wire for each of the pins of the RJ-45 modular connector when assembled using the TIA/EIA 568B standard:

Pin 1: _____

Pin 2: _____

Pin 3: _____

Pin 4: _____

Pin 5: _____

Pin 6: _____

Pin 7: _____

Pin 8: _____

FIGURE 14-1 The TIA/EIA 568A and 568B standards

Step 3 Using wire strippers (often the crimping tool has wire strippers and snips built in), carefully remove approximately 0.5 inch of the outer insulating jacket of each end of the UTP cable.

→ **Note**

After removing the outer insulating sheathing, look for any damaged or cut wires. This is a very delicate procedure, so finesse is required. If any of the eight wires have been damaged, use the wire snips to cut off the entire end (all eight wires and insulation) and repeat Step 3.

Step 4 Separate each pair of wires and align them in the correct sequence according to the TIA/EIA 568B standards defined in Step 2. The next step, where you insert the wires into the RJ-45 connector, will go more smoothly if you take your time during this procedure. Once the sequence is correct, grasp the wires firmly between your thumb and forefinger, and carefully snip the edges of the wires to make them even, as shown in Figure 14-2.

Step 5 With the pins of the RJ-45 connector facing up and away from you, slide the wires all the way into the connector. The outer insulating sheath should be just past the first crimping point in the connector, and you should be able to see the copper of all eight wires if you look at the head of the RJ-45 connector, as shown in Figure 14-3.

Step 6 Place the RJ-45 connector into the crimping tool. Firmly squeeze the handle of the tool until the wires are crimped into place. The crimp should bind each of the wires tightly, and the connector

Figure 14-2 Aligning the wires and evening the ends

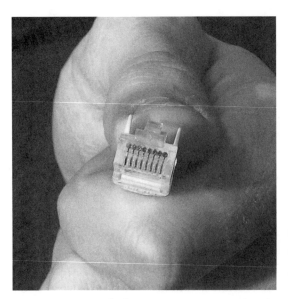

FIGURE 14-3 Head of an RJ-45 connector showing all eight wires firmly inserted

should bind the outer jacket. If any of the wires can be pulled from the connector with a gentle tug, the connection is incorrect. Snip the RJ-45 connector off and return to Step 3.

Step 7 To complete the assembly of the patch cable, repeat Steps 3–6 to add a connector to the other end of the cable.

 30 MINUTES

Lab Exercise 14.02: Verifying TCP/IP Settings

As you are probably aware, TCP/IP has emerged as the standard transport protocol for network communication. Microsoft operating systems normally use the Dynamic Host Configuration Protocol (DHCP), which automatically retrieves and assigns client TCP/IP settings from a DHCP server. This makes it easy to set up a small home or business network of PCs. All systems in the network will communicate with each other using these settings. The problem is that most businesses have their own set of TCP/IP settings (either automatically configured through DHCP or manually configured) that must be used for all new or repaired systems introduced into the network. Your responsibility as a PC technician is to verify the TCP/IP settings.

✔ **Cross-Reference**

To review additional details of TCP/IP, re-read the "Configuring TCP/IP" section in Chapter 14 of *Mike Meyers' CompTIA A+ Guide to 801: Managing and Troubleshooting PCs.*

Learning Objectives

In this exercise, you'll access and verify the TCP/IP settings for a given PC system.

At the end of this lab, you'll be able to

- Define Automatic Private IP Addressing (APIPA)

- Use the ipconfig command-line utility

- Manually configure the TCP/IP settings on a PC

Lab Materials and Setup

The materials you need for this lab are

- A PC system that's properly configured for LAN access using Windows

- A list of TCP/IP settings provided by the instructor

Getting Down to Business

Typically, in corporate environments, the network protocol configuration scheme has been defined by the senior systems administrators. Unless you've had some experience with the configuration, you would not automatically know all of the TCP/IP settings for a network. For instance, even when you're setting up a small network (one that connects to the Internet), you'll need to contact your Internet service provider (ISP) to set up your router's TCP/IP settings. So don't worry if you have no idea what settings to use. The trick is to learn how to get them.

TCP/IP requires each system to have two basic settings for accessing a LAN and two additional settings for accessing other LANs or the Internet. You can configure your system to automatically obtain the following settings when you log on (Microsoft's default settings), or you can specify them, depending on the requirements of your network:

- IP address (unique to the PC)

- Subnet mask (identifies network information)

- Default gateway (address of the router to the external realm)

- Domain name service (DNS)

Step 1   First, you'll locate and verify your current TCP/IP settings.

a.   You can accomplish this by going to the Control Panel. If you have a Windows Vista/7 system, open the Network and Sharing Center applet. In Windows Vista, click on *Manage network connections*, and in Windows 7, click *Change adapter settings*. Go to the Properties dialog box of the appropriate adapter. If you are on Windows XP, open the Network Connections applet, then open the Properties dialog box of the appropriate adapter. Highlight the Internet Protocol (TCP/IP) entry and click the Properties button. When the Internet Protocol (TCP/IP) Properties dialog box appears, one of the setting options shown in Figure 14-4 will be selected.

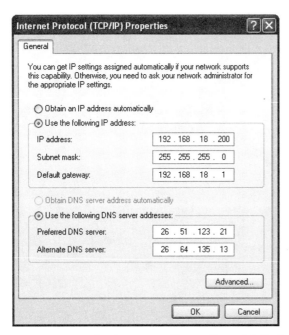

FIGURE 14-4 Viewing manually configured TCP/IP Properties in a Windows XP system

b. If the settings are manually configured, you will be able to verify them in the TCP/IP Properties dialog box. Write the settings down and verify them with the settings given to you by the instructor.

IP address _____

Subnet mask _____

Default gateway _____

Preferred DNS server _____

c. If the system is configured to use the Microsoft Automatic Private IP Addressing (APIPA) settings or if the network has a DHCP server (ask the instructor), the *Obtain an IP address automatically* and *Obtain DNS server address automatically* radio buttons will be selected. You will not be able to verify the values of the TCP/IP settings from this window. Close this window by clicking OK. To verify the settings, launch a Command Prompt window and, at the prompt, type the following command:

```
C:\Documents and Settings\%USERNAME%\>ipconfig /all
```

This produces a listing similar to the one shown in Figure 14-5. Use these values to fill in the following settings and then verify them with your instructor.

IP Address _____

Subnet Mask _____

Default Gateway _____

DNS Servers _____

Step 2 You should be familiar with one final configuration: Automatic Private IP Addressing, or APIPA. If Windows is configured to obtain an IP address automatically and no DHCP server is available, Microsoft will automatically configure an address in the 169.254.0.0 network. Follow these steps to explore APIPA:

a. In a classroom lab environment, have the instructor disable the DHCP server if applicable. Alternatively, you can disconnect the DHCP server's UTP cable from the hub or switch.

b. Verify that your TCP/IP Properties settings are set to *Obtain an IP address automatically* and *Obtain DNS server address automatically*. Close all windows and reboot the system.

c. Launch a Command Prompt window and, at the prompt, type the following command:

```
C:\Documents and Settings\%USERNAME%\>ipconfig /all
```

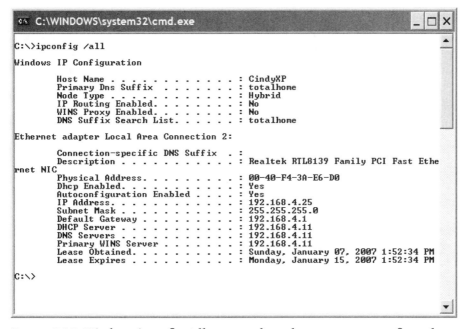

FIGURE 14-5 Windows ipconfig /all command results on a system configured to use DHCP

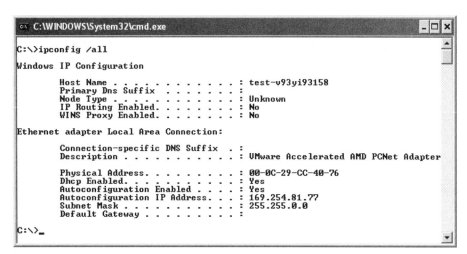

FIGURE 14-6 Windows ipconfig /all command results on a system using APIPA

This produces a listing similar to the one shown in Figure 14-6. Use these values to fill in the following settings and then verify them with your instructor.

IP Address _____

Subnet Mask _____

Default Gateway _____

DNS Server _____

d. Exit the Command Prompt window and launch the TCP/IP Properties dialog box again. Return all settings to the normal classroom configuration. Click OK to finish, and close all the windows. Reboot the system, and verify that it's working properly and that you have reestablished network communication to its prior state.

 30 MINUTES

Lab Exercise 14.03: Sharing Resources

With the network all set up properly, the next thing to do is decide how you want to share resources. You can share any folder or other resource. Optical drives, hard drives, and printers can all be shared.

Learning Objectives

In this lab, you'll set up file sharing for others to access information from their system.

At the end of this lab, you'll be able to

- Enable and configure shared directories and other resources

Lab Materials and Setup

The materials you need for this lab are

- A PC system that's properly configured for LAN access using Windows

Getting Down to Business

Whew! That last exercise was interesting, but the job is only half done. Now you'll find where to set up sharing for a particular resource.

Step 1 Open My Computer/Computer, double-click the C: drive, and create a new folder on the C: drive. Name it **Shared**. Right-click the Shared folder icon to see the folder options, and select Properties. This will open the folder's Properties dialog box. Select the Sharing tab (see Figure 14-7).

✔ **Hint**

If the Sharing tab isn't there, you probably forgot to enable the File and Printer Sharing option in the Networking applet. Go back and do that.

FIGURE 14-7 A folder's Properties dialog box with the Sharing tab selected in Windows XP

✔ Hint

If you're running Windows XP Home Edition or Windows XP Professional Edition in a workgroup environment, the Sharing tab is much simpler. It contains *Do not share this folder* and *Share this folder* buttons and a space to provide a share name.

Step 2 Try sharing and unsharing the folder. Note that the share name and permissions are grayed out when you select *Do not share this folder*. Share the folder again, change the share name, and look at the various levels of permissions: Full Control, Change, and Read.

Step 3 When you're done, click OK to close the dialog box.

 30 MINUTES

Lab Exercise 14.04: Testing Your LAN Connections

Various tools are available that will help you test and troubleshoot your new network. The textbook covers using these tools in detail. Some of these tools will be beneficial to you as a CompTIA A+ certified technician and are covered on the CompTIA A+ 220-801 exam. This lab exercise lets you practice using several key network troubleshooting tools.

Learning Objectives

In this exercise, you'll be introduced to troubleshooting tools for determining proper installation of the network components. These tools are covered in order of importance. First, you'll verify the local settings. Next, you'll try to access other systems on the same LAN. Finally, you'll test the Internet connectivity.

At the end of this lab, you'll be able to

- Use the ipconfig command to determine local network settings
- Use the net config command to check the local system name and who is logged on as a user
- Use the ping command to test the local TCP/IP software and adapter
- Use the net view command to check for other computers on the network
- Use the ping command with switches to test connectivity to other computers
- Use the nslookup command to translate IP addresses and domain names
- Use the tracert command to check the path to other computers

Lab Materials and Setup

The materials you need for this lab are

- A PC system that's properly configured for network access using Windows

- Access to the Internet

✔ **Hint**

The commands vary slightly, depending on the operating system you use. You should practice with each operating system if possible. Test the LAN first by accessing another computer on the network using My Network Places/Network.

Getting Down to Business

As a PC technician, you should be familiar with several networking tools, both for your own good and because they're covered on the CompTIA A+ 801 exam. You'll begin by looking at ipconfig.

✔ **Hint**

Since you have already used the ipconfig /all command, run through the steps again, either on your own system or on a different lab machine. Ask the instructor if any different networks or system configurations are available to explore.

Step 1 You have already examined ipconfig in Lab Exercise 14.02. You'll now use the ipconfig command again to determine local network settings. As you have already learned, checking the automatic TCP/IP settings given to you by a DHCP server and verifying your manual settings is easy: just open a Command Prompt window, type **ipconfig /all**, and press ENTER. The details of your local network connection appear on the screen.

Does the display contain the settings that were automatically assigned by the DHCP server or the ones you entered manually?

_____

Record your settings here:

IP Address _____

Subnet Mask _____

Default Gateway _____

DNS Servers _____

Leave the Command Prompt window open; you'll use it throughout the rest of this exercise.

Step 2 You'll now use the net config command to check the local system name and to see who is logged on as a user. To confirm the computer name and discover who is currently logged on, you'll again use the command line.

Type **net config workstation** at the command prompt and press ENTER. You'll see how the identification is set up for your local PC. There's a lot of information listed, but you're only interested in a couple of items (see Figure 14-8).

How are these listed?

Computer name _____

User name _____

Workstation domain (workgroup) _____

Software version _____

Step 3 You'll now use the ping command to test the local TCP/IP software and adapter.

At the command prompt, type **ping 127.0.0.1** (including the periods) and press ENTER. This is known as the IPv4 loopback or localhost address and will test the TCP/IP software and the internal part of the local network card. Look at Figure 14-9 to see a successful test. If you don't see the test results, there are serious problems with the software. Reinstall your network drivers, and reconfigure the TCP/IP settings.

→ **Note**

Want to see some IPv6 action? At the command prompt, type **ping ::1**. The IPv6 loopback address is ::1. When you ping it, it's just like running ping using 127.0.0.1, but it uses IPv6 instead.

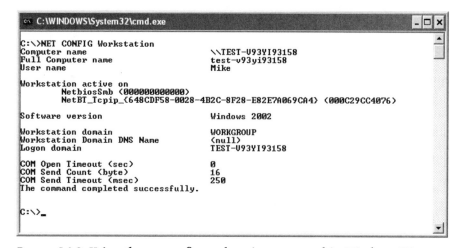

FIGURE 14-8 Using the net config workstation command in Windows XP

```
C:\WINDOWS\system32\cmd.exe

C:\>ping 127.0.0.1

Pinging 127.0.0.1 with 32 bytes of data:

Reply from 127.0.0.1: bytes=32 time=8ms TTL=128
Reply from 127.0.0.1: bytes=32 time<1ms TTL=128
Reply from 127.0.0.1: bytes=32 time<1ms TTL=128
Reply from 127.0.0.1: bytes=32 time<1ms TTL=128

Ping statistics for 127.0.0.1:
    Packets: Sent = 4, Received = 4, Lost = 0 (0% loss),
Approximate round trip times in milli-seconds:
    Minimum = 0ms, Maximum = 8ms, Average = 2ms

C:\>
```

FIGURE 14-9 A successful ping test

Step 4 You'll now use the net view command to check for other computers on the network.

You want to establish that other computers are available on the network so that you can test that your network card can transmit and receive data in Step 5.

At the command prompt, type **net view** and press ENTER. You'll see which other computers are on the network by a listing of their computer names (see Figure 14-10).

Step 5 Now you'll use the ping command to test your ability to connect to other computers on the network.

In Step 4 you obtained the names of other systems on the LAN, so now you want to check whether you can actually communicate with them.

At the command prompt, type **ping** *computer name*, where *computer name* is another PC's host name on the network you found in Step 4, and press ENTER. The results will look the same as when you used ping to see your own computer, but with the other computer's IP address (see Figure 14-11). Be sure to put a space between the ping command and the computer name. If you get errors, use the net view command again to be certain of the computer name's spelling. If the DNS is down, you can adjust by pinging the other computer's IP address instead of its name.

```
C:\WINDOWS\system32\cmd.exe

C:\>net view
Server Name            Remark
-------------------------------------------------------------------------------
\\DOUGJ-PC
\\VISTAULTIMATEUM
\\VM-WIN2K
The command completed successfully.

C:\>
```

FIGURE 14-10 Using the net view command

```
C:\WINDOWS\system32\cmd.exe                                    _ □ ×

C:\>ping mikespc

Pinging mikespc [192.168.4.74] with 32 bytes of data:

Reply from 192.168.4.74: bytes=32 time=2ms TTL=128
Reply from 192.168.4.74: bytes=32 time=2ms TTL=128
Reply from 192.168.4.74: bytes=32 time=1ms TTL=128
Reply from 192.168.4.74: bytes=32 time<1ms TTL=128

Ping statistics for 192.168.4.74:
    Packets: Sent = 4, Received = 4, Lost = 0 (0% loss),
Approximate round trip times in milli-seconds:
    Minimum = 0ms, Maximum = 2ms, Average = 1ms

C:\>
```

FIGURE 14-11 Pinging a computer by its name

→ Try This: Ping Switches

The humble ping command is one of the most frequently used troubleshooting tools for TCP/IP. As you saw in Step 5, you can actually use ping to test whether DNS is working. If you do not receive a response from the computer using its host name, but you do receive a response when using the IP address, this points to a problem with DNS.

Ping also has a number of switches that add to the functionality of the command. If you need to explore the switches, type the following at the command prompt:

C:\>**ping /?**

This will list all of the available switches and their functions. The following combination is typically used for a connection that seems to drop packets intermittently. You would run the command indefinitely and increase the packet size to overload the connection. Type the following command:

C:\>**ping -t -l 65000 computername**

To stop the continuous ping, press CTRL-C to break the program.

Step 6 You'll now use the nslookup command to translate an Internet domain name to an IP address or an IP address to an Internet domain name.

This is a good command for finding out the IP addresses of Web sites. Why do I want this, you ask? Well, when you use a URL in your browser, it has to be translated somewhere to an IP address. This slows down your access time. If you know the IP address and type that into the address of your Internet browser, the site will pop up faster. Follow these steps:

    a.   Type **nslookup microsoft.com**, and then press ENTER.

         What's the IP address(es) of http://www.microsoft.com? _____

         Try **nslookup totalsem.com**.

         What's the IP address(es) of http://www.totalsem.com? _____

    b.   Now enter the IP address you got when you did a lookup for http://www.microsoft.com. If you get a different result, it could be that a Web site is being hosted by someone other than the original domain you looked up.

Step 7   You'll now use the tracert command to check the path to other computers or Web sites on the Internet.

This command will show you where the bottlenecks are in the Internet. The tracert command will list the time it takes to get from your PC to the Web site or other system you're accessing. Follow these steps:

    a.   Type **tracert google.com**, and then press ENTER.

         Was it successful? _____

         How many hops did it take? _____

         What's the IP address of the first hop? _____

    b.   Use the nslookup command with the IP address of the first hop to see where your first server is located.

Go ahead—have fun with this! Part of the learning process with PCs is to dive in and tackle a subject that you're not completely familiar with. As long as you remember to write down any information you want to change before you change it, you can enjoy exploring the amazing world of computers and still have a recovery point.

Lab Analysis Test

1.   A user complains that after you installed the new NIC in her system, she can see everyone on the network but can't access the Internet. What did you forget to do? Are there any other configuration problems that could cause this to happen?

2.   What command would you use to test the NIC's internal TCP/IP capabilities? What would the "human readable" address be?

3. Jerry is attempting to make a crossover cable for a customer. Jerry has forgotten the wire pattern to create the cable. Remind Jerry of what the TIA/EIA standards are along with the color arrangement of the wires from left to right.

4. How do you access the Local Area Connection Properties dialog box in Windows 7?

5. Tanner has replaced his old 100BaseT NIC with a new 1000BaseT NIC. The office network is set up and works fine for everyone else. Now he can't see anyone on the network or access the Internet. Where should he start checking and in what order?

Key Term Quiz

Use the following terms to complete the following sentences. Not all terms will be used.

568A

568B

APIPA

crimpers

crossover cable

default gateway

DHCP

DNS

dynamic

IP address

ipconfig

net view

Network and Sharing Center

Network Connections

nslookup

ping

RJ-45

snips

static

straight-through cable

subnet mask

tracert

1. The _____ and _____ are the minimum addressing requirements for setting up a network card using the TCP/IP protocol.

2. A(n) _____ address is an address that is self-assigned by the computer to make local communication in the event that a DHCP server can't be reached.

3. A user should go to the _____ in Windows 7 to view and manage all of their network settings.

4. A(n) _____ is used to connect two similar devices together for communication, such as connecting two switches together.

5. The _____ command is used to query the state of DNS servers.

Chapter 15
Wireless Networking

Lab Exercises

It's a bad time to be in the wire business. Home networks, once the domain of bird's nests of tangled coaxial cable, have cast off the antiquated notion of physical connectivity and embraced wireless technology. As a CompTIA A+ technician, it's your responsibility to understand the various standards and security measures that make wireless networking possible. If your boss asks you which wireless standard to implement in your office, you had better be quick with an answer! And when you set up a wireless network, it's your job to understand which security features to use.

 30 MINUTES

Lab Exercise 15.01: Buying Wireless Equipment

As a CompTIA A+ certified technician, there's a good chance that you'll eventually find yourself purchasing wireless networking equipment, whether for yourself, a family member, or an employer. It's important that you know how to search the Internet for networking equipment and how to stay within a budget when making purchases. For the purposes of this lab, imagine that you're helping your boss set up a wireless network in some new office space. He's given you a $500 budget to set up a network for ten PCs, none of which have wireless NICs. The office that the PCs are going into is spread out over 150 square feet, so range could be an issue. You'll need a wireless router, wireless NICs for the PCs, and possibly a wireless repeater to extend your network's range.

Learning Objectives

In this lab, you'll identify various wireless networking standards.

At the end of this lab, you'll be able to

- Describe the differences between various wireless networking standards

- Research and purchase wireless networking equipment in order to set up a home or small office network

Lab Materials and Setup

The materials you need for this lab are

- Access to a working computer with Internet access to research wireless networking equipment

- A notepad and pencil to document the specifications

- Optional: A word processor or spreadsheet application to facilitate the documentation

Getting Down to Business

In the following steps, you'll search the Internet for high-quality networking equipment within a given budget.

Step 1 Log on to a computer with Internet access and point your browser to www.google.com. Your goal to start with is to do a bit of Internet research on the available wireless hardware. Do searches for things like "best wireless router" or "wireless NIC reviews." Use the following table to keep track of the hardware you find, as well as the pros and cons for each piece.

Device Name	Pros	Cons

After you've filled out the table, use the available information to create a tentative ranking of the devices you'll want to look at further.

Step 2 Once you've decided which wireless devices you'd like to investigate further, it's time to start looking at prices. Check sites like www.newegg.com, www.amazon.com, and www.tigerdirect.com to see where you can get the best deal on the hardware you want. You can also use shopping aggregators like Google Shopping (www.google.com/shopping) to search many sites at once. You should also try hitting a site that lists various coupons and sales from all across the Internet, such as www.slickdeals.net. If you're using the Chrome or Firefox Web browsers, you can use the InvisibleHand add-on to compare prices across a wide selection of Internet stores. (To get this add-on, just search for InvisibleHand in the Chrome or Firefox add-on stores.)

When you've found the best price on each piece of equipment you want, use the following table to calculate the total cost.

Device Name	Price
Total Cost	

If you come out over budget, go back to the table you filled out for Step 1 and see if you can find some cheaper alternatives to some of the devices you chose. When you've picked out the right wireless devices to cover the network's needs and stay within budget, it's time to show your boss the cost table and purchase your devices!

 20 MINUTES

Lab Exercise 15.02: Wireless Security Features

Wireless networking has become incredibly popular, but despite its wide adoption, many users remain alarmingly ignorant about wireless security. With wired networks, a troublemaker would have to physically plug a computer into your network in order to gain access, but there's little stopping someone from parking their car next to your home or office and secretly tapping into your wireless network. Because of this, it's vitally important that you understand how to configure a wireless network to be as secure as possible. In this lab, you'll enable several different security features on a wireless router.

Learning Objectives

In this lab exercise, you'll configure a wireless router to be as secure as possible.

At the end of this lab, you'll be able to

- Set up a secure wireless network

- Understand different wireless encryption standards

- Set up a MAC filter list

- Disable SSID broadcasting

- Change the default user name and password of a wireless router

Lab Materials and Setup

The materials you need for this lab are

- A working Windows PC

- A working wireless router

- Your wireless router's documentation (it's possible to find a PDF copy on the manufacturer's Web site if you don't have a physical one)

Getting Down to Business

In the following steps, you'll configure your wireless router to be as secure as possible. Because no two routers are the same, you'll have to use a bit of inference to follow along. Most consumer-grade routers are similar enough that you should be able to find the necessary settings.

Step 1 Access your wireless router using its default IP address, usually 192.168.1.1 or 192.168.11.1. You'll have to enter the administrator user name and password, which can be found in the router's manual. If you don't have access to the manual, you can find the default user names and passwords for any wireless router by doing a Web search for the model of router, plus the phrase "default password."

Step 2 The very first thing you want to change is the default user name and password of your router. Not every router enables you to change the user name, but you can change the password on any router out there. The exact process varies from router to router, so check your router's documentation. Usually, you'll find these settings under an "Administration" or "Admin" tab, though they are sometimes found under "Tools" or "Advanced" (Figure 15-1). Once you've changed the password, make sure to save the change (many routers have a "Save Changes" button somewhere).

Step 3 Once you've changed the default router password, it's time to get cracking on some Wi-Fi security. You're going to start off by disabling SSID broadcast for your network. You'll find this setting under the "Wireless" or "Wi-Fi" tab in your router's Web configuration program. SSID broadcast will probably be enabled by default, so disable it and save your changes.

Step 4 As you'll see in Lab Exercise 15.03, disabling the SSID broadcast doesn't necessarily keep people off your wireless network, so you've also got to encrypt your network. This setting gets put in all kinds of weird places, but look for something that says "Wireless Security" or even just "Security" (Figure 15-2). Depending on your router, you'll have several options here, so the general rule to remember is that WEP < WPA < WPA2. You can refer to Chapter 15 of *Mike Meyers' CompTIA Guide to 801: Managing and Troubleshooting PCs* for the skinny on the different wireless encryption standards. Once you've chosen an encryption type, you'll also have to configure a password. Any wireless client wishing to access your network will have to enter this password.

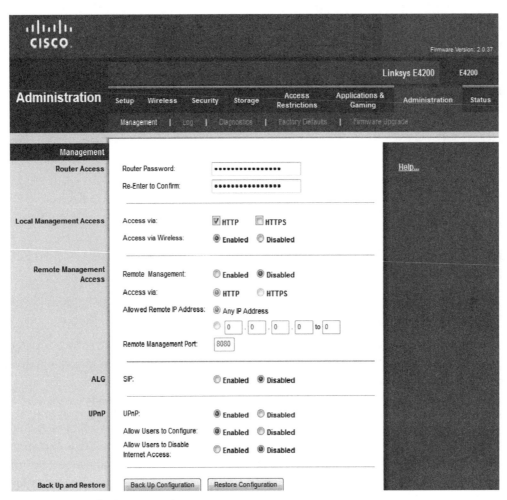

Figure 15-1 Default password settings

Step 5   The final, perhaps somewhat extreme, step in securing your wireless network is setting up a MAC address filter. A MAC address filter only allows devices that you specify to join the network. Refer to your router's manual for where to find this setting. To add a computer to the MAC filter, you'll first have to get its MAC address, which you can get by running an **ipconfig /all** command at the command line. Some routers enable you to either allow or disallow a device on the MAC filter list from joining the network, so for our purposes, make sure you're allowing the devices to connect and not preventing them from connecting. When you've finished adding all the devices that you want on your network to the MAC address filter, save the changes and you're done! If you've got a computer that you *didn't* add to the filter, try connecting it to your wireless network and see what happens.

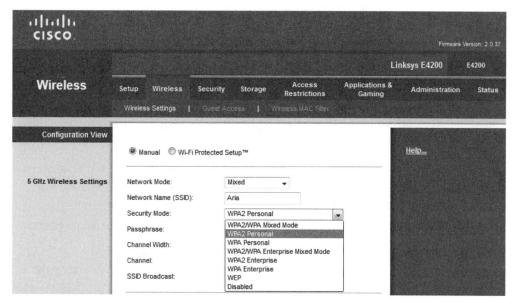

Figure 15-2 Changing your Wi-Fi encryption

 10 MINUTES

Lab Exercise 15.03: Scanning for Wireless Networks

Apart from simply setting up wireless networks, an A+ certified technician may occasionally be asked to figure out why someone's wireless network signal isn't as strong as they'd like it to be. One of a tech's best tools for this job is wireless network scanning software. You're going to use a popular Windows-based Wi-Fi scanner called inSSIDer to monitor the wireless networks in your area.

Learning Objectives

In this lab, you'll first download and install inSSIDer, and then you'll use it to scan for wireless networks in your area.

At the end of this lab, you'll be able to

- Use inSSIDer to scan for wireless networks

- Determine wireless signal strength based on location

Lab Materials and Setup

The materials you need for this lab are

- A working laptop with an Internet connection and a wireless NIC

- (Optional) A wireless router set up not to broadcast its SSID

Getting Down to Business

In the following steps, you'll discover how WAP placement can affect wireless signal strength for your wireless devices. You'll also see how to observe the statistics of wireless networks around you, such as signal strength, encryption type, and SSID.

Step 1 Open a Web browser and navigate to www.metageek.net/products/inssider. Once there, click the large Download inSSIDer button. Once the download finishes, double-click the .msi file and follow the instructions to install inSSIDer. When the installation is complete, open inSSIDer.

Step 2 When inSSIDer starts up, you're immediately greeted with a list of all the wireless networks around you (Figure 15-3). To the far right, you'll see a column for the SSIDs of the various networks. Next to that, you'll see which wireless channel the networks are using. This is important to note, since you can often improve your wireless network's coverage and speed by switching it to an unused channel.

To the right of the channel column is the RSSI, or received signal strength indication, column. This is the column that shows you the signal strength of all the networks around you. The higher the RSSI value (or, at least, the less negative), the stronger the network. inSSIDer, by default, lists the wireless networks in order from strongest to weakest signal, though you can reorder them by clicking any column header.

To the right of the RSSI column is the security column, which shows what kind of security the networks are using. This is a good way to find open networks in your area. To the right of that is the MAC address of the WAPs, and then next to that is the maximum speed of every network, measured in megabits per second. Next to that is the network type (either infrastructure or ad hoc) and then the vendor.

Figure 15-3 inSSIDer's main screen

Take a look at the listed wireless networks and fill out the following:

Do you see any unencrypted networks? _____

Which network has the strongest signal strength? _____

Which channel has the most wireless networks on it? _____

Step 3 Another great use for inSSIDer besides finding open wireless networks and checking for unused channels is to do a wireless site survey of your home or office. To do this, fire up inSSIDer on your laptop and then just walk around, checking to see how your signal strength changes as you move. It might be helpful when you do this to uncheck every wireless network except for the one you're monitoring to make it easier to see. You should also switch to the Time Graph tab on the bottom half of the screen to see the signal strength over time. Be careful not to drop your laptop as you're moving around!

Lab Analysis Test

1. What is the difference between 802.11g and 802.11n?

2. What is MIMO and why is it important?

3. Eustace just set up a wireless network and is concerned that the signal doesn't reach into his kitchen. Name some ways he can improve his wireless coverage.

4. How would you secure a wireless network?

5. Helga wants to install a wireless network for her home, where she has two laptops, a desktop, and a tablet. Write a paragraph describing the equipment she might need.

Key Term Quiz

Use the following terms to complete the following sentences. Not all terms will be used.

802.11a

802.11b

802.11g

802.11n

Ad hoc mode

Infrastructure mode

MAC address filtering

Multiple in/multiple out (MIMO)

Service set identifier (SSID)

WEP

Wi-Fi

Wireless access point (WAP)

WPA

WPA2

1. The newest wireless standard covered on the 220-801 exam is _____.

2. With a(n) _____ network, you don't need a central access point.

3. _____ is an upgraded version of the _____ encryption standard.

4. To create a list of devices allowed on your network, you would use _____.

5. To keep others off your network, you should disable _____ broadcasting.

Chapter 16

The Internet

Lab Exercises

The Internet is a complex system of communication that enables computers, in-business networks, mobile computers, and home PCs to share information worldwide. Today we even have smartphones, tablets, and other personal devices that we can use to connect to the Internet and access e-mail, download MP3s, and do other tasks.

Because nearly everyone wants access to the Internet, implementing and troubleshooting Internet connectivity is a PC technician's bread and butter. The CompTIA A+ 220-801 exam recognizes this and tests you on the details of installing and configuring a connection to the Internet. It may be a legacy dial-up analog modem used to connect to an ISP through a phone line, or a broadband cable modem using the local cable company as the provider. This heightened usage brings with it a new task for the PC technician: Internet security!

Since most computers are now communicating with the world through the Internet, the exposure to malicious intruders and programs has greatly increased. Two components that go hand-in-hand with the Internet are firewalls and wireless network security. You just finished setting up and configuring the hardware portion of a wireless network in the last chapter, so now you'll look at the software side of network security. This chapter's lab exercises first guide you through the properties of the current wide area network (WAN) connection technologies and then take you through the steps needed to perform the installation and configuration of these technologies. You'll also explore the configuration of Windows Firewall and Windows Internet Connection Sharing and learn how to upgrade to the latest version of the Internet Explorer browser.

✔ **Cross-Reference**

Computer security is such an important component of a PC technician's training that the topic receives its own chapter in both the textbook and the lab manual. Refer to Chapter 20 in *Mike Meyers' CompTIA A+ Guide to 801: Managing and Troubleshooting PCs*. Chapter 20 of this lab manual also includes additional lab exercises to build your security awareness.

30 MINUTES

Lab Exercise 16.01: Identifying Internet Connectivity Properties

A new client has signed up with your firm, requesting that you evaluate their current Internet connectivity and recommend the best upgrade path for their 12-person office (six desktop PCs and two laptops). Your first job is to assess what method they are currently using to connect to the Internet and what methods are available in their location, and to make a recommendation for upgrades if necessary.

Learning Objectives

This lab exercise tests basic assessment skills. Every technician should be able to go into a situation and quickly understand the state of the technology in question—in this case, an Internet connection. You should also feel comfortable telling your clients about any concerns with aging technology and feel confident recommending upgrade paths to higher-performance technology.

At the end of this lab, you'll be able to

- Verify the Internet connectivity method

- Check the properties of the connection

- Perform an Internet search to learn about the performance of various connectivity methods

Lab Materials and Setup

The materials you need for this lab are

- A working computer running Windows with some form of Internet connection

- Internet connectivity to perform your research

Getting Down to Business

First, you will visually inspect your computer and its surroundings for the method used to connect to the Internet. Then you will run an Internet utility to determine the speed of your connection and appropriate upgrade paths.

Step 1 Look at the back of your computer:

- Is there a phone cable (RJ-11) plugged in? This could indicate that this computer is using an analog modem for the Internet connection.

- Are there any USB or network (RJ-45) cables plugged into the system? Trace the wires. Do they connect to a cable modem or DSL modem? This could be your connectivity method.

- Is there a network patch cable plugged into the NIC? You may be connecting to the Internet through the corporate LAN.

- Are you on a laptop with wireless connectivity? You could have access to the Internet through a wireless access point (WAP) connected to a cable or DSL modem.

These are the possibilities a technician is faced with today, so the more you can explore the various methods of connectivity, the more knowledgeable you will be. Figure 16-1 depicts a typical PC using a wired LAN patch cable to connect to a broadband cable modem.

Examine the physical components that constitute the method your system uses to connect to the Internet, and then record the details of the hardware/connectivity type here.

_____

_____

Step 2 Once you have determined the connectivity method, boot your system and launch your Internet browser (popular browsers include Microsoft Internet Explorer, Mozilla Firefox, and Google Chrome). In the address bar, type **http://reviews.cnet.com/internet-speed-test/** and press ENTER. This will take you to CNET's Bandwidth Meter Online Speed Test. Follow the onscreen instructions to test the speed of your connection.

What is the speed of your connection? _____

Step 3 Using the Bandwidth Meter Online Speed Test results (where possible), fill in the approximate data transfer speeds of the various Internet connection types:

Dial-up 56 Kbps modem _____

DSL _____

Cable _____

T1 _____

T3 _____

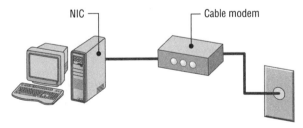

FIGURE 16-1 A PC and cable modem Internet connection

Step 4 Based on the results of the analysis of your client's Internet connection method and performance, are there any recommendations you would make to improve the performance of the connection?

_____

_____

_____

 30 MINUTES

Lab Exercise 16.02: Installing and Configuring an Internet Connection

You determine that the client is currently using dial-up networking through analog modems to access the Internet. Though this is probably acceptable for occasionally connecting to the Internet, these folks have a business to run! You decide to recommend either high-speed DSL or cable. You explain to the client that unlike the analog modem they're currently using, the other methods use a standard network interface card (NIC) and an external device to interface between the DSL or cable lines. Ironically, this device is usually referred to as a DSL or cable _modem_. You will evaluate the current PCs and select one that will act as the interface to the Internet. If required, you'll add a PCI or PCIe NIC, connect the DSL or cable interface, and then configure the interface in Windows.

Learning Objectives

Installing DSL or cable high-speed Internet access requires four steps. First, you should verify whether your system is already equipped with an NIC, either integrated into the motherboard or as a PCI/PCIe card, and if not, physically install such a device. Second, verify that this device is operating properly and has the latest drivers installed. Third, connect the DSL transceiver or the cable modem, and finally, configure the proper settings required by the ISP.

At the end of this lab, you'll be able to

- Install a network interface card (if not already present)
- Verify proper operation, and install or update the drivers
- Install the DSL transceiver or cable modem
- Configure the connection in Windows

✔ **Cross-Reference**

Refer to the "DSL" and "Cable" sections in Chapter 16 and the "Installing Expansion Cards" section in Chapter 8 of *Mike Meyers' CompTIA A+ Guide to 801: Managing and Troubleshooting PCs* for help installing and configuring NICs. It's a good idea to have the textbook handy while you progress through this lab.

Lab Materials and Setup

The materials you need for this lab are

- A PC system with or without an NIC

- A PCI or PCIe NIC

- Access to the proper driver software (either built-in Windows drivers or a separate disc)

- A copy of the Windows installation media (may be needed, depending on the system)

- A Phillips-head screwdriver

- An anti-static wrist strap

Getting Down to Business

Break out your trusty screwdriver and anti-static wrist strap. It's time to install an NIC! The process for physically installing an NIC is functionally identical to the process you've used to install expansion cards in the past, but the software side of things has a few differences that you should pay attention to.

✔ **Hint**

You can skip Steps 1–3 if the system is already equipped with a network interface card, as most systems are today. The steps are included here for completeness. You will be asked to install a second NIC in Lab Exercise 16.04, "Configuring Windows Internet Connection Sharing," so if you have that second NIC handy, go ahead and install it now.

Step 1 Make sure the PC is off and unplugged. While following proper ESD avoidance procedures, remove the cover of the PC. Choose any free PCI or PCIe slot to install the NIC. Remove the back plate if one exists.

Step 2 Plug the NIC into the PCI or PCIe slot (see Figure 16-2). Physically inserting the NIC into the PC is the easiest part of the task. Take care to avoid touching the pins or any of the chips on the NIC. Once the card is inserted, secure it by putting the proper screw through the metal tab of the card and screwing it to the case. Put the cover back on and restart your computer.

Figure 16-2 Inserting a PCI NIC

Step 3 Now that you have physically installed the NIC, turn on your PC. Windows should automatically detect the NIC. The operating system reports success installing the new device with a small balloon from the system tray.

✔ **Hint**

Every Windows operating system has a good selection of network interface drivers built in at the time of release, but your driver may not be one of them. For example, if the NIC you're installing was manufactured after the release of software you're using, the drivers may not be part of the operating system and will need to be manually installed or updated.

Step 4 Now that the drivers are installed, you should confirm the NIC properties and verify what drivers are installed.

    a.   Open the Control Panel. In Windows XP, open Network Connections. In Windows Vista/7, open the Network and Sharing Center. In Windows Vista, click *Manage network connections*. In Windows 7, click *Change adapter settings*.

    b.   Right-click Local Area Connection (note: if this is the second network interface, choose Local Area Connection 2) and click Properties. In the Local Area Connection Properties dialog box, click the Configure button next to the network interface adapter.

c.   In the network interface adapter Properties dialog box, click the Driver tab (see Figure 16-3). Record all the information provided about the driver you installed.

_____

_____

Step 5   Now examine the physical device that has been provided by your ISP to connect the computer to the Internet. If the device is a DSL transceiver, it will typically have an RJ-45 Ethernet connection to connect to the NIC of the computer, an RJ-11 connector to connect to the telephone wall jack, and some sort of power adapter. If the device is a cable modem, it will typically have an RJ-45 Ethernet connection to connect to the NIC of the computer, an F-connector to attach to the cable, and some sort of power adapter (refer to Figure 16-1). Both interfaces may provide a USB connection, but for the purposes of the lab exercise, this will not be used.

✔ **Hint**

If you are in a classroom lab environment, you may not have access to the actual DSL transceiver or cable modem. Follow the instructor's directions to connect the computer to the Internet. You should conduct an Internet search or make a trip to the local technology store to explore the specifications of common DSL and cable interfaces. For the most part, going through the full configuration of the actual connection is beyond the scope of this book, but you should at least know where to go to follow instructions from your ISP; that's the purpose of these last steps.

Figure 16-3 Network interface adapter driver properties

Connect the interface device by following the instructions provided with the device or by your ISP. The layout and configuration of the device may differ somewhat from device to device, but you should be able to confirm that the device is working properly by observing the various indicator lights on the device.

Step 6 To finish this installation and gain high-speed access to the Internet, you will most likely have to follow specific directions from your ISP to configure Windows to communicate through the DSL or cable device. A technician may need to come to your home or office to configure some settings. Windows also provides a generic wizard to configure this communication. The following list walks you through this generic configuration by operating system:

- **Windows XP**   Open Network Connections and select *Create a new connection*. Click Next. Choose the Connect to the Internet option and click Next. Select the option to set up your connection manually and click Next. Pick the appropriate option on the next screen, most likely *Connect using a broadband connection that is always on*. Click Next, then Finish.

- **Windows Vista/7**   Open Control Panel. Open the Network and Sharing Center and select *Set up a new connection or network*. Select Connect to the Internet and click Next. Choose Broadband as your connection. Type in the relevant information and click Connect. Windows will then attempt to set up your Internet connection. When it is finished, click Close.

If you have followed these steps (and actually have installed a DSL or cable interface), you should now have high-speed access to the Internet.

 30 MINUTES

Lab Exercise 16.03: Enabling Windows Firewall

Your client is very pleased with how the rollout of the office's Internet connection upgrade is progressing. They have been surfing around a little, and are impressed with the speed at which the Web sites are loading. You explain that you must now configure a firewall to protect them from outside intrusion through the high-speed connection. Windows offers a very competent built-in firewall. In this lab you will enable Windows Firewall and explore some of the services (ports) that you can allow or block.

Learning Objectives

Completing the following steps, you will explore Windows Firewall and associated TCP and UDP service ports.

At the end of this lab, you'll be able to

- Enable Windows Firewall

- Identify various protocols and associated service ports

Lab Materials and Setup

The materials you need for this lab are

- A working computer running Windows XP, Windows Vista, or Windows 7

- Optional: A machine connected to the Internet

Getting Down to Business

Enabling the firewall is as simple as a few clicks of the mouse and verifying that you can communicate with the trusted sites that you prefer. Windows Firewall is practically self-configuring, but if you want to allow access to Web servers or e-mail servers in your organization, you will have to open some TCP ports. The CompTIA A+ 220-801 exam expects you to know some of these "well-known ports," so you'll explore them in Windows Firewall.

✔ **Hint**

If you are configuring a single machine for Internet access, you will want to implement Windows Firewall on that machine to protect it from malicious intrusion. However, if you are configuring machines as part of a LAN and using a proxy server or Internet Connection Sharing (as you will in the next lab exercise), you will only want to configure a firewall on the machine that connects directly to the Internet. Assume the computer in this lab is the machine connected to the Internet.

Step 1 In Windows XP, return to Network Connections. Right-click the Local Area Connections icon of the external connection (the one connected to the Internet) and select Properties. Click the Advanced tab, and then click the Settings button in the Windows Firewall box. This opens the Windows Firewall dialog box (see Figure 16-4).

In Windows Vista/7, open the Control Panel, then open Windows Firewall. In Windows Vista, select *Change settings*. In Windows 7, select *Turn Windows Firewall on or off*.

Step 2 Turn on the firewall to protect the PC from unwanted access through the Internet connection.

Step 3 In Windows XP, select the Advanced tab of the Windows Firewall dialog box and click the Settings button for the Network Connection Settings (see Figure 16-5).

➜ **Note**

The following advanced options have been removed from the Windows Firewall settings in Windows Vista/7 in an attempt to make the OS more secure; thus, the following steps will only work in Windows XP. There are still methods for setting up exceptions (see the Exceptions tab in the Windows Firewall dialog box, specifically the Add Port button), but most of the advanced features have been moved to Administrative Tools. Windows 7 uses the *Allow a program or feature through Windows Firewall* link to enable you to set firewall settings for each installed application.

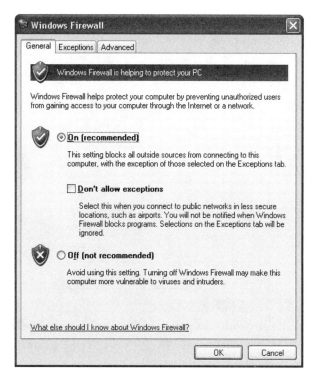

FIGURE 16-4 The Windows Firewall dialog box

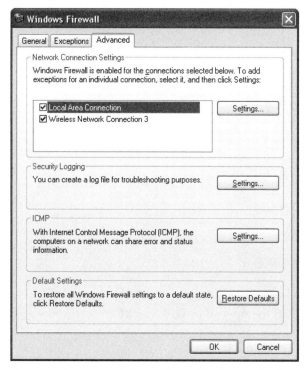

FIGURE 16-5 The Windows Firewall Advanced tab

Step 4   This opens the Advanced Settings dialog box, where you can allow various services to pass through the Internet connection and access dedicated servers on your internal network. For instance, if you have an FTP server that you have technicians update from the field, you will want to enable external communication by allowing TCP service port 21 to pass through the firewall (see Figure 16-6).

Using the Edit button, identify the service ports for the following protocols (I have completed the first one for you; see Figure 16-7):

   a.   File Transfer Protocol (FTP Server): __**TCP Port 21**_____

   b.   Internet Mail Access Protocol version 4 (IMAP4): _____

   c.   Simple Mail Transfer Protocol (SMTP): _____

   d.   Post Office Protocol version 3 (POP3): _____

   e.   Secure Sockets Layer (HTTPS): _____

   f.   Hypertext Transfer Protocol (HTTP): _____

Step 5   To complete this lab, check with your instructor to obtain the proper configuration of the firewall to allow the completion of further labs. You will probably disable the Windows Firewall for normal classroom use.

FIGURE 16-6 Allowing FTP traffic to pass through the firewall in Windows XP

FIGURE 16-7 Service Settings showing the TCP port number for the FTP server in Windows XP

 30 MINUTES

Lab Exercise 16.04: Configuring Windows Internet Connection Sharing

Now that the main PC is secure from external threats and attacks, it's time to configure this machine so that all of the PCs can take advantage of the secure Internet connection. Welcome Internet Connection Sharing (ICS)! With ICS, you will be able to set up a small LAN that allows all the client machines to access the Internet through the ICS host computer (this PC).

Learning Objectives

In this lab, you will implement the steps to use ICS. It will take some extra hardware to actually test the configuration, but you can still learn the basic concepts through the configuration exercise.

At the end of this lab, you'll be able to

- Configure Internet Connection Sharing

✔ **Cross-Reference**

To further explore ICS, refer to "Windows Internet Connection Sharing" in Chapter 16 of *Mike Meyers' CompTIA A+ Guide to 801: Managing and Troubleshooting PCs*.

Lab Materials and Setup

The materials you need for this lab are

- A working computer running Windows

- An additional network interface card for the ICS host computer

- A network switch

- A second computer running Windows to be configured as the client

- Optional: A machine connected to the Internet

Getting Down to Business

ICS allows a small workgroup of computers to connect to the Internet through one of the workgroup computers acting as an ICS host computer. There are a few items that need to be configured on both the ICS host computer and the clients. The host will have two communication devices installed (in this case, two NICs). The network will need a switch to allow multiple computers to communicate. Finally, the client machines will have to be configured to obtain their TCP/IP settings automatically.

→ **Note**

It may seem convoluted to connect an Ethernet cable coming from your Internet source to your computer just so you can connect another Ethernet cable to a switch—why not just connect the switch to the Internet source? But ICS is perhaps at its most beneficial when dealing with dial-up connections. In that case, you'd use a single NIC and a modem. Since most dial-up modems don't offer an Ethernet output, the only way to share the Internet connection would be with ICS!

Step 1 To use ICS, you will need two communication devices installed in the computer: either a modem connected to the Internet and an NIC connected to the internal network, or an NIC connected to a broadband interface and an NIC connected to the internal network. (If you need to install a second NIC to facilitate this lab exercise, perform Lab Exercise 16.02, Steps 1–3.)

Step 2 Open the Local Area Connection Properties dialog box for the network device connected to the Internet, as you did in previous lab exercises. Click the Advanced tab in Windows XP and the Sharing tab in Windows Vista/7 (see Figure 16-8). Under Internet Connection Sharing, check the *Allow other network users to connect through this computer's Internet connection* checkbox. Click OK.

Step 3 Once you've clicked OK, a hand icon (representing sharing) should appear under the Local Area Connection that has just been configured with ICS (see Figure 16-9).

Step 4 Test the ICS feature by following these steps:

a. Verify that the ICS host computer is capable of communicating with the Internet. Connect the external Local Area Connection NIC to the broadband interface (DSL or cable).

b. Power up the switch, and connect the internal interface from the ICS host computer to the switch.

FIGURE 16-8 The Advanced tab of the Local Area Connection Properties dialog box showing Internet Connection Sharing in Windows XP

c. Connect the network interface card of the client PC to the switch.

d. Open the Local Area Connection Properties dialog box, as you did in previous lab exercises. On the General/Networking tab, select Internet Protocol Version 4 (TCP/IPv4) and click Properties. In the Properties dialog box, verify that *Obtain an IP address automatically* and *Obtain DNS server address automatically* are selected (see Figure 16-10).

FIGURE 16-9 A shared Local Area Connection

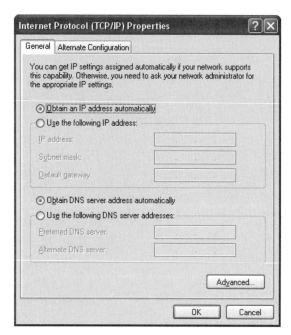

FIGURE 16-10 Internet Protocol (TCP/IP) Properties dialog box

Launch Internet Explorer on the client machine; verify that the connection is set up to use the LAN connection. Type **www.comptia.org** in the address bar and press ENTER. If there are any problems, shut down both machines and check all of the connections. Boot the ICS host computer first (allow all of the services to start), then boot the client machine.

 20 MINUTES

Lab Exercise 16.05: Upgrading and Tweaking Internet Explorer

Now that you have improved and protected your client's Internet connectivity, you will want to make sure that the method they use to interact with the Internet is the most current. Mozilla Firefox, Google Chrome, and Microsoft Internet Explorer are currently the three most popular browsers. The following steps will help you upgrade your client to the latest version of IE (version 9 as of this writing) and introduce you to some of the configuration areas that you should be aware of.

Learning Objectives

When it comes to applications—and this includes Internet Explorer—the computer technician is looked to as the Master or Mistress of All Things Computer. For this reason, a knowledge and awareness of applications, in addition to learning and practicing your craft as an IT technician, will enhance your reputation as an expert. In this lab, you'll briefly explore the upkeep of a networking application.

At the end of this lab, you'll be able to

- Evaluate and upgrade the IE application

- Fine-tune IE settings

Lab Materials and Setup

The materials you need for this lab are

- A working computer running Windows XP (at least SP2), Windows Vista, or Windows 7

- Internet access, preferably high-speed to facilitate downloads

Getting Down to Business

Internet Explorer is one of the most popular browser applications. You and your client may launch an Internet search engine such as Google or Yahoo! to locate and visit manufacturers' Web sites to research and, in some cases, purchase new hardware and software. You'll want to make sure that IE is up to date and working efficiently to make your client's browsing more pleasant.

✖ Warning

The following lab steps have you update Internet Explorer and change some of the configuration settings. If you are in an instructor-led class, or performing these operations on machines in your organization, verify you have permission to perform the upgrades.

Step 1 Open your current browser and navigate to the Microsoft Windows Internet Explorer page (http://windows.microsoft.com/en-US/internet-explorer/products/ie/home) as of this writing. Examine the new features and requirements. Near the large download link, find a separate link for downloading other versions of IE9. Does IE9 work with all versions of Windows? _____

Verify that your system and OS meet the requirements, and then download Internet Explorer 9.

Step 2 When the download has finished, open Internet Explorer. It looks very different from Internet Explorer 8. Microsoft has changed a lot of the old labeled buttons to just icons. Click on the cog wheel in the upper-right corner and select Internet Options.

On the General tab (see Figure 16-11), you can set the home page (or home pages), set browser history settings, change search defaults, and adjust tab settings. There are also options to set the appearance of Web pages displayed by the browser.

Figure 16-11 The General tab of the Internet Options dialog box in Internet Explorer 9

Step 3 Click the Advanced tab and explore the many settings that can be configured to modify how the browser deals with components and content. Navigate down to the Security heading and locate *Empty Temporary Internet Files Folder when browser is closed*. I like to enable this setting.

Explore some of the other tabs available in Internet Options and experiment with the different items you can configure. Microsoft has done a good job of setting the browser up with default settings that will work in most installations, but as the expert, you will want to be familiar with customizing the browser.

Lab Analysis Test

1. Tanner wants to configure his wireless network so that if Andrew just happens by with a laptop and a wireless card, he will not be able to gain access to the network without Tanner's approval. What component(s) does Tanner need to configure?

2. Brandon is using his school's computer to do some research for a term paper. He attempts to surf to a Web site he has found on Google, only to receive an *Access Denied* message from the browser. What could cause this to happen?

3. Andrew has configured his four-computer network to use Internet Connection Sharing. He has double-checked the ICS host computer, and it can access the Internet. All of the physical connections between the computers and the switch seem to be in good shape. Yet, he still cannot access the Internet from a client machine. What might he have missed?

4. Mary has stated that when she used the CNET Bandwidth Meter Online Speed Test, she achieved Internet transfer speeds around 7.5 Mbps. What type of Internet access do you think Mary has?

5. Cindy is installing a high-speed connection to the Internet. What are the four components she will need to verify and have on hand?

Key Term Quiz

Use the following terms to complete the following sentences. Not all terms will be used.

analog

dial-up

digital

drivers

HTTP

ICS

ISP

PnP

POP3

RJ-11

RJ-45

SSID

transceiver

Windows Firewall

1. When connecting to the Internet using a high-speed digital subscriber line, the DSL _____ is often referred to as a DSL modem.

2. The protocol that is synonymous with the World Wide Web is _____.

3. If the NIC isn't detected automatically, you'll need to install _____ manually.

4. Every wireless network has a network name that all of the machines accessing it must configure. This network name is known as a(n) _____.

5. The slowest means of accessing the Internet still in use today is _____.

Chapter 17
Multimedia

Lab Exercises

You have been hired as an entry-level tech for a public school district. Your first day on the job, the technology manager asks how familiar you are with the recording, storing, and playback of audio files on computer systems. It turns out that the history department wants the students to be able to record audio documentaries on historical events, store the files on the network, and produce podcasts of the documentaries. Demonstrating your enthusiasm, you respond that you are somewhat familiar with sound and will tackle the project. You are tasked with researching the sound card, building the prototype system, and providing some basic audio recording and storage training to the history instructors.

As a competent PC tech, you need to understand not just the tasks of installing the physical sound card and associated drivers, but also the applications that take advantage of the PC's sound capabilities. As such, the CompTIA A+ certification exams expect you to know about sound cards and their workings. The following lab exercises introduce you to sound card hardware and drivers, as well as the basic use of some of the popular Windows audio applications.

 30 MINUTES

Lab Exercise 17.01: Installing Sound

The first task on the agenda is to do a little research on sound cards and choose a few that meet the needs of this project. There are a number of different sound chips, and the "card" can be anything from the onboard sound capability of a mid-priced system to professional multichannel (input/output) devices used in recording studios. After you assemble a few candidates, you will select a sound card and then install, configure, and test that card. For the purpose of completing this lab, it is perfectly acceptable to use any working card, or an onboard sound device if that's what you have available.

Learning Objectives

This lab teaches you the basics of installing and configuring a sound card.

At the end of this lab, you'll be able to

- Identify features of sound cards
- Remove and install a sound card and associated devices (speakers and microphone)
- Configure a sound card

Lab Materials and Setup

The materials you need for this lab are

- A working computer system running Windows

- A removable sound card, microphone, and speakers properly installed and functioning (the sound drivers must either be part of the operating system in use or be available on disc or online)

✖ Warning

Different versions of Windows handle the drivers differently, to say the least. You should have a current driver for your sound card handy, just in case Windows decides it cannot remember your sound card when you go to reinstall!

Getting Down to Business

This lab will step you through removing, researching specifications for, installing, and configuring a sound card.

✔ Cross-Reference

For more information on sound cards, review the "Getting the Right Sound Hardware" section in Chapter 17 of *Mike Meyers' CompTIA A+ Guide to 801: Managing and Troubleshooting PCs*.

Step 1 Take a moment and look up the specifications of your current sound card online. Identify the following:

Resolution _____

Sampling rate _____

Dynamic range _____

Signal-to-noise ratio _____

Now see if you can find this information online for some other cards—try M-Audio Audiophile 192, Creative Sound Blaster X-Fi Xtreme, and Turtle Beach Audio Advantage Amigo II.

Step 2 Now that you've seen some of the relevant specifications, the next step is to practice removing and reinstalling the sound card.

✔ **Hint**

This lab assumes that you have a removable sound card, not onboard sound. If all you have to work with is a system with onboard sound, go into the CMOS setup utility and turn off the onboard sound. Make what observations you can and resume the exercise with Step 3. When the time comes in the second half of Step 3 to reinstall the sound card, just go back into CMOS and enable the onboard sound again.

    a.   Shut down your system properly. Unplug the power cord.

    b.   Remove the case cover from your system and locate the sound card (see Figure 17-1).

          What type of slot does the card use? _____

    c.   Disconnect any cables that are attached to the sound card (both internal and external), take out the screw that secures the sound card to the case, and then carefully remove the card. Make sure you're properly grounded before you touch the card!

          What sort of internal connectors does the card have? _____

    d.   What sort of external connectors does it have? _____

    e.   Does the card have jumpers? What are they used for? Again, look on the Internet for the answers. Find the name of the card manufacturer and search that company's Web site for information on your specific model. This information is also available in the documentation for the card, if you still have it around.

_____

_____

Figure 17-1 A typical sound card

f. What is the brand name of the sound-processing chip?

_____

g. Is the name on the chip different from the name of the manufacturer of the card? (For example, the chip might have *ESS* printed on it, while the board is marked *Creative Labs*.)

_____

Step 3 With the card out of your system, turn on the machine and let it boot to the Windows desktop. Then go to Device Manager and see if your sound card is still listed.

Did Windows automatically remove the device when the card was removed? _____

If the sound card is still listed, highlight its icon, right-click, and select Uninstall. (Am I sure? Yes, I'm sure!)

Save your changes and shut your system off properly.

The next steps will confirm that the device has been removed:

a. Reboot your system, go to Device Manager, and confirm that the sound device is no longer listed.

b. Shut down your system and disconnect the power cord. Insert the sound card in the slot where you originally found it, secure the card to the case using the screw you removed, and reconnect all the cables.

c. Reboot the system. When plug and play (PnP) kicks in, your system should recognize that you have added a card.

Windows will now locate the software drivers for the new hardware you installed. In fact, unless you uninstalled them, the drivers should still be on your system.

Step 4 Return to Device Manager. Find your device and open the Drivers tab and confirm that Windows installed the same drivers in the system. If necessary, use the driver disc to reinstall the correct drivers.

Step 5 To confirm that sound is working properly, start by ensuring that the speakers are powered and connected, and that the volume is set at a comfortable level.

Make sure your speakers are plugged into the proper jack on the sound card.

Is the speaker pair plugged into a working AC outlet, or does it have good batteries?

_____

Is there a volume adjustment knob on your speakers? _____

If you have a volume knob, adjust it to the middle position, and then access the Control Panel.

Now place a Volume icon in the taskbar's system tray/notification area so that volume adjustments will be more convenient. Follow the procedure that matches your operating system.

- In Windows XP, open the Sounds and Audio Devices Control Panel applet, and check the *Place volume icon in the taskbar* box.

- In Windows Vista, right-click the taskbar and select Properties. Then, click the Notification Area tab and make sure Volume is checked under *Select which system icons to always show*.

- In Windows 7, right-click on the taskbar and select Properties. Under Notification area on the Taskbar tab, click on Customize. Next to Volume, select *Show icon and notifications*.

Once you have the Volume icon in the taskbar's system tray/notification area, right-click it and select Open Volume Mixer, then follow these steps:

a. In Windows XP, check to be sure that the *Mute all* or *Mute <device name>* option is not selected (see Figure 17-2). In Windows Vista/7, make sure the speaker icon beneath each audio device is not covered by a red circle with a line through it (the symbol for mute).

b. Adjust the slider(s) to the center position.

You now have a good starting point to play sounds. Once you have ensured that the speakers are successfully putting out sound, you can go back and customize the levels to your liking.

Step 6   Test the speakers, and adjust the sound volume to a comfortable level. A good tool to use to test your sound card is the DirectX Diagnostic Tool. In Windows XP, click Start | Run and type **dxdiag** to launch the DirectX Diagnostic Tool (see Figure 17-3). In Windows Vista/7, go to the Start Search bar and type **dxdiag**. Press ENTER.

a. Click the Sound tab, and examine the information displayed about your sound card and drivers.

b. Click the Test DirectSound button (Windows XP only). This takes you through a series of tests to confirm the operation of your sound system.

c. Switch to the Music tab and click the Test DirectMusic button (Windows XP only). This tests whether your system supports the DirectMusic component of DirectX.

FIGURE 17-2 Setting the volume controls in Windows XP

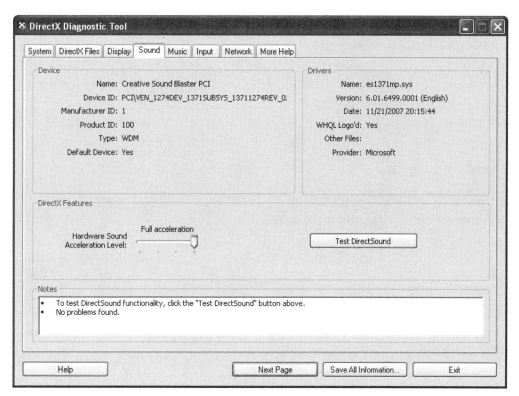

FIGURE 17-3 Using the DirectX Diagnostic Tool in Windows XP

Step 7 You've learned how to remove, install, and configure a sound card. You've also learned how to test the various parts of the sound system. Now it's time to talk about troubleshooting.

Your sound system is working, but your speakers sound a little rough. Are they "blown" out because they were overdriven with poor adjustments? You can go to Eminent Technology's Multimedia Speaker Test Web site and test the response of your speakers at different frequencies:

www.eminent-tech.com/music/multimediatest.html

These tests will help you confirm whether your speakers can still handle all the frequencies they are designed to handle.

 30 MINUTES

Lab Exercise 17.02: Recording Sound

With the sound card installed, configured, and tested, it's time to get the project really rolling with recorded sound. It is expected that each student's documentary will last from eight to ten minutes and will encompass typical current events. Each student has a microphone, sound card, and speakers. What you want to do is get the speech recorded digitally, maybe add some music, and choose the audio quality based on the expected delivery method.

Learning Objectives

The purpose of this lab exercise is to guide you in the recording of sound.

At the end of this lab, you'll be able to

- Use the microphone to record a WAV file

- Fine-tune the quality of the recording

Lab Materials and Setup

The materials you need for this lab are

- A working computer system running Windows

- A sound card, speakers, and a microphone properly installed

Getting Down to Business

Once you have installed, configured, and tested a sound card, you need to run some applications to see if this is going to work. This lab steps you through recording sound into the computer and saving the recording as a WAV or MP3 sound file.

Step 1 To check your system's ability to capture audio so that you can record the documentaries, you will use Windows Sound Recorder. Make sure your microphone is plugged into the proper connector before you proceed.

Access Sound Recorder in Windows XP by selecting Start | All Programs | Accessories | Entertainment | Sound Recorder. In Windows Vista/7, select Start | Accessories | Sound Recorder. In Windows XP, you'll see something similar to an audio cassette player. The buttons are the same—Record, Play, Fast Forward, Rewind, and Stop—but they're labeled with icons instead of words. In Windows Vista/7, however, Microsoft has stripped almost every control from the Sound Recorder, leaving only a Record button (see Figure 17-4). You can't even use Sound Recorder to listen to what you just recorded. You'll only be able to record at a single quality level, and the only format available is WMA (Windows Media Audio).

→ **Note**

To best complete this lab, use a Windows XP computer.

Figure 17-4 Using Windows Sound Recorder

Step 2 Using Sound Recorder from Windows XP, let's explore three different levels of recording. Open Sounder Recorder and load a sound file of any format. When working with digital audio files, the balance between sound quality and sound file size is driven by the project. If you were recording a project for CD, you would want the highest quality. For streaming audio and podcast audio, the MP3 file format is probably acceptable. Telephone quality, while achieving small file size, is not considered production quality.

    a.   To set the recording quality, select File | Properties and then click the Convert Now button. In the Sound Selection dialog box, click the Name drop-down menu and select CD Quality. Click OK and then OK again to return to the Sound Recorder window.

    b.   Click the red Record button and start talking into the microphone. Watch the graph to see that your voice is being recorded. If nothing seems to be happening, check your microphone connections.

    c.   Record a full 60 seconds of CD-quality audio, and then click Stop (the button with a square icon, next to Record). To hear your recording, click Play (the single right arrow).

    d.   To discover how much space this sound file uses, select File | Properties and observe the file's data size. Record the file size here:

        _____

    e.   Create a subfolder named **podcast** in your My Music folder and save the sound file as **cdquality.wav** in the podcast folder.

✔ **Hint**

As you've probably figured out, our scenario for the history department would require a more sophisticated digital audio recording application. One minute is not going to be a very lengthy documentary! Sound Recorder is a good application to demonstrate the steps required to record audio, and you could use it to set up custom sound files to play during events. An example would be the infamous sound file that announces: "You've got mail." If you would like to explore digital audio recording and playback further, you can find and download the open source program called Audacity at http://audacity.sourceforge.net.

Step 3 Telephone quality is very low resolution and frequency response, meaning that it will probably sound muffled and dull. Follow these steps to convert the CD-quality sound file to a telephone-quality sound file:

    a.   Select File | Properties, click Convert Now, and change the Name setting to Telephone Quality. Click OK and then OK again to return to the Sound Recorder window.

    b.   Now check out the data size of the file and record it here: _____. Has the size of the sound file changed? How does it sound? _____

    c.   Save the sound file in the podcast folder as **telephonequality.wav**.

Step 4   Finally, you will explore saving a recording as an MPEG Layer-3 (MP3) sound file. This is probably the best balance between audio quality and file size.

    a.   Launch Sound Recorder and open the cdquality.wav file.

    b.   To set the recording quality to the MP3 format, select File | Properties and then click Convert Now. In the Sound Selection dialog box, click the Format drop-down list and select MPEG Layer-3, then click OK.

    c.   Note the file's data size and record it here: _____. Has the size of the sound file changed? How does it sound? _____

    d.   Open the podcast folder and save the sound file as **mp3quality.mp3**.

✔ **Hint**

In the Sound Selection dialog box, you can also set more specific attributes for an MP3 file; just click the Attributes drop-down list after selecting MPEG Layer-3 and you'll see a number of options to fine-tune the quality of your recording.

---

 30 MINUTES

Lab Exercise 17.03: Exploring Windows Media Player

Now that you have successfully recorded the project, you will have to look at some of the methods used to play the files and create an archive of the documentary on CD. The Windows environment has used Windows Media Player since the introduction of version 6.1 in 1998. In this exercise, you will learn some of the basic navigation steps for using Windows Media Player 12, and burn your recordings to an audio CD.

Learning Objectives

In this lab exercise, you'll learn how to navigate and play audio files, and then you'll learn how to burn an audio CD using Windows Media Player 12.

At the end of this lab, you'll be able to

- Open and play sound files of various formats
- Navigate Windows Media Player 12
- Burn a CD of your recording

Lab Materials and Setup

The materials you need for this lab are

- A working computer system running Windows

- Three or more audio files to burn

- A sound card, speakers, and a microphone properly installed

- Windows Media Player 12 or newer (WMP12 is used in the lab exercise)

- A commercially produced music CD of your choice

- A blank CD-R or CD-RW

Getting Down to Business

Once you've recorded the sound and saved it as a WAV or MP3 sound file, you need a method to audition the finished product and package the sound file for distribution. You may want to make an MP3 file for portable players or streaming audio over the Internet, or you may want to distribute high-quality audio CDs.

✔ **Hint**

There are a number of paths you could take to accomplish the playback of your recordings and archive them to a CD. This lab exercise steps you through one method that explores some of the features of Windows Media Player 12. Some of the steps, windows, and icons may look different depending on the version of Windows Media Player you use.

Step 1 Launch Windows Media Player and then follow these steps:

    a. Open Windows Media Player 12 (see Figure 17-5).

    b. Click on the Play tab in the upper-right corner. This tab enables you to create playlists. Use the navigation tree on the left side of the program to locate your files, and then drag them to the playlist tab (labeled "Play") on the right. The first song you drag will start playing automatically. Click on the Save list button to save the selected files as a playlist (see Figure 17-6). Save the list as **Podcast**.

    c. Click the Burn tab, and then drag and drop Podcast into the Burn List pane on the right side of the Windows Media Player window.

    d. Insert a blank optical disc into an optical drive on your system with recording capabilities, and then click the Start Burn button.

    e. Wait while the podcast audio file is burned to the optical disc, completing the task of archiving your recordings.

FIGURE 17-5 Windows Media Player

Step 2   While you have Windows Media Player open, explore the other options available to you as you work with sound files. One of the most popular uses of the computer when it comes to working with audio is to convert your CDs to MP3 sound files for use on portable MP3 players. Complete the following steps to calculate how many CDs you could fit onto a 8-GB MP3 player:

   a.   Insert a music CD into the optical media drive.

   b.   Click Tools | Options to open the Options dialog box for Windows Media Player. Click the Rip Music tab.

FIGURE 17-6 Creating a playlist

c. Under Rip Settings, click the Format drop-down list and select WAV (Lossless). Use the information at the bottom of the dialog box to calculate the number of CDs that would fit onto an 8-GB MP3 player at this bit rate.

_____

d. Click the Format drop-down list again and select MP3. Experiment with the Audio quality slider (which ranges from 128 Kbps to 320 Kbps), and calculate the number of CDs that would fit onto an 8-GB MP3 player at various quality settings.

_____

Lab Analysis Test

1. Suddenly and for no apparent reason, the speaker icon no longer shows up in the taskbar/notification area. In Windows Vista, where would you check to be sure it is enabled?

2. John replaced his motherboard with one that has built-in sound. He still wants to use his Creative Labs Audigy sound card. What must he do to prevent conflicts?

3. Theresa has been using her system for a long time to visit with friends in chat rooms. Lately her friends are complaining that her sound quality is getting worse. What should she check first?

4. Karl is not getting any sound from his speakers. What three things should he check?

5. John complains about annoying sounds when he opens and closes certain programs and sometimes when he clicks his mouse. He asks you if you can make them go away. Can you?

Key Term Quiz

Use the following terms to complete the following sentences. Not all terms will be used.

aux

compression

line-in

.mid

MP3

sound card

sound file

Sound Recorder

speaker

WAV

1. Joe wants to record himself singing the '50s classic "Hound Dog" to honor the birthday of Elvis Presley. He plugs a microphone into his sound card and opens _____, the recording software that comes with Windows.

2. Joshua is the keyboard player for a local band. He records some of the band's songs into a sequencer using MIDI. When he looks for the files on the computer, he can only find files with the _____ extension.

3. The MP3 format is popular because of the _____ scheme it uses.

4. The most common sound file format for portable sound players today is _____.

5. By default, the Windows XP Sound Recorder saves audio recordings as _____ files.

Chapter 18
Portable Computing

Lab Exercises

The world has gone mobile, and accomplished technicians travel right along with it. General technicians have always worked on the software side of portables, tweaking power management options to optimize battery life for the users. Working on the hardware side of portable computing devices of all stripes, however, used to be the realm of only highly specialized technicians. As portable computing devices become increasingly common and the technology inside becomes more modular, however, frontline general technicians (think CompTIA A+ certified technicians here) increasingly get the call to upgrade and repair these devices.

Most laptops and netbooks have parts that a user can easily replace. You can swap out a fading battery for a newer one, for example, or add a second battery in place of an optical drive for long airplane trips. Lurking beneath access panels on the underside or below the keyboard on some models are hardware components such as RAM, a hard drive, a network card, and a modem—just like laptop batteries, these units can be easily accessed and replaced by a technician. Some laptops even have panels for replacing the video card and CPU.

In this series of labs, you'll do four things. First, you'll use the Internet to research the upgrades available for portable computing devices so you can provide proper recommendations to employers and clients. Second, you'll open a laptop and gut it like a rainbow trout—removing and replacing RAM, the most common of all hardware upgrades. Third, you'll perform the traditional task of a portable PC technician, tweaking the power management options to optimize battery life on particular models. Finally, you'll tour a computer store to familiarize yourself with the latest and greatest portable offerings.

 30 MINUTES

Lab Exercise 18.01: Researching Laptop Upgrade Paths

Your boss just sent word that one of your most important clients wants to extend the life of their sales force's laptop computers by upgrading rather than replacing. You've been asked to provide an upgrade track for your client. This requires you to research the laptops used by the company to determine which upgrades you can make, and to verify that the laptops themselves are not so old that the cost to upgrade them outweighs the cost of new laptops with new technology. You have to determine whether you can add RAM, replace the hard drives, or replace the aging batteries. Get to work!

Learning Objectives

Given the manufacturer and model number of a notebook computer, you'll figure out how to upgrade your client's computers.

At the end of this lab, you'll be able to

- Determine the replacement price of a battery

- Determine memory upgrades, including the quantity and type of RAM

- Determine hard drive upgrades, including the capacity and price of a hard drive

Lab Materials and Setup

The materials you need for this lab are

- A working PC with Internet access

Getting Down to Business

Limber up your surfing fingers because you're about to spend some time on the Web. Researching information about hardware and software is something technicians do all the time. The better you are at it, the better you are at your job!

When you're searching for replacement and upgrade parts and information, always take a look at the device manufacturer's Web site. Most major PC manufacturers, such as Dell and Lenovo, have comprehensive product specification sheets available to the public on their sites. You can even order replacement parts directly from them! A popular tactic for researching upgrades is to grab the upgrade specs from the manufacturer's site and then search the Internet for the best prices. Not only are you doing your job well, but you'll be saving your company money too!

In the following steps, you'll navigate the tumultuous seas of the Internet in a quest to find the Golden Fleece of laptop battery, memory, and hard drive upgrades.

Step 1 Fire up your Web browser, and surf over to the device manufacturer's Web site. Try www.dell.com, or do a Google search for **laptop battery**. Many sites sell every laptop battery imaginable. The goal of this exercise is to become familiar with using the Internet to identify parts, confirm the specifications, and purchase replacement batteries. Once you reach a suitable Web site, answer the following questions:

You need replacement batteries for several Dell Precision M4400 laptops. What's the vendor's part number and price for this battery?

_____

What's the voltage and power capacity of the battery?

_____

✔ **Hint**

Just like any other electrical power source, batteries are rated according to voltage (9.6 V, for instance), current capacity (2600 milliamps per hour, or mAh), and sometimes power capacity (72 watts per hour, or WHr). When purchasing laptop batteries from third-party vendors (that is, vendors other than the laptop manufacturer), make sure to buy a battery that matches the voltage recommended by the manufacturer. Depending on the type of battery (Ni-Cd, Ni-MH, or Li-Ion), the current or power capacity of replacement batteries may be greater than that of the original battery. This is not a problem—increased current/power capacity means longer run times for your portable PC.

Step 2   Search the manufacturer's Web site for information on memory. If that isn't available, flip your browser over to www.kahlon.com to check RAM prices and availability. If the site isn't available, perform a Google search to find other Web sites that sell **laptop memory**. Then answer the following questions.

Your client has a Dell Precision M4400 with 1 GB of RAM. How much RAM can you install? How many sticks of RAM will it take to upgrade this machine to a respectable 4 GB of memory, and how much will it cost?

_____

_____

Step 3   Stay where you landed in your search for memory upgrades. Does the vendor have replacement or additional hard drives available as well? If not, try www.kahlon.com, but now research possible hard drive upgrades for the Dell Precision M4400 the client owns. Answer this question:

The client's Dell Precision M4400 laptops have 160-GB hard drives plus a currently unused modular media bay that could be used to house a second hard drive. How much would it cost to add a second 320-GB hard drive to the Dell?

_____

30 MINUTES

Lab Exercise 18.02: Replacing and Upgrading RAM

Your client settled on the RAM upgrades as the first step for making their laptops more usable, and you get tagged as the person to remove the old RAM and install the new. Upgrading RAM is the most common technician-performed upgrade on portable PCs and something you're likely to run into in the real world.

Learning Objectives

In this lab, you'll learn essential skills for upgrading portable PCs.

At the end of this lab, you'll be able to

- Access the RAM panel in a laptop
- Remove RAM in a laptop
- Install RAM properly in a laptop

Lab Materials and Setup

The materials you need for this lab are

- A working portable computer
- A very tiny Philips-head screwdriver
- An anti-static mat

> ✖ **Warning**
>
> Opening a portable computer can result in a nonfunctional portable computer. Don't use the instructor's primary work laptop for this exercise!

Getting Down to Business

You're about to open the sensitive inner portions of a portable computer, but before you do, it's a great idea to refresh your memory about avoiding electrostatic discharge (ESD). The inside of a laptop looks different from the inside of a desktop or tower case, but the contents are just as sensitive to static electricity. Watch out!

Step 1 Using your handy screwdriver or other handy tool, open the access panel for the RAM. Every portable PC offers a different way to access the RAM, so I can't give you explicit directions here. Most often, you'll find a removable plate on the bottom of the laptop secured with a tiny Philips-head screw. Some laptops require you to remove the keyboard, unscrew a heat spreader, and then access the RAM. Figure 18-1 shows a typical panel, accessible from the underside of the laptop.

FIGURE 18-1 Opening the access panel to find RAM

Step 2 Once you have the panel open, push outward on the restraining clips on the RAM stick(s). This will cause the RAM to pop up partially (see Figure 18-2).

Step 3 Remove the RAM gently, gripping only at the noncontact edges. Place the stick(s) on an anti-static pad or in an anti-static bag.

FIGURE 18-2 Releasing the RAM

Step 4 Install the replacement RAM into the laptop, reversing the process of removal. Place the stick(s) at an angle into the RAM slots and push firmly. Once the contacts have disappeared, press the body of the RAM into the restraining clips.

✔ **Hint**

If you don't have new RAM to install, simply install the RAM you removed in Step 3. This gives you the opportunity to practice!

Step 5 Replace the access panel.

Step 6 Power on the laptop to confirm that the new RAM is recognized and functioning properly.

 30 MINUTES

Lab Exercise 18.03: Adjusting Power Management to Optimize Battery Life

Several of your sales staff members have to attend a conference on the other side of the country. The conference came up on short notice, so everyone needs time to prepare, even while on the flight to the conference. You've been tasked with configuring power management on their laptops to optimize battery life so they can work as long as possible while on the plane.

Learning Objectives

In this lab, you'll adjust the power management features for a PC, a task that's vital to proper support of portable PCs.

At the end of this lab, you'll be able to

- Enable and disable power management in the CMOS
- Change power management settings in Windows

Lab Materials and Setup

The materials you need for this lab are

- A working computer with Windows installed
- A BIOS that supports power management

Having a notebook computer available is a plus. Performing these steps on a notebook computer will allow you to configure the settings for the Portable/Laptop power scheme and then remove the power cord, running on battery power to experience the actual results. If you're practicing on a regular desktop PC, keep in mind that a notebook will have two options for each adjustment: one for when the notebook is using battery power, and one for when it's connected to the alternating current (AC) source.

Getting Down to Business

Windows PCs have two separate areas for power management: the CMOS setup program and the Control Panel. You'll start with CMOS and then go to the Control Panel.

Step 1   Boot your system, and enter the CMOS setup program.

Refer to the "Power Management" section in Chapter 18 of *Mike Meyers' CompTIA A+ Guide to 801: Managing and Troubleshooting PCs* for more information on power management on portable PCs.

Now follow these steps:

a.   Go to the Power Management Setup screen.

b.   Enable power management if it's currently disabled.

c.   Look at each option for common-sense settings. For example, when operating on battery power, the portable should be configured for maximum energy efficiency, thus increasing run time.

d.   Make sure the ACPI setting is enabled if the BIOS supports it.

e.   Save your settings, and boot the system to the Windows desktop.

ACPI is short for Advanced Configuration and Power Interface, a power management specification developed by Intel, Microsoft, and Toshiba. ACPI enables the operating system to control the amount of power given to each device attached to the computer. With ACPI, the operating system can turn off peripheral devices, such as optical drives, when they're not in use.

Step 2   Access the Power Options applet in the Control Panel, and make a note of your current power management settings.

Check out the different power schemes available (this will depend on your specific system) and change the settings to see how they affect when the monitor and hard drives turn off. Each of these schemes has adjustable times. The tabs and settings will differ depending on which version of Windows you're running. Be sure to look at them all. To see more detailed power scheme settings in Windows Vista/7, be sure to click *Change power/plan settings* and then *Change advanced power settings*.

✔ **Hint**

The Windows XP Power Options Properties dialog box (on a notebook) has five tabs: Power Schemes, Alarms, Power Meter, Advanced, and Hibernate (see Figure 18-3). You can use the Alarms tab to set the time when the battery alarm is activated. The Power Meter tab shows the percent of charge remaining in the battery.

✖ **Warning**

Some PCs and some components don't like standby and suspend modes. They can cause your computer to lock up. Be aware of that, and if your computer locks up, turn those settings off.

Step 3 Once you've finished experimenting, enable or disable power management as you prefer.

FIGURE 18-3 Accessing the Windows XP power options on a portable computer

Open

Lab Exercise 18.04: Field Trip to Play with the Latest Portable PCs

The best way to understand portable PCs (laptops, netbooks, tablet PCs, and smartphones) is to play with one. If there isn't one available in the classroom, then this exercise is for you.

Learning Objectives

This lab will take you into the field for a little computer browsing—for educational purposes, of course!

At the end of this lab, you'll be able to

- Recognize the variations in key features among different portable PCs

Lab Materials and Setup

The materials you need for this lab are

- A local computer store or other retailer with a good selection of portable PCs you can examine

✔ Hint

If you don't have a store nearby, use the Web to browse a computer store such as CompUSA (www.compusa.com), or go to a manufacturer's Web site such as Dell's (www.dell.com) and customize a laptop to your heart's content. Be sure to explore all the options and customizations you can add to it. Just make sure you don't click Buy!

Getting Down to Business

Portable PCs are manufactured by a wide variety of companies, and no two notebooks are created equal. Some notebooks feature a slim and lightweight profile and are designed for the busy traveler; others feature a full complement of ports and rival desktop PCs in their power and features. Netbooks are smaller, compact versions of laptops that are ideal as long-term traveling companions. They can fit in a purse or backpack and thus are handy for browsing or doing e-mail on the road. Tablet PCs have pen-based interfaces that allow you to use them like a paper notepad. Smartphones are great for staying connected everywhere you go. Take a look at all the available models and compare their features.

Step 1 Go to your local computer store or office supply store and check out the portable PCs on display. Try to find a store with a variety of brands. Bring this lab manual (or a copy of the following chart) with you to record the different specs you find.

Step 2 Pick out three portables, preferably from different manufacturers. For each portable, record the following information.

Feature	Portable 1	Portable 2	Portable 3
Size/weight			
Screen type/size			
CPU			
RAM			
Pointing device(s)			
I/O ports			
ExpressCard(s)			
Hard disk drive/solid-state drive			
Floppy/optical drive(s)			

Lab Analysis Test

1. Bill wants to upgrade his memory from 2 GB to the maximum amount of RAM his notebook can take. He has a Lenovo ThinkPad T500 notebook. How much RAM does he need to buy?

2. Teresa complains that her Windows XP notebook turns itself off without any warning. What should she adjust?

3. Maanit will be traveling from the United States to India. He'll use his laptop to watch DVDs on the way, usually on battery power. Lately, the battery seems to run out of juice well before the battery specifications indicate. What could possibly cause this recent development? Are there any recommendations you would make to Maanit to improve his laptop's performance?

4. During your research earlier in these exercises, which did you discover to be the most expensive—hard drives, memory, or batteries? Which component was the most inexpensive to replace?

5. Would the LCD screen or hard drives turn off, for energy conservation, if you set your power scheme to Always On and you walked away for a long period of time? Why or why not?

Key Term Quiz

Use the following terms to complete the following sentences. Not all terms will be used.

ACPI

battery

hard drive

hibernate

memory

netbook

notebook

Power Meter

Power Options

Power Scheme

standby

1. The amount of time the hard drive will continue to spin once it's no longer being accessed is determined by the _____ setting in Windows XP and the advanced power settings in Windows Vista/7.

2. You can use the _____ applet in the Control Panel to set the power conservation options for the notebook computer.

3. The battery, _____, and _____ are all upgradeable laptop components.

4. The amount of power remaining in a battery can be determined by looking at the _____.

5. Software can control power consumption if _____ is turned on in the CMOS setup program.

Chapter 19

Printer Technologies and Installation

Lab Exercises

Printers continue to be a major part of the day-to-day working environment, both at home and in the office, despite attempts to create a "paperless office." What this means is that the PC technician will have to understand the operation of several types of printers and be able to keep them in good working order. Many companies have service contracts for their more expensive printers (they're usually leased property anyway!), but there will always be printers that need a good technician's love and care.

This chapter's lab exercises will take you through a scenario in which your boss walks into your office and tells you five printers are being delivered to you—two impact printers using legacy parallel ports, two USB inkjet printers, and an HP LaserJet laser printer using a network interface. You need to install them and make sure they work properly so that they're accessible by anyone in the company who needs them. You'll learn about some of the key differences between the two most popular types of printers (inkjet and laser printers), and you'll load printer drivers. Finally, you'll look at some of the maintenance issues that are required to keep the printers up and running and some of the techniques to follow when they stop.

 30 MINUTES

Lab Exercise 19.01: Examining Types of Printers

There's an enormous amount of information on the Internet about printers. All of the top printer manufacturers—HP, Lexmark, Canon, and so forth—have Web sites that can provide insight about modern printers. As a PC technician, you'll need to visit these sites for information about your new printers, and to download the most current drivers for those printers.

✖ Warning

You must have access to the Internet for this exercise. If you don't have access, refer to Chapter 19 of *Mike Meyers' CompTIA A+ Guide to 801: Managing and Troubleshooting PCs* for a review.

Learning Objectives

In this lab, you'll compare the features of impact, inkjet, and laser printers using the Internet.

At the end of this lab, you'll be able to

- Recognize the key differences between impact, inkjet, and laser printers

- Identify and visit Web sites on the Internet dedicated to printers and printer troubleshooting

Lab Materials and Setup

The materials you need for this lab are

- A working computer with Windows

- A connection to the Internet

- Access to either an inkjet printer or a laser printer

✔ **Hint**

A trip to your local computer store or other retailer with a good selection of printers would be beneficial for a general knowledge of printers.

Getting Down to Business

Fire up your favorite Web browser and head out on the old Information Superhighway. The Internet is just brimming with helpful information about printers.

✔ **Hint**

Web sites have the annoying tendency to either disappear or drop the information that was once relevant to a particular subject. If any of the links in this exercise are no longer active or don't seem to contain the relevant information, you may need to do a little Web research of your own. As always, practice safe surfing! There are thousands of online forums available, and they can contain questionable hyperlinks, poor-quality information, and in some cases, outright wrong information. Try to stick with legitimate manufacturer and technical Web sites, examine where that hyperlink is going to reroute your computer, and visit multiple sites to verify information you discover in the forums. Consider it excellent practice for real-world tech work!

Step 1   To find information about inkjet printers, access the following Web site to complete this step: http://computer.howstuffworks.com/inkjet-printer.htm/printable. If this link doesn't work, you can also do a Google search and look for information about how inkjet printers work.

a.   What's the major difference between impact and non-impact printers?

_____

_____

b.   What part of an inkjet printer moves the print head back and forth across the page?

_____

c.   List the two ways in which the droplets of ink are formed in inkjet printers.

_____

_____

d.   The type of paper used in an inkjet printer greatly influences the quality of the image produced. What are the two main characteristics of inkjet printer paper that affect the image the most?

_____

_____

Step 2   For information about laser printers, access this site to complete this step: www.howstuffworks .com/laser-printer.htm/printable. Do a Google search or refer to the textbook if this site isn't available.

a.   What's the primary principle at work in a laser printer?

_____

_____

b.   What moves the image from the drum to the paper?

_____

c. Printer Control Language (PCL) and PostScript are both examples of what?

_____

_____

d. What's toner? Is it an ink, wax, or something else?

_____

Step 3 Put these steps in the printing process of a laser printer in the correct order (don't forget to reference the textbook as well):

Charge: _____

Clean: _____

Develop: _____

Fuse: _____

Transfer: _____

Expose: _____

Process: _____

Step 4 If you have access to a laser printer, open it and carefully examine the insides. Also read the printer manual for details on the specifications. Access the manufacturer's Web site for additional information.

If you don't have access to a laser printer, go to your local office supply or computer store and ask a salesperson to show you the differences between various impact, inkjet (black and white as well as color), and laser printers.

Look inside your laser printer.

a. What parts are easily removable and replaceable?

_____

b. Practice removing and reinserting the toner (see Figure 19-1) and paper.

Figure 19-1 A toner cartridge with its photosensitive drum exposed

✖ Warning

Remember to turn the printer off before removing anything but the toner or paper. Also, be careful not to spill any toner inside the printer.

Look at the manual or the manufacturer's Web site for these specifications.

c.   How much RAM can it hold? _____

d.   How much effect does the amount of RAM have on the cost of a new printer?

_____

e.   Are the drum and toner separate, or are they one replaceable part?

_____

f.   What is the speed of the printer (pages per minute)? _____

g.   What is the quality of the output (resolution)? _____

_____

h.   What are the number and types of ink cartridges? _____

_____

i.   What is the price of a new printer? _____

j.   What is the cost per page? _____

✔ Hint

Most inkjet (and even laser) printers are priced very low, so they're affordable to buy initially. Using them is another question. Calculate the cost of the ink and how many pages it'll print. This calculation will amaze you. They're not so cheap after all.

k.   What can you conclude from your research about the true total cost of printing, including consumables? _____

_____

30 MINUTES

Lab Exercise 19.02: Installing a Printer

The key to a successful printer installation is having the correct software drivers and understanding how the printer will interface with the computer. You'll most likely need the drivers when you install those five printers your boss is having delivered to you, and you'll also have to configure the printers you are installing to use parallel, USB, and network interfaces. A common practice in multiple-user environments—companies considered to be small office/home office (SOHO)—is to use a printer with its own network interface card (NIC), so that computers from anywhere in the network can print directly to the printer through the network interface.

Learning Objectives

In this lab, you'll install a printer, first as a directly connected device, and then as a network device. You will then explore and change its settings.

At the end of this lab, you'll be able to

- Recognize the variations in key features of laser printers

- Install a laser printer in Windows

- Change laser printer settings in Windows

- Configure a TCP/IP port for a network printer

Lab Materials and Setup

The materials you need for this lab are

- A working computer with Windows installed

- An inkjet or laser printer for installation (or you can skip Step 1)

- Optional: A print device with a network interface card

Getting Down to Business

These days, installing a printer is a fairly straightforward task. This is good news, because you'll probably do your fair share of it as a computer technician.

Step 1   To install a plug-and-play printer:

   a.   Connect the printer to your system via a parallel or USB port.

   b.   Turn on the printer, and then turn on the PC.

   c.   As the boot sequence progresses, the plug-and-play feature will locate the printer and install it for you. Follow the instructions on the screen.

✔ **Hint**

Here's the twist. If your printer is older than your operating system, the OS should install the printer drivers with little interaction on your part. If the printer is newer than your OS, then you'll need to have the driver disc handy because the system will stop and ask you for it. Some printer manufacturers actually require you to start their own printer installation programs even before connecting the printer to a system. As always, consult the manufacturer's instructions first.

Step 2 To install a printer that is not plug and play:

    a.   Access the Printer applet. In Windows XP, select Start | Printers and Faxes. For Windows Vista, select Start | Control Panel | Printers. In Windows 7, go to Start | Devices and Printers.

    b.   Click the Add a Printer button or link. A wizard should pop up on the screen. Click Next to proceed (Windows XP only).

    c.   You want to install a printer attached to your PC, so select the local printer option (see Figure 19-2). In Windows Vista/7, clicking on the option will advance the wizard automatically. In Windows XP, select the local printer option and click Next.

    d.   Follow the steps through the Add Printer Wizard by selecting LPT1 and then a printer from the list of printers or your driver disc. Finish the installation by printing a test page.

✖ **Warning**

If you weren't able to install an actual print device for this exercise, don't print a test page when it asks. You'll receive some interesting messages if you do.

Figure 19-2 Installing a local printer

Step 3 In the following steps, you will set up a TCP/IP printer interface port for a Hewlett-Packard LaserJet printer with a built-in NIC (a technology Hewlett-Packard calls JetDirect). If you have access to a printer with a network interface, or your classroom is equipped with one, use the IP address or printer name of the printer when configuring the port. This will allow you to actually test the installation.

   a. In Windows XP, open the Printer & Faxes folder by way of Start | Control Panel | Printers & Faxes and launch the Add Printer Wizard by clicking *Add a printer* under Printer Tasks. On the welcome screen, click Next. In Windows Vista, go to Start | Control Panel | Printers. Right-click in the window and select Add Printer. In Windows 7, go to Start | Devices and Printers and click on *Add a printer*.

   b. While it may seem counterintuitive, select the local printer installation option again. Windows considers installing a printer via IP address as installing a "local" printer because it uses a "local" port.

   c. Click the *Create a new port* radio button and select Standard TCP/IP Port from the drop-down menu.

   d. In Windows XP, this launches the Add Standard TCP/IP Printer Port Wizard (see Figure 19-3). You'll see the same options in Windows Vista/7, but without the extra wizard. Click Next.

   e. In the Add Port dialog box, enter the IP address of the network printer. The Add Standard TCP/IP Printer Port Wizard (XP)/Add Printer Wizard (Vista/7) automatically creates the port name (see Figure 19-4). Click Next.

   f. If the IP address is fictitious, for the purpose of completing the lab steps, the Add Standard TCP/IP Printer Port Wizard (XP)/Add Printer Wizard (Vista/7) will be unable to identify the printing device. In the Additional Port Information Required dialog box, click the drop-down menu for Standard and select (in this case) Hewlett Packard JetDirect (see Figure 19-5). Click Next.

Figure 19-3 The Add Standard TCP/IP Printer Port Wizard

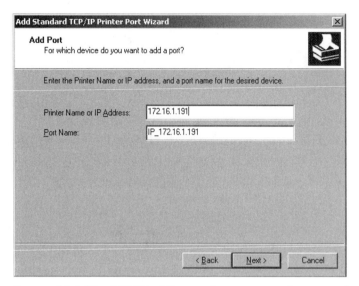

FIGURE 19-4 The TCP/IP address and port name of a network printer

g.   Review the port characteristics and click Finish (see Figure 19-6).

h.   You will now follow the steps through the Add Printer Wizard by selecting a printer from the list of printers or your driver disc as you did when directly connecting to the printer in Step 2.

✖ Warning

Again, if you are unable to install an actual print device for this exercise, don't print a test page. You'll receive some interesting messages if you try.

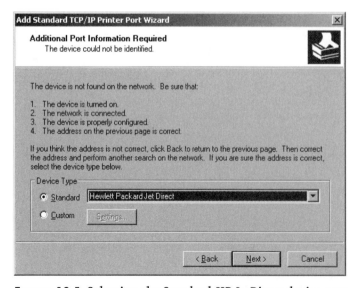

FIGURE 19-5 Selecting the Standard HP JetDirect device type

FIGURE 19-6 Port characteristics

 30 MINUTES

Lab Exercise 19.03: Maintaining and Troubleshooting Printers

It is estimated that technicians, especially those working for the help desk or desktop support group for a small- to medium-sized organization, spend approximately 30 percent of their time on printer issues. If you think about it, of all the components used in computing technology, printers have the highest percentage of moving parts. Moving parts are more likely to need maintenance than are static components.

Printers also like to be finicky and stop printing, usually resulting in a phone call from the client to the help desk for quick resolution. The following exercises will help you develop some understanding of laser printer and inkjet printer maintenance, and what steps to take when they stop printing.

Learning Objectives

In this lab, you'll research laser printer maintenance kits, clean dirty inkjet nozzles, and troubleshoot a failed print job.

At the end of this lab, you'll be able to

- Select a proper maintenance kit for various laser printers
- Clean and verify operation of inkjet nozzles
- Manage print jobs in Windows
- Restart a stalled print spooler

Lab Materials and Setup

The materials you need for this lab are

- A working computer with Windows installed

- A connection to the Internet

- Access to an inkjet printer

Getting Down to Business

The following exercises will round out your activities as you finish with the rollout of the five new printers in your office. You will want to get your Internet connection fired up again and research the maintenance kit available for your laser printer. Then you'll check the print-head nozzles of the inkjet printers and run the cleaning routine if necessary. Finally, you should prepare for any print errors so that you can correct them quickly and efficiently.

Step 1   Laser printers are, by design, highly precise machines. They typically move thousands of sheets of paper per month through the printing mechanism, placing 1200–1600 dots per inch (DPI) of toner on each page. As such, toner cartridges need to be replaced from time to time and parts that wear out need to be refurbished. Most manufacturers offer a maintenance kit for the printer to assist in the upkeep of the printer when these common parts age or fail. It would be a good idea to have a maintenance kit on hand for each model of laser printer in your organization.

✔ **Hint**

Most of the current manufacturers of laser printers—HP, Lexmark, Kyocera, Canon, and so forth—offer some form of maintenance kit for their printers. You should be able to find via an Internet search the available kits, their contents, and competitive pricing. Don't be surprised to find the maintenance kits somewhat costly, though they should still be only a fraction of the cost of replacing the printer.

Select a laser printer make and model, and perform an Internet search to identify the appropriate maintenance kit, its contents, and the average cost of the kit. Use this information to fill in the following items:

Printer model: _____

Maintenance kit: _____

Contents: _____

_____

Price: _____

Step 2 Though you have just installed new inkjet printers, if the printer sits idle for an extended period of time (a few weeks or months), or the ink cartridges have been replaced, you may need to check the print quality and clean the nozzles. The following steps were performed on an Epson Stylus PHOTO 890 in Windows XP but are similar to the steps required on HP and Lexmark inkjet printers. Consult the manual for specific instructions. Note that available maintenance options vary widely from printer to printer, so you will need to read the documentation that came with your printer.

✖ Warning

The nozzle cleaning process uses a fair amount of the expensive ink. If you are working on a personal inkjet printer, or one in the classroom, after printing the nozzle check page, run the nozzle cleaning process only if required.

a. Open the printer applet (whatever your version of Windows happens to call it) and select your inkjet printer.

b. In Windows XP, right-click the printer and select Properties. In Windows Vista/7, right-click the printer and select Printing Preferences.

c. In Windows XP, click the Printing Preferences button (see Figure 19-7).

Figure 19-7 Properties window showing Printing Preferences button

d. Select the Utility tab (see Figure 19-8) and click Nozzle Check. This will print a test pattern using the cyan, yellow, magenta, and black ink nozzles.

e. If the printout is not clear or there are dropouts, click Head Cleaning to clear the nozzles and then return to the Nozzle Check to verify performance.

Step 3 When you are called upon to troubleshoot a failed print job, you should follow a logical step-by-step process to make sure that no obvious, possibly simple failure has occurred. If the power cord has been kicked out or the paper tray is open, troubleshooting the network connectivity or the printer driver would waste valuable time. Once you know the print device is online and ready and there are no paper jams or mechanical errors, it might be time to open the Print Manager and attempt to restart the document.

The following steps are meant to be a rough guideline to troubleshoot and diagnose a failed print job:

a. First, check the physical print device:

- Is the printer plugged in, and is the power turned on?

- Is the printer out of paper or is there a paper jam?

- Is the toner low or in need of replacement?

FIGURE 19-8 Utility tab under Printing Preferences

- Are there any error messages on the printer's LCD readout or any error indicator lights flashing?

- Is the printer online and ready to print?

If you examine all of these areas and find everything appears to be in working condition, then you may have a problem with the connectivity between the computer and the printer, or there may be problems with the document or drivers.

b. Make sure that the connections between the computer and the printer are in good condition and securely fastened. These may be USB, Firewire, parallel, or UTP using RJ-45 connectors.

✔ Hint

To create a failed print job, disconnect the printer cable, shut the power off on the printer, or open the printer paper tray. If you do not have a physical printer, create a printer, following the steps in Lab Exercise 19.02. Send a print job to the printer; the printer icon should appear in the system tray and indicate that the print job has failed. Then continue with Step 3.

---

c. After checking all of the physical components, try to resend the document. Open the Print Manager by clicking the icon in the system tray/notification area.

In the Print Manager, select the failed print job by highlighting the job with *Error* in the Status column (see Figure 19-9).

Select Documents | Restart. If you are creating the printer problem, the printer icon in the system tray/notification area indicates that the print job has failed once again.

d. Highlight the document once again, and then select Documents | Cancel to delete the document.

If this were a real scenario, you would verify that the print drivers were installed and are the correct drivers for the operating system. You would then perform Step 4 to see if the problem is related to the print spooler.

FIGURE 19-9 Print Manager showing error status on a Word file

Step 4   If the print device is online and ready, there are no paper jams or mechanical errors, and restarting the document is of no help, you can check to see if the print spooler is stalled. The print spooler is a holding area for print jobs and is especially important for network printers. If the print device runs out of paper while printing a document, you may have to stop and start the print spooler before the print device will receive jobs again.

You will use the Services snap-in for the Microsoft Management Console (MMC) to complete this task.

   a.   Launch the Services console by opening Administrative Tools in the Control Panel and then double-clicking Services.

   b.   Scroll down and highlight Print Spooler. Select Action | Properties. You should see that the print spooler is started and running (see Figure 19-10).

   c.   Click the Stop button. The print spooler indicates that it has stopped.

   d.   Click the Start button. The print spooler indicates that it has started.

   e.   Alternatively, you can highlight Print Spooler in the Services console and select Action | Restart. You'll see a message stating that the print spooler is stopping, and then another message indicating that the print spooler is starting.

In the real-world scenario, your print spooler service would be restarted, and you should have a healthy, functioning print server once again.

Figure 19-10 Print Spooler Properties dialog box

Lab Analysis Test

1. Patrick and Erik are having a small disagreement. Patrick says that printers can use numerous different interfaces, while Erik says that there are only two: parallel and USB. Who is correct? List the interfaces you are aware of and a typical use of each interface.

2. Theresa is using Windows and just purchased a printer from a friend. When she installs it using the original driver disc that came with the printer, it won't install properly. Why?

3. Danyelle has just joined a large organization as a level II tech and is tasked with the evaluation of all the laser printers in use. The business managers are concerned that all of the units will need to be replaced because of frequent paper jams and poor print quality. Danyelle makes her recommendations, and is actually awarded a bonus for saving the company money. What is her recommendation?

4. Brandon has sent a document to the printer, but the document never actually prints. Where can Brandon check to see the status of the document?

5. Why are laser toner cartridges so expensive?

Key Term Quiz

Use the following terms to complete the following sentences. Not all terms will be used.

dpi

ECP

IEEE 1284

impact

inkjet

laser

primary charge roller

primary corona

TCP/IP port

toner

transfer corona

transfer roller

USB

1. The part of the laser printer that actually causes the toner image to be created on the paper is the _____ or _____.

2. To use a printer that's attached to the network with its own NIC, you must configure a(n) _____.

3. The resolution of a printer is measured in _____.

4. The printer that spits ink onto the paper is a(n) _____ printer.

5. Printers with platens are _____ printers.

Chapter 20
Securing Computers

Lab Exercises

Obviously, keeping your computer secure is important. Several chapters have already been devoted to securing Windows and networks. But there are still a few more helpful tools you should know about to keep things running smoothly. Local Security Settings (also labeled Local Security Policy, sometimes in the same version of Windows) enables you to set a variety of rules about using the system; Event Viewer shows you information about events you didn't even know were happening; and Microsoft Security Essentials is a free tool that enables you to clean your system of, and protect your system against, viruses and other malicious software. Each of these tools increases the power you have over your own security and the security of your computer. You'll also learn how to handle a computer that has illegal materials on it or is part of a criminal investigation.

 15 MINUTES

Lab Exercise 20.01: Configuring Local Policies

NTFS permissions are powerful tools to control with great detail what users and groups can do to folders and files. However, NTFS does not cover a number of important security issues that don't directly involve the file system. For example, what if you don't want a particular user group to shut down the computer? What if you want to make sure all accounts use a password of at least eight characters? What if you want to prevent certain users from reformatting the hard drive? These types of security settings are all controlled under the umbrella term of *local policies*.

> ✔ **Hint**
>
> There are hundreds of different policies that you may configure for a system. This lab only covers a few of the most basic policies!

Learning Objectives

At the end of this lab, you'll be able to

- Locate and open the Local Security Policy/Settings utility
- Create, modify, and delete local policies with Windows

Lab Materials and Setup

The materials you need for this lab are

- A Windows PC with the C: drive formatted as NTFS

- Access to the local administrator password

Getting Down to Business

Local Security Settings is a very powerful applet that enables you to adjust all sorts of settings for and details about your system. Simply put, it is a series of rules you define, ranging from how many attempts to log on a user is allowed, to who can change the time on the clock!

Step 1   Log on using an account with administrator rights. From the Control Panel, open Administrative Tools. Double-click Local Security Policy. When opened, it should look something like Figure 20-1.

Double-click (or single-click in Windows Vista/7) the Account Policies icon to expand its contents: Password Policy and Account Lockout Policy. Click Password Policy in the left column, right-click *Password must meet complexity requirements* in the right column, and select Properties. Enable this policy, as shown in Figure 20-2, and click OK.

Create a normal user account and call it **Janet**. Try making a simple password like **janet** and see what happens. Keep trying to make a password until you get one that is accepted. What do you need to do to make an acceptable password? Hint: Use the help in the User Accounts Control Panel applet to get some ideas as to what you need to do.

FIGURE 20-1 Local Security Settings in Windows XP

Figure 20-2 Enabling password complexity

Step 2   Head back to the Password Policy in Local Security Settings and enable Enforce Password History. Open the User Accounts applet from the Control Panel and try to change a password to the same password you already have. What happens?

_____

Step 3   In Local Security Settings, click Account Lockout Policy under Account Policies in the left column. An account lockout is when the operating system no longer allows a certain account the right even to _try_ to log on. Try to change the properties on the _Account lockout duration_ setting—it is disabled until you set the _Account lockout threshold_ to something other than the default of 0. Try changing the _Account lockout threshold_ to 3 attempts. Note that Windows now automatically sets the _Account lockout duration_ and the _Reset account lockout counter after_ settings to 30 minutes.

Log off the computer. Use the Janet account and intentionally attempt to log on using incorrect passwords. What happens after the third try?

_____

 20 MINUTES

Lab Exercise 20.02: Reviewing Security Events

With all the pop-ups, dialog boxes, and little message bubbles that Windows throws at you all day long, you would think it's telling you everything that happens every minute of every day—Windows Vista, doubly so. But it isn't. Of course, there are many processes that go on in the background, but even when Windows alerts you of an event, there may be more to the story. Perhaps an application crashes unexpectedly and Windows provides little or no feedback. It's possible that one tool in Administrative Tools took notice and can help—Event Viewer.

→ **Note**

You learned about Event Viewer in Chapter 19 as a troubleshooting tool. This lab shows you how it can also be used as a security awareness tool.

Learning Objectives

In this lab, you'll practice using Event Viewer.

At the end of this lab, you'll be able to

- Work with Event Viewer to track events on your system

Lab Materials and Setup

The materials you will need for this lab are

- A PC with Windows

Getting Down to Business

Think about your actions on a computer as a series of events: you log on, you open an application, you close it, you log off, and so forth. This is how Event Viewer sees things, but in a lot more detail. If something goes wrong, Event Viewer usually records it. It also records a lot of things that are perfectly normal—the trick is being able to sort through all the information, which Windows makes fairly simple.

Step 1 Access Event Viewer by going to the Control Panel and opening Administrative Tools. Double-click Event Viewer to open it (see Figure 20-3).

Step 2 Windows Vista/7 adds the extra step of expanding the Windows Logs folder in the left column and adding an Actions panel on the right side, but otherwise Event Viewer is very similar in each version of Windows. Four or five logs should be listed. The important one for now is Application; the events in this log all concern the operation of applications on your system. Click it in the left column and a long list of events should appear on the right.

Step 3 Scroll through the list and look at the different levels used by Windows to describe events (the Type column in Windows XP; the Level column in Windows Vista/7). Click the column label at the top of the list to sort the events by level. You should see a lot of events labeled Information. These are your everyday events—any successful operation, such as proper use of a driver, is marked as Information.

Figure 20-3 Event Viewer

Step 4   There might also be a few events labeled Warning or Error. Warnings do not indicate that something bad *is* happening, but rather that something bad *will* happen. An example of a Warning event is when Windows is low on resources, such as disk space. Errors are more serious. These events occur when there is a failure or loss of functionality, such as when an application crashes.

Go through the list and see if you can find any Warnings or Errors. Double-click one and look at the Event Properties dialog box that pops up for more information on what happened. A lot of Event Viewer's reports can be very cryptic, which is why Windows Vista/7 now has a handy Event Log Online Help link built into Event Viewer. Clicking the link opens a dialog box asking for permission to send information about the event over the Internet. Your browser will open and take you to the Microsoft TechNet database. There isn't information available on every single event, but it can be very useful in tracking down problems.

If you don't have Windows Vista or Windows 7, you can always record the Event ID number that is listed with the event and search for it on the Internet. For example, if it is Event ID 1002, simply search for **"Event Viewer ID 1002"** and see what comes up. You're likely to find out at least a little more than you knew before.

Step 5   Search through the Security and System logs to see what sorts of events they record. In the Security logs, use the Task Category detail to see what each event records. Write down three Task Categories recorded by the Security log.

_____

_____

_____

Lab Analysis Test

1.   Jason is working on a document when Word crashes. Which log in Event Viewer will give him more information? Which level would it be most likely identified as?

2.   In the Local Security Policy/Settings applet, what does *Account lockout threshold* control?

3.   What is the path used in Windows 7 to access the Security log in Event Viewer?

4.   What are two methods of learning more about a particular event in Event Viewer?

Key Term Quiz

Use the following terms to complete the following sentences. Not all terms will be used.

chain of custody

event auditing

Event Viewer

incidence reporting

Local Security Policy/Settings

object access auditing

phishing

1.   The _____ is a list of everyone who has had control of a PC.

2.   _____ is a type of social engineering attack where a malicious person calls pretending to be someone they're not.

3.   Telling your supervisor after you've gathered data about a computer or dealt with a PC or network problem is called _____.

4.   _____ keeps track of every event that occurs on your system and assigns it a level, such as Information or Warning.

5.   When Event Viewer makes a new entry after certain things happen (such as when a user logs on), this is called _____.

Chapter 21
The Right PC for You

Lab Exercises

Picking the right PC is a very personal choice, but the number of PCs available can make the search overwhelming. CompTIA, in their infinite wisdom, has decided to break down and categorize the different types of computers that users can choose from. Depending on the type of work that a user does, you need to be able to point them to a PC that can fill that role. Think of it as being similar to picking out an automobile. Some people need a truck with four-wheel drive and a huge bed for hauling equipment, while others need a small, compact car for city driving. In this chapter, we'll research a few different types of computers using the Internet and explore their differences.

 30 MINUTES

Lab Exercise 21.01: Building a Thick Client

The thick client is a strange beast, mostly because techs rarely use the term "thick client." Techs only refer to a thick client when comparing it to its smaller sibling, the thin client. Both thin and thick clients exist in a client/server network environment, where PCs connect to a central server to access resources. Depending on the workload, you may want to let your local workstation bear some of the burden of processing, keeping your applications locally stored on your thick client. On the other hand, the thin client can be very light on processing capability. It relies heavily on the server to store the applications and, in some cases, even process the data. In reality, a thick client is just the good old-fashioned PC we all love. It can run the Windows operating system and just about any standard desktop application you throw at it.

Learning Objective

In this exercise, you'll research what it takes to create a standard thick client.

At the end of this lab, you'll be able to

- Find parts for a standard thick client by using the Internet

Lab Materials and Setup

The materials you need for this lab are

- An Internet-capable PC for research

Getting Down to Business

By Chapter 21, you've had quite an adventure, learning about all the different aspects of computing. You've seen everything from microprocessors to power supplies, from Microsoft Windows to video cards. Now it's time to put all that experience to the test. You will research the parts for a fully functional thick client. Here is the list of criteria your PC must meet to qualify as a thick client:

- Runs the latest Windows operating system
- Runs standard desktop applications such as Microsoft Office and Internet Explorer
- Network connectivity
- Storage (SSD or HDD)
- Monitor
- Keyboard and mouse

Step 1 Open a Web browser and visit a Web site from which you can purchase computer parts. Suggestions include:

- www.newegg.com
- www.tigerdirect.com
- www.cdw.com

Your instructor will set a price limit for you. You don't want to make a high-end gaming machine—at least not yet! If this is a self-guided course, then set a limit of $650. That should keep you in the realm of the thick client.

Step 2 Shop for the parts listed in the following table and complete the other columns for each component you choose.

Part	Model/Version	Web Site	Price
Motherboard			
CPU			
RAM			
Hard drive			
Optical drive			
Power supply			
Case			
Mouse			
Keyboard			
Monitor			
Windows OS			
Video card (optional)			

Step 3   Add up all the prices for your parts.

Grand total: _____

If you went over budget, find less expensive parts for your components and try to cut some corners to make that perfect thick client computer.

 30 MINUTES

Lab Exercise 21.02: Building a Gaming PC

In Lab Exercise 21.01, you priced the parts for a standard thick client computer. Now let's have a little more fun and see what we need to build a gaming PC. Everything will be very similar to the previous exercise when picking out your parts, but with a special twist: your PC will need to be able to handle some of the most hardware-intensive applications on the market.

Learning Objective

In this exercise, you'll research what it takes to create a gaming PC.

At the end of this lab, you'll be able to

- Find components for a gaming PC by using the Internet

Lab Materials and Setup

The materials you need for this lab are

- An Internet-capable PC for research

Getting Down to Business

Creating a gaming computer takes all the knowledge you gained from creating a thick client, plus the following additional requirements to make it a gaming PC:

- Runs the latest Windows operating system
- Powerful CPU (high clock speed and multiple cores)
- Network connectivity
- Storage (SSD or HDD)
- 22-inch monitor
- Keyboard and mouse

- High-capacity RAM

- High-end graphics card

- High-end sound card

- High-end cooling system

Step 1 Open a Web browser and visit a Web site from which you can purchase computer parts. Suggestions include:

- www.newegg.com

- www.tigerdirect.com

- www.cdw.com

Just like in the previous lab exercise, the instructor will set a price limit for you. If this is a self-guided course, then set a limit of $1500. In a perfect world, I would give you an unlimited budget to get all the highest-end components in the world, and while it's always fun to be a dreamer, I want to show you a realistic, everyday gaming machine.

Step 2 Shop for the parts listed in the following table and complete the other columns for each component you choose.

Part	Model/Version	Web Site	Price
Motherboard			
CPU			
After-market CPU cooler			
RAM			
Hard drive			
Optical drive			
Power supply			
Case			
Mouse			
Keyboard			
Monitor			
Windows OS			
Video card(s)			
Sound card			
Speaker/headphones			

Step 3 Fill in the following table with any additional parts you might need to purchase, such as fans, lights, or fans with lights!

Model	Web Site	Price	Qty.

Step 4 Now, add up all the prices for your parts.

Grand total: _____

Did you go over the price limit of $1500 or the price set by your instructor? If you went over your budget, maybe you need to get some lower-capacity RAM or let go of a graphics card, if you went with an SLI or CrossFire setup. Do what you need to do to fall within the price limit.

Step 5 Now, let's take a look and see if the power supply you chose will actually power your computer. There are many power supply calculators online that will show you how much wattage you need to power your components. Open your Web browser, go to your favorite search engine, and search for "power supply calculator." You can also just go to this Web site, which I use all the time: http://extreme.outervision .com/psucalculatorlite.jsp. Fill in the calculator with your gaming PC's specifications.

Does the power supply you chose supply enough wattage for your gaming rig? If so, how much wattage do you have left over?

_____

→ **Note**

When building your gaming PC, you'll need a power supply that can properly power all of your high-end components.

 30 MINUTES

Lab Exercise 21.03: Building a Home Theater PC

These days, computers are used not only to check e-mail, create documents, and play video games, but also to view pictures, listen to music, and watch TV shows and movies. To really take advantage of your media collection, you need a PC that can integrate with your home theater setup (if you have one).

The market for home theater boxes is still young, but there are a lot of options. Apple TV, Roku, Windows Media Center, and XBMC are all designed to take your media and put it on your television. With so many options, your client might need help picking out the right parts. This lab exercise explores the criteria of what comprises a home theater PC.

Learning Objective

In this exercise, you'll research what it takes to create a home theater PC.

At the end of this lab, you'll be able to

- Find components for a home theater PC using the Internet

- Use Windows Media Center and XBMC

Lab Materials and Setup

The materials you need for this lab are

- An Internet-capable PC for research

- A Windows operating system with Media Center installed

Getting Down to Business

To create a home theater PC, you will use many of the components that you used in the previous lab exercises in this chapter. I am not going to list all of those parts again here, but rather just list the specific components necessary to build a home theater PC:

- Sufficiently powerful CPU and RAM to run your operating system

- Enough storage for your OS and media

- Network connectivity

- Wireless keyboard/mouse combo

- Graphics with HDMI output

- HTPC case (ATX, microATX, ITX)

- TV tuner card

- Blu-ray Disc drive

Step 1 Open a Web browser and visit a Web site from which you can purchase computer parts. Suggestions include:

- www.newegg.com

- www.tigerdirect.com

- www.cdw.com

Step 2 Shop for the parts listed in the following table and complete the other columns for each component you choose.

Part	Model/Version	Web Site	Price
HTPC case			
Motherboard with built-in HDMI			
TV tuner			
Surround sound speakers with receiver			
Blu-ray drive			
Wireless keyboard			
Wireless mouse			
Video card with HDMI (optional)			

Step 3 Now that you have found the components for your home theater PC, you need a way of getting your media onto that 70-inch flat screen TV you own (right?)! I want to show you two different options. One is included with some versions and editions of Windows, while the other is a free download that works with any copy of Windows. Let's first take a quick tour of Windows Media Center.

→ Note

Don't confuse Windows Media Center with Windows Media Player. They are entirely different.

To use Windows Media Center, you need one of the following operating systems:

- Windows XP Media Center Edition
- Windows Vista Home Premium or Ultimate
- Windows 7 Home Premium, Professional, Enterprise, or Ultimate

→ Note

Microsoft has announced that they will drop built-in DVD playback in Windows 8 and that Media Center will only be available as a paid add-on.

a. Using the appropriate version of Windows, open Windows Media Center. When you open it for the first time, you are given the choice of an Express or Custom installation (see Figure 21-1). Click on Custom.

b. Click Next at the Windows Media Center setup screen.

FIGURE 21-1 The Windows Media Center Get Started screen

c.   Choose whether or not you want to join the Customer Experience Improvement Program. This sends data back to Microsoft so that they can improve Media Center. Click Next.

d.   The next screen asks if you want to download periodic updates to your cover art collection and TV listings. Click Yes, and then click Next.

e.   Media Center will tell you that you have finished installing the required components. Click Next.

f.   Media Center will prompt you with a choice to set up several features further. You can configure these options later, so click the option to finish, and then click Next.

g.   You have now configured Windows Media Center. You can visit the Settings area to configure additional options, such as where your media libraries are located, and to configure your TV tuner to get a signal to watch what is on TV. Media Center guides you through it all.

Step 4   Another popular option for how to present your media is called XBMC (unofficially known as the Xbox Media Center). Some crafty people modified the original Xbox to add a media center, hence the name. It has since grown into an open source project that can be run on just about any operating system available. (It can even run as a live CD.) To get XBMC, visit www.xbmc.org and follow these steps:

a.   Move your mouse pointer over the Downloads link then click Get XBMC.

b.   Choose the operating system on which you are installing XBMC and wait for the download to finish. It's a pretty big file. Depending on your Internet connection speed, it might take a while.

FIGURE 21-2 XBMC running with the default skin

c. Once it has finished downloading, run the setup file and follow through the installation instructions. Then run XBMC (see Figure 21-2).

d. At first glance, XBMC looks overwhelming—you can change just about anything in XBMC. Take some time to get acquainted with the interface. I don't use the mouse in XBMC. Using the keyboard feels more like using a remote control as you would in a traditional home theater. Highlight SYSTEM using the arrow keys and press ENTER.

e. The System menu hides the real power of XBMC. It has so many configurable options, I could write an entire book on just this menu! Go to Add-ons and press ENTER (see Figure 21-3).

FIGURE 21-3 The Add-ons screen in XBMC

f. Add-ons are exactly what they sound like. They add extra functionality to XBMC, such as watching YouTube or Hulu within the media center. Select Enabled Add-ons and press ENTER.

g. Select Skin and press ENTER. What is the name of the default skin in XBMC?

_____

h. Press BACKSPACE twice to return the Add-ons screen. Select Get Add-ons and press ENTER. Press ENTER again for XBMC.org Add-ons.

i. Go to Skin and press ENTER to view the choices (see Figure 21-4).

j. Look at all the skins available! And these are just the ones that are built into the default add-on packages. There are countless users out there who are making skins that might suit your personal taste. This, right here, is where XBMC shines. Find a skin that fits your style, press ENTER, then select Install. Press ENTER again. XBMC will download and install the skin.

k. Once the skin has downloaded, answer the prompt by selecting Yes to switch the skin. Press the BACKSPACE key as many times as needed to return to the main screen.

l. If you don't like the skin you chose, go back to Step 4d and try again.

m. Which skin did you like the most?

_____

Figure 21-4 The list of available skins in XBMC

n. Once you have found your skin, take some time to experiment and explore by adding folders to the VIDEOS and MUSIC menus.

o. Remember, XBMC is an open source project. You can find documentation and walkthroughs for this application with a quick search in your favorite search engine. Have fun with it!

→ **Note**

The creators of XBMC release regular updates for the media center software. The steps outlined in this lab exercise may not lead to the same options in future updates.

Lab Analysis Test

1. Bruce wants to build a computer that specializes in audio/video editing. What can you tell him about that type of workstation that makes it unique?

2. Tony wants to build a home server PC. What features will it need to have in order to be a good home server?

3. Natasha is trying to decide if she should have thin clients or thick clients attached to the network. Explain the similarities and differences between thin and thick clients.

4. Steve wants to watch TV, broadcast over the air, on his computer in his living room. What hardware and software does Steve need to accomplish this?

5. Clint wants to build the ultimate gaming PC. What are some of the requirements he'll need as far as hardware is concerned for have the gaming PC of his dreams?

Key Term Quiz

Use the following terms to complete the following sentences. Not all terms will be used.

audio/video editing workstation

gaming PC

graphics workstation

home server PC

home theater PC

thick client

thin client

TV tuner

virtualization workstation

Windows Media Center

XBMC

1. A(n) _____ is a type of computer that connects to a server on a network. It offloads much of the processing to the server. In many situations, this computer doesn't even have a hard drive.

2. A(n) _____ is a powerful computer that is used with applications like Adobe Photoshop, Adobe Premiere, and Autodesk SketchBook Pro.

3. A(n) _____ is a computer that can run a second "guest" operating system on top of another operating system, sharing the hardware resources of one computer.

4. A computer that has RAID functionality along with the ability to stream media to other workstations on the network is most likely a(n) _____.

5. By installing a(n) _____, you will have the ability to watch over-the-air television on your computer.

Index